7/00

THOMAS JEFFERSON
Man on a Mountain

Thomas Jefferson at sixty-one, shortly after his reelection to the presidency.

THOMAS JEFFERSON
Man on a Mountain

by Natalie S. Bober

ATHENEUM   NEW YORK

For Larry
and for Steve.
Their love "has made all the difference."

Picture Credits: L. H. Bober: 45, 70, 179, 230, 232, 245; Colonial Williamsburg Foundation: 88; Diplomatic Reception Rooms, United States Department of State, Photograph by Will Brown: 203; Free Library of Philadelphia: 31; French Cultural Services: 164; Harvard University Art Museums (Fogg Art Museum); Given in memory of Thomas Jefferson Newbold, Harvard Class of 1910, by Mrs. T. Jefferson Newbold and Family, June 1960: 217; Independence National Historical Park Collection: 199; Library of Congress: 112; L. Sykes Martin: 237; Metropolitan Museum of Art: 94 (Bequest of Michael Friedsam, 1931, The Friedsam Collection), 200 (Gift of Henry G. Marquand, 1881); Joseph and Margaret Muscarelle Museum of Art, College of William and Mary, Virginia; Gift of Dr. R. C. M. Page: 23; National Archives: 92, 95, 106, 168; New York Historical Society: frontispiece; New York Public Library Picture Collection: 18, 20–1, 180; New York Public Library Print Collection: Miriam and Ira D. Wallach Division of Art Prints and Photographs, Astor, Lenox and Tilden Foundation: 174, 193; Pennsylvania Historical Society: 105; Smithsonian Institution: 103; The Thomas Jefferson Memorial Foundation, Inc., Charlottesville, VA: 54, 228–9, 240 (Photograph by Edwin S. Roseberry © 1980); Ellen Eddy Thorndike: 239.

Atheneum
Macmillan Publishing Company
866 Third Avenue, New York, NY 10022
Collier Macmillan Canada, Inc.
Printed in the United States of America

10 9 8 7 6 5 4 3
Library of Congress Cataloging-in-Publication Data
Bober, Natalie.
Thomas Jefferson: man on a mountain/by Natalie S. Bober.
—1st ed. p. cm.   Bibliography: p.   Includes index.
Summary: The life of the author of the Declaration of Independence and third president of the United States, who was also a noted inventor, architect, farmer, statesman, and educator.
ISBN 0–689–31154–0
1. Jefferson, Thomas, 1743–1826—Juvenile literature.
2. Presidents—United States—Biography—Juvenile literature.
[1. Jefferson, Thomas, 1743–1826. 2. Presidents.] I. Title.
E332.79.B63 1988   973.4'6'0924—dc19 [B] [92] 87–37462 CIP AC

CONTENTS

PREFACE

In the introduction to his sixth and final volume on the life of Thomas Jefferson, the late Dumas Malone, eminent Jefferson scholar, said, "I have left out much I would have liked to include and cannot hope to have done full justice to a virtually inexhaustible subject." Reading this, we wonder how one could have the audacity to attempt to compress the rich diversity of Jefferson's life into one volume.

There are many tributaries to the flow of a river, but we cannot hope to explore every stream. For our purposes here we must stick to the main stream, excluding many side trips, however interesting and important, that contributed to Jefferson's growth, only because space does not permit more.

There is no end to the discoveries to be made about Jefferson. He himself never ceased to grow. So much has been written about him, and the depth and breadth of his mind was so vast, that one even wonders who may dare to interpret it. Jefferson, perhaps more than any other person of his time, changed the shape of his country and "became one of the most notable champions of freedom and enlightenment in recorded history." Yet this multitalented man who, in the words of another biographer, "could calculate an eclipse, survey an estate, tie an artery, plan an edifice, try a cause, break a horse, dance a minuet, and play a violin," was a very real human being—a young boy afraid to go to class because he hadn't prepared his lessons, later an eager young law student, a devoted friend, an adoring—and adored—husband, father, and grandfather.

Throughout his life, even after he had become a prominent figure on the national stage, it was the pull of family that tugged at him relentlessly. He considered none of his public accomplishments worthy of note. Rather, it was as the philosopher on Monticello surrounded by his children and his grandchildren that he attained his greatest happiness. Indeed, it is in the bond that developed between him and his grandchildren that the real Thomas Jefferson steps out of the history books and becomes a living man. I have tried to paint a picture of this man.

I have tried to relate the man and his career to the era in which he lived, to the thought currents of his time, to the historical circumstances that surrounded him and the part he played in them. But it has not been my intention to deal fully with the politics of the time. I have attempted to relate them only in so far as they shed light on Jefferson the man and move his story forward.

As we explore the development of his mind, we can see how his personal code of living was reflected in his writing of the Declaration of Independence. We can see him as the perennial optimist who once told John Adams that he steered his bark with hope in the head, leaving fear astern; as a man who lived with the taunt of cowardice but had a passion for peace; as a man to whom subtlety and understatement were a way of life; and as a man who believed in the illimitable freedom of the human mind.

He was a rare blend of prophet and practical statesman, a reluctant rebel who saw the possibilities of the times in which he lived but recognized the importance of the past. He could adapt the classical models to the needs of his own time and to the future he envisioned.

He never lost his faith in the worth and dignity of the common man. He believed in an aristocracy—but an aristocracy of talent, not of wealth. He was a constant seeker after knowledge—an eternal student who was "bold in the pursuit of knowledge," and a teacher who took "supreme delight" in communicating the knowledge he so boldly pursued.

It is my hope that as Thomas Jefferson calls to us across the ages, young people will recognize his insatiable curiosity about everything, his willingness to say, "I don't know" and then to turn to books to find the answers. When called upon to recommend a program of study for a young man, Jefferson could say, "The only help a youth wants is to be directed what books to read, and in what order to read them."

It is my hope, too, that this book will help to dispel the myths that surround Thomas Jefferson and will "ungrave" him and bring him to life for all the young people who read it. Perhaps then they will be ready to study him in greater depth.   N. S. B.

ACKNOWLEDGMENTS

Research for me is always a joy, but it became even more so as many people graciously gave of their time and expertise during the various stages of researching and writing this book. To them I express my appreciation.

At Monticello, Bill Beiswanger, Architectural Historian, and Peter Hatch, Superintendent of Grounds Restoration, spent the better part of a day with me, bringing into sharper focus the relationship between Jefferson's development and the development of Monticello. Seeing the house and gardens through their eyes brought to life the "human" Jefferson.

At the Colonial Williamsburg Foundation Library, Eileen Parris furnished me with valuable material on the Williamsburg that Jefferson knew, and made it possible for my husband to photograph the original *Journals of the House of Burgesses*.

Margaret Cook, Curator of Manuscripts and Rare Books at the Swemm Library, College of William and Mary, made the library's holdings available to me.

At the National Gallery of Art in Washington, D.C., Morris Robinson allowed me to view privately the film *The Eye of Thomas Jefferson*. At the National Museum of American History, Dr. Harry Rubinstein, Curator, Division of Political History, made available the museum's photo files, and Kate Henderson shared with me the excitement of viewing the desk on which Jefferson wrote the *Declaration of Independence*.

At the Library of Congress, James Gilreath, Rare Book Curator, spoke to me of Jefferson's passion for books and made me tremble with joy as he unlocked the door to the little room that holds the books Jefferson first gave to the Library of Congress, then placed in my hands Jefferson's own copy—annotated in his own precise handwriting—of the writings of Tacitus.

David Dutcher, Chief Historian at Independence National Historical Park in Philadelphia, made the meetings of the Continental Congress in Carpenter Hall and the Pennsylvania State House come alive. Roy Goodman, Reference Librarian of the American Philosophical Society, provided much material—and food for thought—as he spoke of Jefferson's recognition of the eighteenth century as a century of possibilities.

The librarians at the Massachusetts Historical Society, the New-York Historical Society, and the New York Society Library were all extremely cooperative.

For his help on several levels, I thank Thomas Fleming, author of *The Man from Monticello*. His many thoughtful suggestions and stimulating conversation proved invaluable. For his final careful reading of the manuscript and his astute judgments, I am particularly grateful.

I owe a special debt of gratitude to my uncle, Mortimer Goodman, whose research and commentary on the Declaration of Independence made this a better book. To him also, and to my aunt, Estelle Goodman, and my friend Sandie Samuels, my gratitude for their meticulous job of proof-reading the manuscript. My gratitude, also, to Jennifer Horowitz, whose help in the final stages became to me a lee port in a storm. Her work on reference notes, on chronology and genealogy charts, on pictures, and on the bibliography spared me much pain. And to Linda Leff, for an extraordinary collaboration on the index, a special note of thanks.

Every book needs an editor, but the true editorial gift is rare. Marcia Marshall, my friend and editor these many years, has that gift. Her never-failing encouragement and support, and the astute eye that enabled her to gently but firmly trim and prune, all the while keeping my vision intact, have endeared her to me all the more.

It isn't often that a mother can work with—and learn from—a son. I have had that joy. My son Stephen read the manuscript at every stage along the way, bringing to it his unique combination of talented teacher of young people and understanding of American history. His willingness to walk with me through the eighteenth century and his thoughtful, incisive suggestions have "made all the difference."

My husband, by his infinite patience, his understanding, and his sharing, multiplies the joy. It is he who makes it all possible.   N. S. B.

Chronology

1743: April 13—Thomas Jefferson born at Shadwell, in Virginia.

1757: August 17—T. J.'s father, Peter Jefferson, dies at age 50.

1760: T. J. enters College of William and Mary.

March 25—King George III of England succeeds George II.

1762: T. J. begins legal study with George Wythe.

1765: January—Stamp Act passed by Parliament.

April 13—T. J. turns 21 and inherits Peter's estate.

T. J. becomes a parish vestryman and justice of peace.

T. J. organizes Rivanna project.

July 20—T. J.'s sister Martha Jefferson marries Tom's school friend Dabney Carr.

October 1—T. J.'s sister Jane Jefferson dies at 25.

1766: Stamp Act repealed.

1767: T. J. admitted to bar.

June 15–July 2—Townshend Acts passed in Parliament.

Work begins on Monticello.

1768: T. J. elected to Virginia House of Burgesses.

1769: Townshend Acts rescinded, except for the tax on tea.

1770: February 1—Shadwell destroyed by fire.

1772: January 1—T. J. marries Mrs. Martha Wayles Skelton.

September 27—daughter Martha "Patsy" Jefferson born.

1773: March 12—T. J. and fellow burgesses urge formation of colonial Committees of Correspondence.

April 20—Dabney Carr dies at age 30; T. J. takes care of his family and affairs.

May 28—T. J.'s father-in-law, John Wayles, dies.

December 16—the Boston Tea Party occurs.

1774: February 21—sister Elizabeth Jefferson dies at age 30.

March 31—Parliament reacts to Boston Tea Party by passing the Boston Port Act, closing the port to trade. To be enacted June 1.

April 3—daughter Jane Randolph Jefferson born.

September 5—First Continental Congress meets.

1775: April 18—Battle of Lexington and Concord begins Revolutionary War.

March 20—Second Virginia Convention meets; Patrick Henry makes speech ("Give me liberty or give me death").

June 8—British governor flees Virginia.

June 22—Second Continental Congress meets.

September—daughter Jane Randolph Jefferson dies at 17 months.

1776: January 1—British burn Norfolk, Virginia, and Falmouth, Maine.

January 10—Thomas Paine publishes *Common Sense*.

March 31—T. J.'s mother, Jane Randolph Jefferson, dies.

June 10—T. J. elected to write Declaration of Independence.

July 2—colonies vote to declare independence.

July 4—colonies sign Declaration of Independence.

Autumn—T. J. and George Wythe begin revision of Virginia law.

1777: May 28—T. J.'s son born.

June 14—T. J.'s son dies at 17 days.

1778: August 1—daughter Mary ("Polly" or "Maria") Jefferson born.

1779: T. J. succeeds Patrick Henry as governor of Virginia.

1780: April—capital of Virginia moves to Richmond for safety from Revolutionary War.

November 30—daughter Lucy Elizabeth Jefferson born.

December—Benedict Arnold leads British Army to invade Virginia coast.

1781: January—Benedict Arnold attacks Virginia; Washington sends the marquis de Lafayette to defend Virginia.

T. J. begins to write *Notes on Virginia*.

April 15—T. J.'s daughter Lucy Elizabeth Jefferson dies at 5 months.

June 3—Jack Jouette's ride warns T. J. of British arrest party.

June—T. J. retires from governorship.

1782: May 8—daughter, also named Lucy Elizabeth Jefferson, born.

September 6—T. J.'s wife, Martha Wayles Skelton Jefferson, dies.

1783: May—T. J.'s sister Anna Scott Jefferson joins household.

June—T. J. elected to Congress. Leaves two younger daughters with his sister-in-law (Martha's half-sister, Elizabeth Wayles Eppes) and her husband in Virginia, then takes Patsy to boarding school in Philadelphia before going to take his new seat at Annapolis. At Congress, T. J. helps form government of the new nation.

1784: May 7—T. J. appointed minister plenipotentiary to France.

July 4—T. J. sails for France. Takes Patsy with him, leaving younger girls with Francis and Elizabeth Eppes.

August—T. J. and Patsy arrive in Paris.

October 13—T. J.'s daughter Lucy Elizabeth Jefferson dies at two-and-a-half-years old.

1785: May 2—T. J. elected to succeed Benjamin Franklin as minister to the French court.

August—T. J. meets Maria Cosway.

October 4—Cosways leave Paris.

1787: February 28—T. J. leaves for southern France.

December—T. J. ends relationship with Maria Cosway.

1788: July—T. J.'s younger daughter, "Polly," arrives in Paris.

1789: April 14—George Washington becomes the first president of the United States.

July 14—Storming of the Bastille in France.

October 8, 1789—the Jeffersons begin journey home to Virginia.

1790: February 23—T. J.'s daughter Martha "Patsy" Jefferson marries Thomas Mann Randolph, Jr., a second cousin.

March 21—T. J. becomes Washington's secretary of state for term ending December 1793.

1791: January 23—T. J.'s grandchild Anne Cary Randolph born, the first of Martha's twelve children.

T. J. helps Washington plan a capital city.

1792: September—T. J.'s grandson Thomas Jefferson Randolph born.

1796: T. J. elected vice president of the United States.

T. J.'s granddaughter Ellen Wayles Randolph born.

1797: March 3—T. J. inaugurated as president of American Philosophical Society.

March 4—T. J. inaugurated as vice president of the United States.

June 18–July 14—Alien and Sedition Acts passed.

October 13—T. J.'s daughter Mary ("Maria" or "Polly") Jefferson marries Jack Eppes, a cousin.

1799: December 31—T. J.'s grandchild born prematurely to the Eppes dies unnamed.

1800: December 3—Thomas Jefferson and Aaron Burr receive equal number of votes for presidency.

1801: February 17—Congress elects T. J. president of the United States.

T. J.'s grandson Francis Wayles Eppes born.

1802: Alien and Sedition Acts expire and are abandoned.

1803: Louisiana Purchase enacted.

Lewis and Clark expedition authorized.

1804: T. J.'s granddaughter Maria Jefferson Eppes born.

April 17—T. J.'s daughter Mary ("Maria" or "Polly") Jefferson Eppes dies at age 25.

1805: T. J. begins second term as president.

1807: T. J.'s granddaughter Maria Jefferson Eppes dies at 3 years.

1809: T. J. returns to Monticello.

1812: June 18—War of 1812 begins.

1814: British burn the Capitol during War of 1812; T. J. donates his library to Congress to replace the destroyed volumes.

T. J. begins work on Albermarle Academy (later University of Virginia).

1825: March—Lafayette visits T. J. as University of Virginia opens.

May 27—T. J.'s granddaughter Ellen Wayles Randolph marries Joseph Coolidge, Jr.

1826: July 4—Thomas Jefferson dies on the fiftieth birthday of the United States.

Family Tree

Peter
Jefferson
(1707–1757)
m.
Jane
Randolph
(1720–1776)

- Jane
Jefferson
(1740–1765)

- Mary Jefferson
(1741–1817)
m.
*Col. John
Bolling*

- **THOMAS
JEFFERSON**
(1743–1826)
m.
*Martha Wayles
Skelton
(1748–1782)*

- Elizabeth
Jefferson
(1744–1774)

- Martha
Jefferson
(1746–1811)
m.
*Dabney Carr
(1743–1773)*

- Peter Field
Jefferson
(1748–1748)

- Son (1750)

- Lucy
Jefferson
(1752–1784)
m.
*Charles L.
Lewis*

- Anna Scott
Jefferson
(1755–1802)
m.
*Hastings
Marks*

- Randolph
Jefferson
(1755–1815)
m.
*1-Anne Lewis
2-Mitchie Pryor*

- Martha "Patsy"
Jefferson
(1772–1836)
m.
*Thomas Mann
Randolph
(1768–1828)*

- Jane Randolph
Jefferson
(1774–1775

- Son (1777)

- Mary ("Polly"
or "Maria")
Jefferson
(1778–1804)
m.
*John (Jack)
Wayles Eppes
(1773–1823)*

- Lucy Elizabeth
Jefferson
(1780–1781)

- Lucy Elizabeth
Jefferson
(1782–1784)

- Jane Barbara
Carr
(1766–1840)

- Lucy Carr
(1768–1803)

- Mary Carr
("Polly")
(1768–?)

- Peter Carr
(1770–1815)

- Col. Samuel
Carr
(1771–1855)

- Dabney Carr
(1773–1837)

- Infant
(1800)

- Francis
Wayles
Eppes
(1801–
1881)

- Maria
Jefferson
Eppes
(1804–
1807)

- Anne Cary
Randolph
(1791–1826)
m.
*Charles Lewis
Bankhead*

- Thomas Jefferson
Randolph
(1792–1875)
m.
*Jane Hollins
Nicholas*

- Ellen Wayles
Randolph
(1794–1795)

- Ellen Wayles
Randolph
(1796–1876)
m.
Joseph Coolidge

- Cornelia Jefferson
Randolph
(1799–1871)

- Virginia Jefferson
Randolph
(1801–1882)
m.
*Nicholas Philip
Trist*

- Mary Jefferson
Randolph
(1803–1876)

- James Madison
Randolph
(1806–1834)

- Benjamin Franklin
Randolph
(1808–1871)

- Meriwether Lewis
Randolph
(1810–1837)

- Septimia Anne
Randolph
(1814–1887)

- George Wythe
Randolph
(1818–1867)

THOMAS JEFFERSON
Man on a Mountain

"I was bold in the pursuit of knowledge, never
fearing to follow truth and reason to whatever results they
led, and bearding every authority which stood in their way."
—*Thomas Jefferson*

Prologue

The young and sensitive new member of the Virginia House of Burgesses, the oldest representative assembly in America, was humiliated. He had been given his first assignment—to draft an address to the royal governor of the colony—and he completed it simply and concisely. He had studied diligently for years to prepare himself for such a task, and now it seemed to no avail. Some of the older members were not satisfied with his paper. They wanted a fuller discussion. One of them rewrote it.

He was convinced that he was beginning his political career with a failure.

This shy, lanky, redheaded young squire, newly sworn in as a burgess amid much pomp and ceremony to represent his county of Albemarle, was Thomas Jefferson. He vowed to himself that he would remain silent for the balance of the legislative session and listen carefully to the ideas that were swirling around him. It didn't take him long to realize that the members of this assembly were highly intelligent, self-confident, and united, and believed strongly in their freedom as lawmakers and in their rights as colonists.

It was spring, the year was 1769, and the spirit of discontent that had been simmering in the colonies over the last few years was beginning to boil over. "The ball of revolution"[1] was starting to roll, and the young man from Albemarle was ready to keep it moving. He had already learned the value of freedom and self-government as he grew to manhood on the edge of the wilderness, in the largest and one of the most important colonies in America.

I
On the edge
of the wilderness

The Virginia into which Thomas Jefferson had been born twenty-six years before was much larger than the state of Virginia as we know it today. The colony stretched from the Atlantic Ocean west to the Mississippi River and north to the Great Lakes, and included what would become the states of West Virginia, Kentucky, Ohio, Illinois, Indiana, Michigan, and Wisconsin. It must have seemed like an empire.

The Piedmont section, where the Jeffersons made their home, had not been settled until more than a hundred years after the colonization of the eastern seaboard. It was a vast wilderness, but enterprising young planters were beginning to move west from the crowded and worn-out lands in the east. Situated at the foot of the Blue Ridge Mountains, Piedmont land was fertile, and the air was free of mosquitoes and free of infection. Tom's father, Peter Jefferson, was among the earliest settlers of the area. It was a time when large tracts of land, called patents, were readily acquired by suitable persons, and Peter was granted title to his first 322 acres in 1730 in what is now called Albemarle County. Soon he added another thousand acres on the south side of the Anna River, referred to as the Rivanna.

Peter was neither rich nor wellborn, but he was ambitious and had a fine mind and a pioneering spirit. He loved the outdoors and was an expert horseman and hunter and a tireless swimmer. His strength was legendary. While still young, in spite of a meager education, he learned the art of surveying,* an appropriate profession in a new country.

* A surveyor laid out boundaries of the patented public lands in order that grants and deeds might be obtained.

While living in Albemarle, Peter met William Randolph, a young aristocrat who owned 2,400 acres adjoining Peter's land. They soon became close friends, and it was through this friendship that Peter met William's lovely and talented cousin Jane.

Jane's father, Isham Randolph, was typical of the Virginia aristocracy—intelligent, well educated, and a gentleman in every sense of the word. He lived in a grand house, staffed by about one hundred slaves, on a large plantation on the James River.

When William Randolph took his friend Peter to visit his Uncle Isham, Peter met and quickly fell in love with the seventeen-year-old Jane. Two years later, on October 19, 1739, they were married. He was thirty-two; she was nineteen. That she would leave the opulence of her father's home to live in a tiny cottage on the edge of the wilderness with the man she loved tells much about her.

With this union, a man without family prestige or social pretense became identified with one of the leading families in Virginia. In eighteenth-century Virginia there were two distinct groups: the aristocracy, typified by Isham Randolph, and the yeomanry, who were generally industrious, belligerently independent, and instinctively democratic. The marriage of Jane Randolph to Peter Jefferson joined the two classes. And of the blending of these two strains would come the unique mosaic that was Thomas Jefferson.

Peter immediately went to work clearing his land and building a house with his own hands. He worked at the task, aided only by a slave family, for several years. As he worked, he came to know the Indians whose trails passed nearby. A feeling of friendship and mutual trust built up between them, and the Indians treated Peter with the respect that they were apt to feel for men who never feared and never deceived them.

When his house was finished, sometime before the spring of 1743, Peter brought his gentle and well-born wife and their two little daughters to live there. They were eagerly awaiting the birth of their next child.

Peter named the house Shadwell, after the parish in London where Jane had been christened twenty-three years before. It was here, soon after, that their first son was born. The child was named

Thomas—after his paternal grandfather and great-grandfather.* Shadwell was a spacious farmhouse, a story-and-a-half high, with a wide entry and four large rooms on the ground floor and many garret rooms above. Jane's interest in gardening was given free reign here, and soon she was supervising the digging of a terraced garden behind the house and was planting purple hyacinths and yellow narcissus.

The house stood in a clearing on a slight rise of ground, with a view of the hazy Blue Ridge Mountains in the distance. The magic of this beautiful land would have a lasting influence on the mind of the little boy who was born there.

Tom's stay in this idyllic setting was interrupted when he was just two years old. At this time the family's life was altered drastically. Peter's friend William Randolph had died, leaving his children orphans. William's wife had died three years earlier, and William's dying wish was that "his dear and loving friend" and family move to his home, called Tuckahoe, to care for his children and manage his estate. This unusual request Peter honored as an act of pure friendship, accepting no compensation for his services. His own lands were left in the care of an overseer.

So it was that Thomas Jefferson's earliest memory was being handed up to a servant on horseback and sitting on a pillow for a long distance. The family traveled by horse and coach. While Tuckahoe was only about fifty miles from Shadwell, the roads then were hardly more than mud tracks, and the journey took three days.

Jane had spent much time in this house as a child and felt comfortable here. And Tom had lots of playmates. In addition to his sisters, there were two Randolph girls and one boy, aged four, also named Thomas. But instead of growing up as the oldest boy in the family, he now found himself the younger.

Peter Jefferson hired a tutor to teach the three Randolph children and Tom's two older sisters, Jane and Mary, as well. When Tom was five years old, he was allowed to join the older children in the

* By the calendar year then in effect, he was born on April 2, 1743. But the new style, adopted when Tom was still a boy, changed the date to April 13. This is the date he would celebrate.

little tree-shaded white frame building that had become their school. Tom later called this "the English school" and spoke of it happily. But he learned early one of the harsh lessons of slavery: One difference between blacks and whites was that only whites went to school. None of his black friends could go to school with him. Years later he would remember this and propose that all black youths be educated "to tillage, arts or sciences" until twenty-one, and all black girls to age eighteen, and this at "public expense."[1]

As Tom was growing up, his father and his father's good friend Joshua Fry, who was a professor of mathematics at the College of William and Mary in Williamsburg, were often partners on surveying expeditions. When Tom was six years old, the two men were commissioned to find and mark the boundary line between Virginia and North Carolina. They were gone for many weeks.

When the men returned, Tom listened wide-eyed as his father told stories of their adventures. As he marveled at his father's courage in fighting wild animals and snakes, he was learning the importance of perseverance in the face of danger.

Now Peter and Joshua Fry were able to use their findings—and their skills—to draw a map of Virginia. It was the first such map ever attempted since Captain John Smith had made a conjectural sketch in 1609. Tom watched his father and Professor Fry bending over the great table in the family room, their surveys, drafting instruments, and broad sheets spread out all over it. When the map was completed, they told Tom, they would send it to London, to Thomas Jeffrys, geographer to the king, to be printed. Tom was still a young boy, but he felt some of his father's excitement at what he had accomplished, his pride in what he had taught himself.

When Tom was nine, Peter decided that the Randolph children were sufficiently grown to allow him to move his family back to their own home in Shadwell. Soon after, Tom was sent to study in the Latin School of the Reverend William Douglas, minister of St. James Parish, in Northam. Once again, he was uprooted from home, this time separated from his entire family (the school was fifty miles from Shadwell), but he would be just five miles from Tuckahoe and his Randolph cousins. He boarded with the Douglas family for the school year and spent summers and holidays at Shadwell.

During the summers, when Tom was back in Shadwell, his father found more time to spend with him. He taught Tom mathematics. Outdoors, he taught him to shoot deer and wild turkey and to paddle a canoe on the Rivanna. He taught him to portage—to carry a canoe overland between two waterways—and when he was satisfied that Tom could handle a canoe properly, he gave him one of his own. Tom learned to watch for logs, rocks, and tree roots in the water and to repair the canoe himself if it needed mending. "Never ask another to do for you what you can do for yourself" was a principle of his father's he never forgot.

When Tom was ten, his father gave him a rifle and sent him into the forest alone on a hunting expedition in another attempt to encourage self-reliance. But try as he might, Tom couldn't shoot anything. Eventually he came upon a wild turkey caught in a pen. Excited, he tied it to a tree with his garter, shot it, and brought it home in triumph. But Tom never learned to enjoy hunting. He preferred to leave the animals in their natural habitat.

Peter also taught Tom to ride and made an expert horseman of him. As he stalked or rode through the southwest mountains or fished on the banks of a stream, he came to know the forest as few did. He learned the names and habits of all the birds, and he knew all the insects of the fields.

The strong bond of love and respect for his father was being strengthened daily. As Tom grew, the physical resemblance between father and son became striking. Tom was fast becoming as tall, sinewy, and agile as Peter. And he was trying harder and harder to emulate him.

Peter's library was small but select. His editions of Shakespeare and the Bible were well-worn. In spite of Peter's lack of formal education, he worked hard to educate himself, and he instilled in this first-born son a passion for books and a love of language that would remain with him all his life.

Evenings at Shadwell were often spent around the fireplace, where the family gathered to sing together, Tom's sister Jane leading the choir. By now there were eight children. Jane, three years older than

Tom, was the oldest and Tom's favorite. Then there were Mary, Thomas, Elizabeth, Martha, Lucy, and finally the twins, Anna and Randolph, who had been born when Tom was twelve. Two other boys, born at Tuckahoe, had not survived.

His sister Jane could read music and had a good ear for tunes. She encouraged Tom to learn and helped him with his reading and his music. When Peter realized that Tom was interested, he bought him a violin.

A violin was called then by its old-fashioned name *fiddle*. It was almost the only musical instrument known in the back countries of the colonies. Larger instruments like the piano and organ were difficult to ship from Europe and almost impossible to transport overland to the western regions. And young gentlemen were not supposed to "puf out the face in a vulgar fashion"[2] in order to play a wind instrument. In Virginia, fiddling and singing contests became a part of rural social life, and almost every farmhouse with a boy in it could boast a fiddle.

During spring holidays, Tom and Jane often wandered together through the woods near Shadwell. Now and then they stopped to rest for a while on a log, and Jane sang folk songs, hymns, or psalm tunes, Tom accompanying her on his ever-present fiddle. Later they returned to Shadwell, their arms laden with bunches of wildflowers.

In the spirit of Virginia hospitality, Shadwell was open to constant guests. Since it was near the main road, it was a stopping-off place for all passersby, including the great Indian chiefs on their way to and from Williamsburg, the colonial capital. A pleasant relationship developed between the native Americans and the Jefferson family, and Tom spent much time with them. He was thrilled when Ontasetté, the chief of the Cherokee people, made a beautifully balanced canoe paddle as a gift for him.

Peter had been enlarging Shadwell since shortly after the family had returned there from Tuckahoe. Tom often stood with his father at the drawing board, watching as he planned new buildings.

He was growing up in a comfortable society that had been created by planters who cultivated tobacco and relied on slave labor. He experienced no physical hardships and no financial worries. His family was the center of his life. The freedom, openness, and simplicity of up-country life were subtly coloring his values.

He saw only the better aspects of slavery in his own home: his father patiently teaching his slaves to be carpenters, millers, wheelwrights, shoemakers, and farmers; his mother in her sitting room in the morning with her daughters and her servants, busy with household tasks—one spinning, one basting, another winding yarn. A plantation had to be almost completely self-sustaining.

At the same time, men like Peter Jefferson faced the perils and adventures of life on a new frontier. These developed their physical strength and their spirit of daring, their sense of industry and responsibility, traits they passed on to their sons. They taught their sons early that every privilege carries with it a duty.

In 1754 Peter was chosen to represent Albemarle in the Virginia House of Burgesses, which was the lower branch of the General Assembly and considered singularly important in colonial government.

Then, in June of 1757, when Tom was just fourteen years old, Peter suddenly became ill. His physician and good friend, Dr. Thomas Walker, visited him professionally on June 25. He called again three times in July and came almost every day during the first two weeks of August, but his efforts were all in vain. He could not save his friend. Peter died on August 17. He was fifty years old.

In the frightening confusion that ensued at home, Tom felt helpless and alone. He wandered off by himself to seek solace in his mountains—the mountains he had climbed with his father—the mountains he had come to know and to love even as he loved and revered his father. With his father gone, Tom would be responsible for himself and, as the eldest son, responsible to some degree also for his mother and his sisters and baby brother. He was overwhelmed by a sense of sadness and of loss. But Virginians didn't cry. He'd heard his mother say that many times. She explained that death was not to be discussed, grief not indulged. "Look to the brighter side," she admonished him. "Gallop over your grief as you gallop over the hills of Albemarle."

Peter took care of his son in death as in life. His dying instruction was that Tom should receive a "thorough classical education," but he cautioned his wife not to neglect the "exercise requisite for his bodie's [sic] development."[3] Physical exercise was as important as mental stimulation. And he had made careful provision in a detailed will, drawn several months before, for the welfare of his wife, his two sons, and his six daughters. He did *not* weigh the scales heavily in favor of his elder son in spite of the fact that primogeniture—the English tradition of the right of the eldest son to inherit the entire estate of his parents—was the law in the colonies.

But to Thomas he did leave "my mulatto fellow Tawney, my books, mathematical instruments, and my cherry tree desk and book-case" and "either my lands on the Rivanna River and its branches, or my lands on the Fluvanna in Albemarle County . . . which of the two he shall choose"[4] when he reached the age of twenty-one.

But it was his father's love of learning more than anything else that was Peter's legacy to Tom. The *only* thing Tom wrote about his father—almost sixty-four years later, when he was seventy-seven—reveals what was most important to Thomas Jefferson throughout his lifetime: ". . . being of strong mind, sound judgement, and eager after information, he read much and improved himself."[5]

Books would become for Tom the means to "improve *himself*," the keys to unlock the mystery of any subject he wanted to learn. Books would become the passion that ruled and shaped his life.

In deference to Peter's wishes, Tom's guardians decided that he should study with one of the most scholarly and prominent clergymen in the colony, the Reverend James Maury. Reverend Maury's home was fourteen miles from Shadwell, in the shadow of what was referred to as "Peter's Mountain." Tom would live with him during the week and return home on Saturday. He would be living in the Piedmont region full time for the first time since he was two years old.

James Madison (cousin of the future president), James Maury, Jr., John Walker, and a boy from nearby Louisa County named Dabney Carr were also students there. The four boys, all between the ages of fourteen and sixteen, soon became close friends. But Tom's special friend was Dabney Carr. Dabney was the same age as Tom, and the two were very much alike in temperament and personality. Dabney often went home with Tom on weekends.

Sometimes they rode the several miles to what they called "Tom's Mountain," an 850-foot peak that soared in lonely splendor above the broad Piedmont valley, climbed a tree there, and looked out at the vast panorama spread out beneath them. To the south and east they could see the heavily wooded forests of the Piedmont with its countless varieties of trees and flowering shrubs. To the west the tiny village of Charlottesville lay between the mountains. North was Peter's Mountain, higher than Tom's, and beyond it, the Southwest Range. Tom thought this had to be the most beautiful place on earth.

At Reverend Maury's Latin School all the boys had horses. They rode every day, following mountain trails. Tom became a fearless rider. But he loved to walk also—this was his favorite exercise—and he often tramped through the woods, alone or with a friend.

Reverend Maury taught them well, and it was here that the world of books and learning was fully opened to Tom. Maury had a library such as Tom had never seen. He owned over four hundred volumes.

In Maury's class Tom learned a "correct" knowledge of Greek and Latin, and developed an appreciation for languages as tools of communication and as a pathway into history and mythology. He often read the Greek poet Homer in his canoe trips down the Rivanna, or the Roman Virgil when he stretched out on the grass in the shade of an oak tree. And he was learning to read these authors in the original.

Tom was a good student, but he did have one bad habit. He frequently avoided preparing his lessons, simply not doing his assigned homework. When the situation became serious, he'd find an excuse for a "holiday." Too shy to request this himself, he would persuade a friend to do it for him. Once the time off was granted, he remained secluded in his room until he had completed his assignments and knew his work perfectly. Then he returned to class triumphantly.

By the age of sixteen Tom was tall and slim, with broad shoulders, a long, thin neck, jutting chin and prominent cheekbones, a wide-winged nose, chestnut-red hair, and an abundance of freckles. He wasn't particularly handsome, but there was a kindness apparent in his expression, an intelligence shining in his soft hazel eyes. He was well over six feet, an unusual height in those days, and he had large hands and feet. His friends called him "Tall Tom." He was strong, and he stood straight as a gun barrel, but his movements were awkward, and he was very shy. He was indifferent to clothes and not at all concerned with his appearance. His awkwardness, though, was more than made up for by his bubbling enthusiasm for everything he did. He loved the outdoors, he was a careful observer of all the plants and animals in the forests, he knew the Bible, a few English classics, was well grounded in Greek and Latin, and had perfected his knowledge of French. He had taken dancing lessons with his sisters and knew the minuets, reels, and country dances that were popular then. He loved to dance, and he loved to play the tunes on his fiddle as well. He carried himself with the bearing of one familiar with a saddle, a gun, a canoe, and a minuet—a country-bred youth who had never been required to till the soil but had the ease and freedom to enjoy country life.

Now it was Christmas, the year was 1759, the last year of the reign of George II of England, and Tom sat easily astride his spirited mare, a fiddle in a light case hung around his neck and a roll of minuets newly arrived from London in his saddlebag. Jupiter, his body servant, rode just behind him, as befitted a wealthy young gentleman of colonial Virginia. Jupiter was just Tom's age and traveled with his young master wherever he went. They were on their way to a party at the home of Colonel Nathaniel West Dandridge, whose son and daughter were close to Tom's age.

As he headed toward Colonel Dandridge's, Tom was a little apprehensive about what he would find there. But, humming to himself as he rode along, he told himself not to worry because he danced well, and the girls seemed to like him. When he arrived, he was immediately welcomed into the large, merry group of young people who had assembled for the festivities, and all his fears dissolved. There was a frankness, an earnestness about him, a friendliness in his tone, that immediately attracted people to him. Besides, he knew all the country fiddle tunes of the day. He kept his friends entertained for hours, although some of the girls would have preferred that he dance with them rather than play the fiddle all evening.

The next morning, another guest who lived nearby arrived. Shabbily dressed in coarse hunting clothes, he seemed older than most of the young people there. Tom learned that he was almost twenty-four, and he was married. He appeared to be popular with the others, though, and was greeted joyously. His name was Patrick Henry.

Tom was drawn to him immediately and discovered that Patrick fiddled also. Patrick didn't know the classical music that Tom did, but he had a keen ear and could follow any tune that Tom played. They made music together all evening.

Christmas then was observed as a season, not just a day, and Virginians celebrated it from Christmas Eve until Twelfth Night with joyful abandon. Fall plowing had been done, and the harvests of tobacco had been gathered. Hogs had been slaughtered and butchered, and sportsmen had brought in abundant supplies of wild game and occasional deer or even black bear from the swamps. Barrels of oysters were in the cellars.

Every house was an open house, and no invitations were necessary for visiting. Slaves never put in less than a cartload of wood for the fireplace, and the doors were open to everyone. Hosts never knew in advance how many guests would share their dinner or sleep in their beds.

The young people remained at Colonel Dandridge's for two weeks—occasionally all moving to a neighboring plantation and then returning—all the while dancing and singing, feasting, and drinking toasts to King George II.

During these weeks a warm friendship began between Tom and Patrick. Patrick had a gaiety that was contagious. He was a favorite of all the young people. They loved his stories, his practical jokes, and his infectious good humor. Tom saw Patrick simply as a fun-loving young man. Patrick Henry probably didn't recognize in this shy, redheaded boy a future political leader. Neither could imagine that a partnership would develop in which Tom would be called the pen of a revolution, and Henry its tongue.

When the festivities at Colonel Dandridge's ended, Tom and Jupiter began the leisurely ride home. But Tom felt restless. He had a vague feeling that he was wasting time. He realized that he had been partying for two weeks, and that when he returned to Shadwell he would be caught up in yet another round of parties. His sister Mary was to be married on January 24. Again, time would be taken away from his studies, and the expenses incurred on the estate would be considerable.

As he rode home through the Virginia hills, he began to ponder the alternatives. At Colonel Dandridge's he had heard talk of the College of William and Mary, and he began to think of the possibility of attending the college himself.

So on New Year's Day, 1760, he visited his guardian and his mother's cousin, Peter Randolph. Together, they agreed that he should attend William and Mary. Then two weeks later, on January 14, he summoned all his courage and wrote a letter to another guardian, John Harvie, who was the manager of his business affairs, requesting permission to attend college:

Sir,

I was at Colo. Peter Randolph's about a fortnight ago & my Schooling falling into Discourse, he said he thought it would be to my advantage to go to the college, & was desirous I should go, as indeed I am myself for several reasons. In the first place as long as I stay at the Mountains the Loss of one fourth of my Time is inevitable, by company's coming here & detaining me from school. And likewise my Absence will in a great Measure put a stop to so much Company, & by that Means lessen the expenses of the Estate in House-Keeping. And on the other Hand by going to the College I shall get more universal Acquaintance, which may hereafter be serviceable to me; & I suppose I can pursue my Studies in the Greek and Latin as well there as here, & likewise learn something of the Mathematics. I shall be glad of your opinion.[6]

It was an awkward letter, with no hint of the graceful prose that would later win Tom such wide acclaim, but it set down the reasons that were important to him then and would remain so throughout his life. It made its point. In the late winter of 1760, Thomas Jefferson bid his mother, his sisters, and his brother good-bye, gave his sister Jane a special hug, mounted his horse, and set off across the country to Williamsburg. His saddlebags were filled with his books and his music. Jupiter went with him.

As Tom turned his mare southeast toward Williamsburg, he was headed toward his first contact with urban life. Williamsburg, 150 miles away, was a compact, civilized town on the edge of a vast, untamed continent. Tom had heard stories about it, but until now his world had been rimmed by the horizon of his little mountaintop. Now he was breaking through that rim, on his first great adventure.

It was cooler than usual when they arrived, and the early spring flowers were unexpectedly covered with snow. He and Jupiter went directly to his cousin Peyton Randolph's home, one of the most beautiful in all Williamsburg, to pay his mother's respects to her family, and had dinner with them. But Tom declined the Randolphs' invitation to stay with them. He wanted to live at the college—in the dormitory.

II
A restless mind

The College of William and Mary kept Tom waiting for two weeks while he was examined for his fitness to enter, since he had not attended the Grammar School there. The hopeful young student-to-be thought the Grammar School "disagreeable and degrading" for serious college students, because it "filled the College with Children."[1] But the delay gave him time to explore his new surroundings. Eighteenth-century Williamsburg was a carefully planned town with some of the handsomest public buildings to be found in the English colonies. It was little more than a village but had many metropolitan attractions similar to those found in New York, Philadelphia, and Boston.

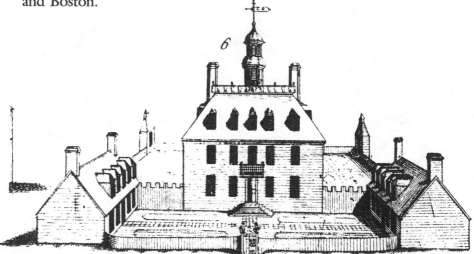

The Governor's Palace. It was here that eighteen-year-old Thomas Jefferson was invited to dine and to play the violin in weekly chamber music concerts. Later, he would live here as governor of the state of Virginia.

The main street, Duke of Gloucester Street, stretched for nearly a mile, with the College of William and Mary at one end and the Capitol at the other. Public buildings lined the street in between. The Governor's Palace, the official residence for the governors, was a handsome and imposing brick building, a symbol of the power and prestige of the crown in colonial Virginia.

The streets of Williamsburg were not paved, so they were very dusty. The soil was chiefly sand, and the breezes from the York and the James rivers raised clouds of dust, but this kept the city free of mosquitoes.

In all, there were about a thousand people living in Williamsburg in about two hundred houses. It was the capital of Britain's largest colony in North America, and its principal function was government. Its ties with England were perhaps closer than those of any other British colonial capital. The aristocracy of the Tidewater liked to think that going to Williamsburg was like going to court in London.

Tom was dazzled by what he saw. The town was well stocked with all sorts of goods and the best provisions and liquors. Students from the college, in their black gowns and tricornered hats, were everywhere. During sessions of the legislature, politicians in velvet coats, frontiersmen in their coonskin caps, and judges trailing scarlet robes all made their way to the Capitol.

Tom, who had never been interested in clothes, began now to notice these things. He saw fashionable clothes he had never seen before. Ladies in imported gowns made of the best silks and damasks from China, satins and velvets from Europe, and fine linen from Ireland, and gentlemen in brightly colored knee breeches, ruffled shirts, and tight-fitting waistcoats attended receptions and dances. There were frequent balls during the fall and winter months at the Raleigh Tavern, but some were also held in private homes or, occasionally, at the Capitol.

To Tom, who had spent his life in the country, Williamsburg offered much that he had never known before. It was here that he saw his first play. From the beginning of the eighteenth century, Williamsburg had been a center for theater. The first theater in America was built there, and, in addition to local troupes, companies came from London and New York to perform. Tom enjoyed them all.

Perhaps most important for Tom, the town offered the intellectual companionship that he craved, as well as the books, bookstores, and library to satisfy him. In colonial America books were the main source of information for educated men and women. Newspapers as well as good conversation at dinner tables and coffeehouses helped to sustain the learned few, but for the most part it was the carefully assembled bookshelf that kept the mind stimulated.

On March 25, 1760, just a few weeks before his seventeenth birthday, when the results of his entrance examinations were finally reviewed, Tom was admitted to an advanced class at the College of William and Mary. Williamsburg would be Tom's chief residence for the next seven years, one of the most important periods of his life.

The College of William and Mary had been founded in 1693. It consisted of four schools: grammar, philosophy (which Tom attended), divinity, and one for Native Americans. All the faculty, except for one professor, Dr. William Small, were Anglican clergymen.

A Scotsman of great learning, Dr. Small was also the only member of the faculty who did not get involved in student brawls. Nor did he believe in the power of a master to inflict punishment on a student. Quiet and dignified, he earned his students' respect. Small was teaching

The College of William and Mary, where sixteen-year-old Thomas Jefferson was introduced to the philosophy of the Enlightenment.

physics, metaphysics, and mathematics when Tom first arrived at William and Mary. Then, because of the dissensions and unrest at the college, several of the professors were dismissed, and Small was appointed interim professor of philosophy.

Perhaps the greatest attribute of William and Mary was its location in the city of Williamsburg and its proximity to the seat of government, for its students were, by birth and station, potential leaders. Their education consisted in part of listening at the doors to the House of Burgesses. As they watched the leaders of the province in action, they came to know and to respect them as people and, unconsciously, to absorb valuable training in the operation of government. The college became the training ground for some of the greatest minds of the Revolution.

At the time that Tom enrolled in William and Mary he was probably more mature than many of his fellow students. No doubt he looked down on them and on some of his teachers, too. But Dixon and Hunter, the bookstore in Williamsburg, had more than three hundred titles in stock, and Tom found himself drawn there regularly. He bought books extravagantly. What he learned that year he learned on his own. The college did not furnish the guidance and direction he had hoped to find.

But he didn't try very hard, either.

During this first term the attractions of the town overwhelmed him. He made friends easily and went to horse races with them,

joined a secret society called the Flat Hat Club (the first college fraternity in British America devoted entirely to fun), attended plays, dined with relatives, and danced at balls at the Raleigh Tavern. He became conscious of all the pretty girls around him, and he began to spend money on his clothes.

He joined his friends in complaining bitterly about the food being served to them in the dormitory, until the housekeeper was finally instructed "to serve fresh and salt meat for dinner, to provide puddings and pies on Sundays and two weekdays, and to see that suppers were not made up of different scraps, but were the same for every table."[2] All of this left him little time for his studies.

Soon after he had arrived in Williamsburg that spring, Tom had an unexpected visitor, Patrick Henry. Patrick told Tom that he had recently been admitted to the bar in Virginia and had studied for only three months to accomplish this. His decision to "read" law had been an impulsive one, he explained, made just after they had been together at Colonel Dandridge's. His country store had gone bankrupt, and he had to earn money to support his wife.

Tom was delighted to see him and immediately invited him to come to his room for dinner that evening. He reminded Patrick to bring along his fiddle. Noticing that Patrick looked thin and hungry under his heavy hunting shirt and deerskin breeches, Tom asked Jupiter to try to get a snack of cold meat and warm corn bread for them. Patrick continued to spend evenings with Tom throughout the school year, often staying the night and regaling Tom with stories of the backwoods. Frequently he borrowed books from him, but Tom soon realized that Patrick always returned them a few days later unread.

At William and Mary, Tom met John Page, who came from a highly influential family. John lived at Rosewell, a magnificent three-storied mansion in Gloucester County built by his grandfather and said to have contained thirty-five rooms. John Page was also the nephew of the wife of William Randolph, who had been Tom's father's friend. Tom and John were in the same class, had many of the same interests, and became good friends. Tom began to spend weekends at Rosewell with John and eventually came to love him as a brother.

They spent many happy evenings together on the great lead rooftop of Rosewell, absorbed in their shared enjoyment of astronomy. Their friendship would last for half a century.

John Page, whom Jefferson met at college. They remained close friends for fifty years.

* * *

Near the end of this first summer in Williamsburg, Tom returned to Shadwell for a short vacation. When he was ready to return to school, he was overjoyed to learn that his friend Dabney Carr was planning to go back with him. As they talked about their studies, Tom suddenly realized how much time he had wasted during his first term. He was appalled—and embarrassed—at what he had done. Characteristically, he wrote a letter to one of his guardians, stating that "the cost [of my schooling] should be taken from my inheritance. It is not fair that it come from the estate."[3] His wise, understanding guardian replied, "If you have sowed your wild oats thus, the estate can well afford to pay the bill."[4]

Tom returned to Williamsburg determined to change his ways. He would study, he would learn, he promised himself. He would justify his guardians' faith in him. And he would behave in a manner he knew would have made his father proud. But he did not give up his friends. Nor did he relinquish all opportunity to have fun. He still attended occasional horse races and fox hunts and frequently attended the balls at the Raleigh Tavern. He was a much sought-after young man and a leader among the young people.

Anne and Betsey Blair, who lived in a beautiful house on Duke of Gloucester Street, became close friends of Tom's. Often, the young people would gather at the Blair house to sit on the steps and sing in the dusk of a warm evening. They were a close-knit group, all of whom loved the gossip, the whirl of social life, the excitement that was "Devilsburg," their nickname for the town.

But Tom's best friends were John Page and Dabney Carr, whom he often called "Currus." Page was a good student with an interest in science and classical literature that matched Tom's, but he was not as determined. Years later Page would say of his friend: "I never thought . . . that I had made any great proficiency in any study, for I was too sociable, and fond of the conversation of my friends, to study as Mr. Jefferson did, who could tear himself away from his dearest friends, and fly to his studies."[5]

Out of the chaos that was the College of William and Mary at that time, Tom managed to secure a university education. He found the *only* man of knowledge and ability, the one skillful and sympathetic teacher at the college, Dr. William Small.

When Tom returned to school for his second year it was Dr. Small who set him on a course of inquiry and learning that would continue for the rest of his life. The two were immediately drawn to one another, the older man recognizing in the eager young student a curiosity and a thirst for learning equal to his own, while Tom found in Dr. Small a friend, a teacher, and a surrogate father.

Unmarried and lonely, Small made Tom his daily companion. The two often went for long walks together. Small had a logical mind, and he loved to talk—and to watch the enthusiasm with which his young student absorbed the ideas he put forth.

In the time he spent at William and Mary, Small did much to liberalize the college. He made a drastic departure from the teaching methods of the day by abandoning the ancient practice of compelling students to memorize lessons and instituting instead the modern lecture system. Dr. Small talked to a group of students, then asked that later, in their rooms, they write out what they remembered and understood of what he had said. Some days Tom wrote for hours.

He was excited by all that he was learning and found that Dr. Small had reawakened in him the love for math that his father had initiated so many years before. Math would remain his favorite subject, and he would use it as a familiar, obedient servant. From that time on, whenever he went on a journey, he carried a box of instruments and a book of logarithms, and he always had a ruler in his pocket. "We have no theories here," he said of math, "no uncertainties remain on the mind; all is demonstration and satisfaction."[6]

Dr. Small taught him also to observe objects with a scientist's eye. But what Tom learned most from this teacher was delight in the exercise of the mind and in the world of ideas.

John Page, too, would call Dr. Small his "ever to be beloved professor" and credit him with inspiring his own abiding interest in all branches of math. Small was one of those rare teachers who spark the imagination of their students and who forge new paths of learning for them. Thomas Jefferson said later of this unusual man that William Small had probably fixed the destinies of his life.

But William Small did more than just introduce young Thomas

to the world of ideas. Perhaps equally important, Small introduced him to a small, brilliant group of people and a way of life he had never known. These men exposed the young boy from Albemarle to the world of culture—the world of taste, refinement, and scholarship that existed beyond the boundaries of Virginia.

First among these new acquaintances was George Wythe (pronounced to rhyme with Smith), at thirty-four a thoughtful and distinguished jurist and one of the most learned men in Virginia. Wythe, in turn, introduced Tom to Governor Francis Fauquier and the extraordinary circle that surrounded him.

Fauquier, who had arrived in Virginia in 1758, when he was almost sixty years old, was a country gentleman from Hertfordshire, England, and a Fellow of the Royal Society. According to rumor, he had lost his entire inheritance to Lord Anson, a famous admiral, in a single night of gambling. Anson, out of compassion for Fauquier, saw to it that he was given an appointment as governor in the New World. All who knew Fauquier knew that, despite his faults, he was a man of high personal and official honor.

When Fauquier first arrived in Virginia, he was astonished to see a hailstorm on July 9 that broke every window on the north side of the palace and left enough ice on the ground for him to cool his wine and freeze cream the following day. He measured the hailstones, and thereafter, he kept a daily record of the Williamsburg weather. Thomas Jefferson would eventually do the same at Monticello and in Washington.

Governor Fauquier, historians tell us, "left an impression of taste, refinement, and erudition on the character of the colony,"[7] and certainly on the redheaded youth whom he made his companion.

Impressed by the soft-spoken and brilliant young man, by his open mind and his willingness to consider both sides of a question, Fauquier invited the eighteen-year-old student to the palace for dinner with Dr. Small and Mr. Wythe. At his table Tom was privileged to hear stimulating conversations and exciting new ideas. The governor was a lover of good music and held a weekly amateur chamber concert at the palace. When he learned that Tom could fiddle, he asked him to join their music group. Tom was delighted.

So it was that once a week he and Dr. Small would be joined by the slender but erect and vigorous Mr. Wythe, always meticulously dressed, his dark gray eyes glowing with warmth and intelligence, in a stroll to the palace. There, in the parlor, while Wythe and Small listened, the young boy and the governor of Virginia would tune up their fiddles and, in the candlelight that illuminated the room, with the portraits of the king and queen of England gazing down at them from the wall, would play some of the music recently arrived from Europe.

There were others in the group, also. Tom, not yet proficient enough to play first violin, played second. Occasionally, he played the cello. His cousin John Randolph played first violin. Robert Carter, a close friend of the governor, lived near the palace and often played the harpsichord or the German flute. At times John Page was invited to join the group. He and Tom frequently practiced together on weekends at Rosewell.

Tom had loved music since he was a young boy, but it was probably during these years in Williamsburg that music became for him "the favorite passion" of his soul. No doubt it was the first time in his life that he heard music performed in concert.

It was after dinner at the palace, as they sat around the table and drank port wine, that Tom absorbed more than any student at William and Mary had ever learned at college. For it was the governor's conversation that did the most to form Tom's mind. Governor Fauquier, whom Tom would later call "a compleat gentleman" and "the ablest man who ever filled the office,"[8] was a man of the world and a scholar, an openhearted and open-minded eighteenth-century gentleman interested in new ideas and good talk. At his table Tom heard talk of the theaters of Old London, of works of art, of the governor's colleagues at the Royal Society. He heard discussions of the problems of taxation and of recent meteorological phenomena. He heard the literary gossip of London, and he heard of strange lands that existed far beyond Virginia. He was learning to judge things by other than Virginia standards—to see the world in perspective.

At the governor's table with Professor Small, George Wythe, and Francis Fauquier, Thomas Jefferson, a shy young man eager to learn and quick to absorb all that these accomplished men had to offer, recognized even then the rare privilege that was being afforded him. This table, he knew, was truly his university.

* * *

Just before Tom's nineteenth birthday, in the spring of 1762, Dabney Carr told him that the great Cherokee Indian chief Ontasseté would speak to his people, who were camped just outside the town, that evening. Ontasseté was about to journey across the sea to England to put his people's needs before the king.

Tom was excited to see his father's old friend. He had always had an interest in the Cherokees and particularly admired Ontasseté, whom he remembered from the chief's earlier visits to Shadwell. Tom still cherished the canoe paddle Ontasseté had made as a gift for him then. Tom was curious about the Cherokee culture and anxious to learn more about it. He had recently become troubled by the sharp contrast between the wilderness that the native Americans represented and the extravagant social whirl that was Williamsburg.

Now he and Dabney walked together to the campsite and, in the splendor of a full moon, they listened spellbound as the great warrior and orator bid his people good-bye. The scene "filled me with awe and veneration, although I did not understand a word he uttered," Tom described it.[9] There was a magic in the air that night. As Tom stood listening, he could feel his own father's presence. He never forgot it.

In April, shortly after he heard Ontasseté speak and just two years after he had arrived in Williamsburg, Tom left the College of William and Mary but continued to study privately with Dr. Small. The two men remained friends until Small's return to England later that year.

It was through Small that Tom became familiar with the pattern of thought called the Enlightenment that was prevalent in Europe at the time. It preached freedom of the mind, and for Tom, it laid the foundation for his own belief in the power of human intelligence. Dr. Small introduced him to the work of Isaac Newton, the English mathematician and astronomer; to the works of Francis Bacon, the brilliant English statesman, essayist, and philosopher who believed that knowledge is power; and to the writing of John Locke, whose ideas were being discussed in Williamsburg then. Locke put forth the revolutionary philosophy that "since reason is the only sure guide which God has given to man, reason is the only foundation of a just government." Accordingly, "since governments exist for men, not men for governments, all governments derive their just powers from the consent of the governed."

Locke had also written: "The state of nature has a law to govern it, which obliges everyone; reason, which is that law, teaches all mankind . . . that being all equal and independent, no one ought to harm another in his Life, Health, Liberty, or Possessions."[10]

Tom considered this simply common sense.

III
Old Coke

At the time that Tom completed his course of study at the College of William and Mary there was no law school in Virginia. Young men interested in pursuing a career in this field "read" law under the direction of an established attorney. Tom's good fortune was that, when he and Dr. Small decided that this was the path Tom should travel, George Wythe consented to take him on as a student.

Wythe was simple and kindly. Considered one of the most learned men in Virginia, he had read widely in English and Roman law and was a distinguished classical scholar. And he loved to teach.

In 1754, Wythe served as acting attorney general for the Colony of Virginia. From then until the outbreak of the Revolutionary War he sat in the House of Burgesses and carried on an extensive legal practice.

George Wythe's first, and most significant, assignment to his young student was to study *Littleton's English Law with Coke's Commentaries*. Sir Edward Coke was an English jurist and the leading authority on the common law. He had been a champion of the common law as opposed to the encroachments of the Crown.

Wythe referred to it as "the lawyer's primer" and told Tom that it had also been the lawyer's primer at the Inns of Court in London for more than a century. Wythe urged him to read it carefully—line by line—and to write down in a commonplace book his understanding of what he was reading. This was easy for Tom. At William Small's suggestion he had been "commonplacing" his ideas all through college.

Wythe recommended, also, that Tom attend any of the courts that were open to him—the General Court when it was in session

George Wythe, Jefferson's "faithful and beloved mentor in youth and most affectionate friend through life."

and the House of Burgesses—and record his impressions of what he heard there. He advised him, too, to continue his study of the classics and of philosophy, impressing upon him the importance to a lawyer of general knowledge.

Tom heeded his advice. He attended sessions at the General Court, as he had been doing whenever he could since he had first come to Williamsburg. He loved to stand at the door and listen to the battles of wit that were waged inside.

Tom also did some clerical work there. He looked up cases in the law library at the Capitol for Mr. Wythe and drew papers in Mr. Wythe's office. At the same time that he struggled to master *Coke upon Littleton,* he delved deeply into history, political science and philosophy. He continued to perfect his French and Latin as well as his science and math. "Variety relieves the mind as well as the eye . . . ," he wrote.

Deciding that a "great inequality is observable in the vigor of the mind at different periods of the day," he divided his own day into five parts: "rise at 5 A.M. (earlier in summer); read til 8: books on agriculture, botany, zoology, chemistry, anatomy, religion; 8–12: read Coke and Littleton; 12–1: read politics; afternoon: read history, then run a mile into the country and back, because 'my father believed that running keeps a man fit,'" he said. "And in the evenings read rhetoric, oratory, literature and language."[1]

Later, he squeezed in the study of Anglo-Saxon since English law came from the Saxons. Tom didn't realize that he had neglected to plan time for meals. But Jupiter saw to that. He put meals in front of him while he was working and hovered till he ate.

Some days Tom studied fifteen hours a day, reading and then abridging and commonplacing what seemed important to him. In this way he found the essence of what he was reading. He kept two separate commonplace books, one containing his ideas on law and government, the other devoted to literary extracts from Greek, Latin, and English classics. He continued this habit for the rest of his life. Often, he rose at dawn and studied until 2 A.M. On those days his only recreation came at twilight, when he ran to a particular stone that stood a mile outside of town.

George Wythe was a systematic man who encouraged Tom to work out a schedule of study. But he didn't expect him to fill every moment from dawn until bedtime with reading. Tom imposed this demanding schedule on himself. "I was bold in the pursuit of knowledge,"[2] he explained to a friend years later.

Tom continued to study law intensely for five years. He did this at a time when one could enter into the practice of law with just a meager understanding of it, as he knew his friend Patrick Henry had done just a short time before. But he was not in a hurry. "For with slight efforts how should one obtain great results? It is foolish even to desire it,"[3] he copied from Euripides into his *Literary Bible*.

In the fall of 1762 Tom met Miss Rebecca Burwell. He was nineteen and a half; she was sixteen.

Rebecca, who had been orphaned at the age of ten, lived with her aunt and uncle, the William Nelsons of Yorktown, good friends of the Pages. William Nelson was a member of the Governor's Council—and often its presiding officer—so the family was frequently in Williamsburg. No doubt Tom and Rebecca met there, within the circle of young aristocrats to which they both belonged. They saw each other at John Page's home also, where both were frequent guests.

Rebecca was referred to then as "enthusiastic," which probably meant that she was a lively and vivacious young lady. On the flyleaf of one of his books Tom wrote:

> Jane Nelson is a sweet girl,
> Betsy Page is a neat girl,
> Rebecca Burwell is the devil:
> If not the devil she's one of his imps.

Tom soon fancied himself in love with her.

In spite of his feelings for her, near the end of December of 1762 Tom decided to leave Williamsburg and return to Shadwell. Dabney Carr went home, also. They remained there for nine months.

Tom worked on his land, but he did not neglect his reading. Many days, he and Dabney, their books under their arms, tramped across the fields and up the hill to their special spot on Tom's Mountain, stretched out on the grass under their favorite oak tree, and read aloud in the shade of its branches. Here they could look out on the world as they discussed the contents of their books, talking about government, politics, philosophy, and literature. And here, one day, they made a pledge that whoever should die first would be buried beneath this tree.

Sometimes they paddled Tom's canoe on the streams of the Rivanna. They spent time, also, visiting their friends on neighboring plantations. The Christmas holidays found Tom visiting Lewis Bur-well, Rebecca's brother, at the great house of the Burwell family. Lewis was one of Tom's classmates. He had inherited the plantation, just two miles from Rosewell, on his father's death. Tom brought with him a roll of new minuets for the ladies. Rebecca was one hundred miles away in Williamsburg.

It was there, on Christmas Eve, that her profile, which she had cut in black paper for him to carry in his watchcase, was ruined.

The ancient house, in a state of decay, had a leaking roof and rats coming out of its thick walls at night to plague the young man. Describing the scene to his friend John Page, Tom wrote: "I am sure if there is such a thing as a Devil in this world, he must have been here last night and had some hand in contriving what happened to me. Do you think the cursed rats . . . did not eat up my pocket-book, which was in my pocket, within a foot of my head? And not contented with plenty for the present, they carried away my jemmy [skillfully]-worked silk garters, and half a dozen new minuets I had just got to serve, I suppose, as provision for the winter. . . . You know it rained last night, or if you do not know it, I am sure I do. When I went to bed, I laid my watch in the usual place, and going to take her up after I arose this morning, I found her . . . all afloat in water, let in at a leak in the roof of the house, and as silent and still as the rats that had eat my pocket-book."[4]

Tom went on to tell his friend that, in attempting to take the soaked picture and watch paper out of the case to dry them, he had torn them both beyond repair.

Soon, Tom returned to Shadwell, and Dabney left to take a job in a law office in Charlottesville. Tom missed him. He missed their walks through the woods to the top of his mountain, and he missed the joy of sharing their thoughts and ideas. "All things appear to me to trudge in one and the same round: we rise in the morning that we may eat breakfast, dinner and supper, and go to bed again that we may get up in the morning and do the same. You never saw two peas more alike than our yesterday and today," he wrote to Page.[5]

Perhaps, far from his friends, from Williamsburg, and from "Belinda," as he often called Rebecca, life lost its interest. In writing to his friends, Tom, as was the custom then, usually tried to disguise her name in case others should read the letter. He referred to her also as *Adnileb, R.B., Becca,* and *Campana in die,* which, in Latin, means *bell in day.* In one letter he used the masculine pronouns *he* and *him* to further mislead any readers.

Tom continued to unburden his heart in long letters to Page and to ask his advice about Belinda. But one letter, written on January 20, was not sent off for two months, a sure indication of the leisurely temper of the times.

And Tom continued to wrestle with "Old Coke"—he was "tired of . . . [the] old dull scoundrel."[6] Nonetheless, he filled his commonplace book with notes on the law. He was beginning to think of the law as something that lives and moves.

Tom remained at Shadwell for many months after Christmas, alternately studying, overseeing the plantation, and writing letters to his friends. In fact, he was already becoming an inveterate letter writer. Family tradition tells us that his mother, too, was an unusually fine writer who composed many lively, intelligent letters. Tom came by his talent naturally.

Thoughts of Rebecca continued to haunt him, but he did nothing more than write to his friends about her. To Page, as Tom addressed him, he asked: "How does R.B. do? Had I better stay here and do nothing, or go down and do less? . . . Inclination tells me to go, receive my sentence, and be no longer in suspense; but reason says, if you go, and your attempt proves unsuccessful, you will be ten times more wretched than ever. . . ."[7] Rebecca knew nothing of his turmoil.

A few months later he wrote to his friend Will Fleming, "I have thought of the cleverest plan of life that can be imagined. . . . you marry S__y P__r [Sukey Potter], I marry R__B__, join and get a pole chair and a pair of keen horses, practice the law in the same courts, and drive about to all the dances in the country together."[8] But in the same letter he told Will how pretty Jenny Taliaferro was and sent greetings to Patsy Dandridge.

Most days at Shadwell, though, he arose in the morning when

the hands of the clock on the mantelpiece in his room could be distinguished in the gray light of early dawn and read until sunset. Then he crossed the Rivanna in his little canoe and walked up to the summit of his beloved mountain. He began to think of someday building a house there.

It was at that time that he began to collect his own library of the best books in every branch of human knowledge. In the eighteenth century a well-educated man was expected to be interested in many things. In this respect, Tom was typical of his generation. The difference lay in degree. He simply went further. He remained a lifelong student and would eventually become the most widely read American of his generation. He studied because he liked to. "Nature intended me for the tranquil pursuits of science,* by rendering them my supreme delight," he would say later.[9]

Tom continued to study independently at Shadwell for the next few years. But he did return to Williamsburg periodically to consult with Mr. Wythe, to attend the sessions of the General Court, to buy books, and, during the winter months, to attend the functions given by the gentry there.

Although Tom spent much time studying, he also loved the fine arts, practiced his violin three hours a day, and often danced away the evenings or spent them with friends at backgammon or chess. He managed to find time for everything.

October 1763 found Tom in Williamsburg again. He had come to attend a ball at the Apollo Room of the Raleigh Tavern on October 6. There he would finally see Rebecca again after almost a year. And there, he decided, he would finally express his feelings to her.

In colonial America the tavern was the heart of the community, and the Raleigh Tavern, built in 1735, was the most famous in Virginia. It was the center of political and social activity, for it was here that many of the distinguished lawyers who came to Williamsburg to attend court and the legislators who came to attend sessions of the House of Burgesses sought accommodations for the duration of their stay in the capital. In addition to the rooms in which the men lodged, the tavern contained the post office at which the burgesses could

* Science meant *all* knowledge.

pick up their mail, meeting rooms, a bar, and game rooms. Advertisements of all kinds were posted on its walls. It was a hub of activity.

Here, the wisest men drank with the abandon of the times. And here in the Apollo Room, ablaze with candlelight, musicians on the balcony played flutes, fifes, and fiddles as the young people danced quadrilles, minuets, and the Virginia reel. At these times, the room echoed with laughter and song.

The day of the dance dawned bright and clear. But Tom spent hours indoors composing what he would say to Belinda, rehearsing it over and over again. He would tell her how he felt about her and of his hopes and plans for them. But when he danced with her in the Apollo Room that evening, she completely disarmed him and he found himself tongue-tied. "Good God! . . . a few broken sentences uttered in great disorder and interrupted with pauses of uncommon length were the too visible marks of my strange confusion," he described it the next day in a letter to Page, who had not yet arrived in Williamsburg. Belinda made no attempt to ease his pain and embarrassment.

"For God sake, COME," he ended the letter.[10] He was filled with despair and shame. Beneath the mask of a gay, aristocratic bachelor lurked a sensitive, shy young man.

A few weeks later, though, when a group of young people were at Carter's Grove Plantation, Tom was a little more successful. At least he was able to talk to Rebecca. He told her, then, that he had to go to England, and while he did not ask her to marry him, he did indicate to her that if she were willing to wait for him, he would ultimately ask the question.

But Belinda was not willing to wait. Perhaps she needed a passionate declaration of love, rather than a carefully thought-out plan that involved waiting. Within six months she was engaged to be married to Jacquelin Ambler, who was somewhat older than Tom and had really made up his mind.

Tom's love affair with Rebecca was carried on mostly in his mind, and we might speculate that at this time he was more in love with the *idea* of love than with Rebecca herself. Early marriage was the rule then, but there was a certain reluctance in Tom's attitude— an unwillingness to settle down before he had had an opportunity to complete his studies and see some of the world.

With Belinda's refusal, Tom turned his back on the social life of Williamsburg and buried himself in his studies. But first, to give vent to his disappointment, he copied into his Commonplace Book several passages disparaging women:

"Mortals should beget children from some other source and there should be no womankind; thus there would be no ill for men,"[11] and "O Zeus, why hast thou established women, a curve deceiving men, in the light of the sun?"[12]

Women in Jefferson's Virginia had few educational opportunities, and so he may have decided, too, that conversations with men were more stimulating. During the next few years his friendships with them, and particularly with John Page and Dabney Carr, intensified.

He copied into his notebook another—very different—passage from Euripides:

"Nothing is better than a reliable friend, not riches, not absolute sovereignty. Nay more, the crowd is not to be reckoned with, in exchange for a noble friend."[13]

Throughout his life he always spoke lovingly about his friends. He wrote to John Page many years later: "But friends we have, if we have merited them. Those of our earliest years stand nearest in our affections."[14]

As Tom continued to read and to study, he continued also his habit of commonplacing his thoughts, making certain that he never used two words where one would do. By now his two commonplace books, one containing his political views and the other his *Literary Bible,* were filled with the maxims and principles that impressed him then and would govern the rest of his life.

He even tried his own hand at writing. Sometimes, late at night when he couldn't fall asleep, he would begin to write a love story. But he complained to Dabney Carr that whenever he did this he always fell asleep before he finished the third page.

He read the Greek classics for their practical value and in order to derive from them a moral lesson. "The moral sense, or conscience, is as much a part of man as his leg or arm,"[15] he would tell a nephew many years later. He learned from Homer and Euripides to look at life with courage, and that man could never justify his existence unless he lived for others as much as for himself.

To the restless minds of Tom and his friends, minds that refused to accept the principle of authority, the classical authors offered new and practical views that they were ready to accept.

As they absorbed the philosophy of the Roman poets, who stressed the need to work for the future without thought of present or personal reward, they were unknowingly preparing themselves for the roles they would play in the coming fight for freedom.

IV
Listening at the door

As Tom approached his twenty-first birthday, he was fast gaining a reputation as the most inquisitive young man in the colony. Tall and quiet, he displayed the varied influences that had been at work shaping him. Physically fit, with the sturdiness of a frontiersman, he was equally at home in the palace drawing room. His love of nature and the outdoors was matched by his eagerness for long hours of reading and study.

On the day he came of age, April 13, 1764, he officially came into the inheritance left by his father. According to the stipulations of the will he was to choose between the lands on the Rivanna and the Fluvanna rivers. He easily chose the 2,650 acres along the Rivanna on which his father had lived, leaving the Fluvanna lands for his brother, Randolph. His lands included Shadwell and his little mountain, as well as 2,500 acres in other locations, and many slaves. Shadwell, however, would not become his until after his mother's death. But he continued to call it home, paying his mother rent, and lived there when he was not in Williamsburg.

Now he stopped charging the expenses of his education against his father's estate and assumed the role of head of the family. He began to keep careful records of what he spent and saw to it that his mother, sisters, and brother were well provided for.

At this point, he had an assured position. He was the sole owner of a fine estate, and, as his father before him, he was honored by being named a vestryman of his parish and a justice of the peace in Albemarle. As a justice, for several days each month, he sat (without pay) with a small group of gentlemen justices on a raised "bench" beneath the royal coat of arms in the handsome brick courthouse of

Albemarle to hear cases dealing with property settlements in their community.

According to an old British custom, Tom had a double row of sapling locust trees planted along the drive to the house at Shadwell to mark this birthday. But he did not spend the day at home. He remained in Williamsburg, involved in a mathematical project. They were about to measure the height of Williamsburg above water. There were two streams, one a tributary of the James River and the other of the York, both navigable to within a mile of the town.

"Everything is now ready for taking the height of this place above the water of the creeks," he wrote to Page from "Devilsburgh" and asked him to come and take part in the interesting affair.[1]

Tom had also recently become concerned with the navigation of the stream that flowed through his own lands. As far as he knew, no tobacco had ever been transported to Richmond via the Rivanna. Passage on the river was obstructed by rocks. Everything grown at Shadwell, therefore, had to be hauled to Richmond by land, a tedious and expensive job. Tom explored the river on his own by canoe, paddling as far as he could. Then, when he was stopped by rocks, he waded into the stream and attempted to dislodge some of them. When these moved easily, he realized that the stream could be made navigable.

He immediately began to raise money for the project and interested his neighbor, Dr. Thomas Walker, a member of the House of Burgesses, in it. By the next summer a channel in the river was opened, and the harvests were floated to market on rafts. This was his first official involvement in a local project, and he was proud of it.

Tom continued his study of law in Williamsburg and paid close attention to what was happening in the legislature. He often stood at the open door of the lobby—for there was no gallery then—listening to the stormy debates that were taking place in the Assembly about the Stamp Act.

The Stamp Act required placing a stamp that certified payment of a tax on all newspapers and most commercial and legal documents, including playing cards, pamphlets, diplomas, bills of lading, and marriage licenses. The tax had been proposed by George Grenville, chancellor of the exchequer, and passed by the British Parliament in January 1765, to take effect the following November. It would be the first direct tax on Americans and was designed to raise revenues to support the new military force in the colonies—some 10,000 redcoats stationed there—ostensibly for the colonists' protection but actually a hint of the strained British-Colonial relations.

But the colonists objected. They called it taxation without representation. Since they were not represented in the British Parliament, they felt that it did not have the right to lay taxes on them.

It was at this time that Patrick Henry was elected a burgess to represent Louisa County. One of the members of the Virginia Assembly resigned his seat in order to bring in Henry because of his "audacity, his tempestuous eloquence, his fighting spirit."[2]

Henry dominated the scene in Williamsburg from the first moment of his arrival there. In spite of his appearance (his clothes were coarse and worn), whenever he pleaded a case, his eloquence on the rights of man soon changed the opinions of the assembly from contempt to admiration. He was poor and a failure as a merchant, but he came from a good family and was far more intelligent and cultured than he appeared. He quickly became "Mr. Henry" to all of Williamsburg, an indication of respect and honor.

May 1765 found Mr. Henry in Williamsburg to take his seat at the spring session of the assembly. As he frequently did when he was in Williamsburg, he stayed with Tom. The Stamp Act had recently become law, and sentiment was running high against it, but no one knew quite what to do. There was no thought of formal resistance. A year before the House had quietly denied the right of Parliament to tax the colonies, but the Stamp Act had been passed in spite of their objections. Now Patrick Henry sat, day after day, waiting for one of the older members to reopen the subject. Only three days of the session remained.

Then, on Thursday morning, May 30, 1765, Patrick and Tom walked to the Capitol together. They were a study in contrasts as they made their way along Duke of Gloucester Street. Tom was dressed in the height of fashion, in a coat of elegant red fabric, its large cuffs trimmed with braid and buttons, a tight-fitting waistcoat, and breeches that stopped at the knee. The buckles on his shoes had been polished till they shone. Patrick was wearing plain hunting clothes. He carried an old copy of *Coke upon Littleton,* borrowed from Tom, under his arm. Tom had noticed his friend hastily scribbling on the flyleaf of the book earlier that morning.

When they reached the Capitol, Patrick proceeded to his seat in the House of Burgesses, and Tom, with his younger friend John Tyler, who was also still studying law, took his place at the door to the Assembly Room.

The other burgesses, all members of the wealthy planter aristocracy, were dressed in the best London had to offer, pointing up even more the shabbiness of Henry's clothes. Some were fearful of what Henry might say and hoped to stop his efforts by humiliating him. But Patrick seemed unconcerned about the impression his appearance made. Shortly after the meeting was called to order, with an unfailing instinct for choosing the right psychological moment, Patrick Henry rose slowly from his seat and began to speak haltingly in a flat, quiet voice. Only his eyes revealed his passion. Tom and John could sense the tension in the air.

Patrick began to read what he had scribbled on the flyleaf of Tom's book:

—Resolved, That the settlers brought with them to this colony all the privileges, franchises, and immunities held by the people of Great Britain.

—Resolved, That the colonists are entitled to all the privileges, liberties, and immunities of citizens and natural born subjects as if they had been born within the realm of England.

—Resolved, That taxation of the people by themselves, or by persons chosen by themselves to represent them is the distinguishing characteristic of British freedom.

—Resolved, That colonists should be governed by their own Assembly in the article of their taxes and internal police.

—Resolved, therefore, That the general assembly of the colony has the sole right and power to lay taxes and impositions upon the inhabitants of this colony. Every attempt to vest such power in any other persons would destroy both British and American freedom.[3]

When the reading of these resolutions was finished, Tom heard his friend begin to speak in his usual faltering way. But as he spoke, he seemed to gain confidence. Gradually, he straightened his shoulders and stood erect, his voice picked up, and soon his words rang through the room. People were hearing for the first time words that they had thought but had been too afraid even to whisper to themselves. "Old Coke's" comments on the Magna Charta were suddenly being transformed from dead law into living truths.

Tom stood spellbound as he heard Patrick thunder, "Caesar had his Brutus, Charles the First his Cromwell and (pausing) George the Third . . ."

"Treason," cried Mr. John Robinson, the speaker. "Treason! Treason!" echoed from every part of the House.

But with amazing presence of mind, and not hesitating for an instant, Patrick calmly concluded, "may profit by their examples. Sir, if *this* be treason, make the most of it."[4]

Here for the first time was the rhetoric of revolution against the king of England. "He speaks as Homer wrote," Tom whispered to John Tyler. Virginia, Tom suddenly realized, was on the road to separation from the mother country.

There was much confusion and wild shouting. Some of the resolutions were passed by a large majority. But the last one, the strongest of all, was passed by just one vote after what Tom thought was a "most bloody" debate.

Distressed by the passage of this resolution, portly Peyton Randolph came puffing out of the door, saying, "By God, I would have given five hundred guineas for a single vote."[5]

With this speech Patrick Henry became a challenge to the ruling class in the colony. He became the spokesman for the common people, the champion of colonial liberty, and caused Virginia to be divided into two parties: the Whigs, or Patriots; and the Tories, who remained loyal to England.

It is probably hard for a reader of this generation to understand the mixture of love, pride, and veneration with which the colonists regarded the mother country—its parliament and king, its church, its literature, its history. Even though many of the members of the House considered themselves Whigs, they could not give up England as long as there was any hope of a just union with her.

* * *

After the vote, Patrick Henry, not used to the politics of legislation and always impatient with detail, assumed his job was done. He put on his buckskin breeches, mounted his horse, and rode home.

Perhaps Tom suspected that the fight was not yet over, for the next morning found him back at the Capitol very early. There, in the Burgesses' chamber, he met his uncle and former guardian, Colonel

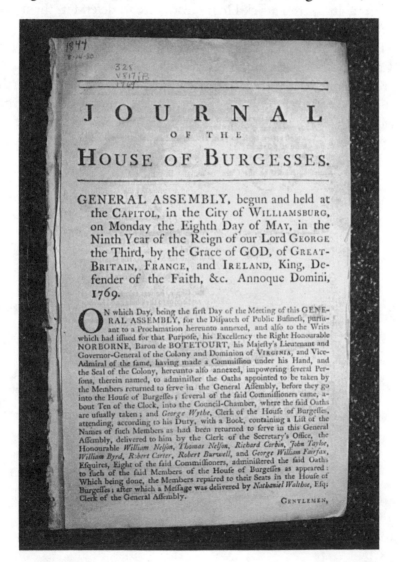

A page in the *Journals of the House of Burgesses.*

Peter Randolph, a Tory member of the House. Tom watched as Randolph sat down at the clerk's table and began to turn over the journals of the House. He had a dim recollection, he told his nephew, of a resolution of the House being *expunged* many years ago. He would like to find the record of the erasure. He wanted a precedent. Then the House bell rang, and the House convened. Tom resumed his stand in the doorway. A motion was made to expunge the last resolution, and with Patrick Henry not there to defend it, the motion carried. The resolution was erased.

Peyton Randolph, George Wythe, Edmund Pendleton, and Robert Carter Nicholas were among the members who were opposed to the resolutions and whose influence in the House had until then been unchallenged. Suddenly, though, the common people, whom Patrick Henry represented, were coming to the forefront—the very people whose rights Thomas Jefferson would later champion.

V
Lawyer on horseback

In the summer of 1765 Tom set aside his studies and his concern about the growing political tensions in the colony and went home to Shadwell for a happy celebration. His sister Martha, then nineteen, was about to marry Dabney Carr.

From the time that Dabney had first come home from the Reverend Maury's school to spend vacations with Tom at Shadwell, Tom, Dabney, and Tom's sisters Jane and Martha had spent much time together on Tom's mountain. Now Dabney would be his brother-in-law as well as his friend.

Soon after the wedding Dabney and Martha moved to a small house in nearby Charlottesville, where Dabney opened an office and began to practice law.

Tom missed them but was happy for the time he was able to spend with Jane. He shared with her a dream that was beginning to take shape in his mind to someday build a home on his mountain. Together they pored over the plans and descriptions of gardens in a book he had recently purchased, *The Theory and Practice of Gardening*.

He talked to her about the Stamp Act, about the worsening relations with England, and repeated conversations he had overheard in the Raleigh Tavern in Williamsburg.

Jane was Tom's equal in intelligence—her mind and her spirit were in tune with his—and the depth of her understanding, the earnestness and simplicity of her nature, endeared her to him.

Now, while they were making the most of their time together, Jane suddenly became sick. Within a few days she died. Tom was devastated. He would never fully recover from this loss. Half a century later he would speak of her to his grandchildren—especially after church when the psalm tunes that they had played and sung together when they were young brought her vividly to mind—as though she had only recently died.

Now he gathered their music books and locked them in a cupboard. He shut her harpsichord and put away his violin. He couldn't play without her. Then, as he would do all through his life, he turned to work as a distraction from sorrow. He went back to Williamsburg and buried himself in his books.

For several years Tom had been dreaming of traveling. He and John Page had often talked of going to Europe together. Now he decided to make a trip to New York. He would stop along the way in Annapolis and in Philadelphia. Spring planting on the plantation was finished, and he felt he could afford the time.

On May 11, 1766, he set out on a journey that would take him out of Virginia for the first time in his life. Jupiter went with him. The day dawned bright and clear and his spirits were high. Filled with excitement and anticipation, he was not prepared for the mishaps that beset him. On the very first day, he told John Page in a letter, his horse ran away with him twice, and he feared his neck would be broken. On the next day, as he rode over the vast countryside in his open carriage, there was a sudden torrential downpour, and not a single house in sight at which to stop and ask for shelter. The rivers swelled from the heavy rains, and on the third day, as he crossed the unfamiliar Pamunkey, he went through water so deep it flowed over the cushion he was sitting on. Then a wheel of his carriage hit a submerged rock with such force that he was almost catapulted into the stream. But the weather finally cleared, the rain stopped, and the sun came out to dry him.

From then on Tom had a leisurely trip through the lovely Virginia spring, stopping along the way, as was the custom, to visit friends.

When Jefferson arrived in Annapolis, the capital of Maryland, he found the people in the midst of rejoicing over the repeal of the Stamp Act. It had been withdrawn in March as a result of fierce colonial opposition and pressure from London merchants interested in American trade, which was being hard hit by a colonial boycott. Other than newspaper reports, this may have been the first sign that he had of the community of interest among the colonies.

From Annapolis Tom rode through Delaware and on to Pennsylvania. There he saw beautifully cultivated fields of grain, clover, and flax, and "luxuriant orchards." Years later he would encourage the growth of crops like these in Albemarle.

Philadelphia, which stretched for almost two miles along the Delaware River, had a population of about eighteen to twenty thousand people. Tom stopped there to be inoculated against smallpox.

Tom was introduced to the celebrated Dr. William Shippen, a specialist in this new form of medicine. Dr. Shippen performed the procedure, and a lifelong friendship between the two men began.

There was at this time much heated debate about the safety of the crude method of inoculation being used. It was against the law in New York and was performed only rarely in Virginia. But Tom's interest in science far outweighed any fear of danger, and he had decided to run the risk. When he was well enough to travel again, Tom continued his journey to New York.

This was the first time that Tom had seen the large cities of the New World. He was fascinated by what he saw, particularly the richness of detail and design in the architecture. But the trip north by horse and carriage had been a difficult one, so he decided to sail home. He went by boat from New York to Norfolk, Virginia, then drove with Jupiter from there to Shadwell.

Patrick Henry had been admitted to the bar after three months of preparation. It took Tom five years from the time he began to "read" with Mr. Wythe to consider himself ready. Early in 1767, shortly before his twenty-fourth birthday, Thomas Jefferson took the necessary examinations and was admitted to the bar of the General Court by George Wythe, his "faithful and beloved mentor in youth and most affectionate friend through life."[1]

The General Court consisted of the governor and his council. It sat in Williamsburg twenty-four days each April and October. Tom practiced also in the county courts. The cases he handled were, for the most part, typical of an agrarian community. They involved problems of the ownership of land: boundaries, partitions, sales and inheritance as well as cases that arose out of the institution of slavery.

In his methodical way Tom kept careful records of these cases, listing them in a notebook by dates and number. He separated the cases by neatly drawn lines, leaving space in between where, in his small, precise handwriting, he could fill in later developments. He built a fine reputation and was retained as counsel by many of the outstanding men of Virginia.

During the five years that he practiced law, he traveled frequently to the county courts and to Williamsburg, where he maintained an office. Generally he went on horseback or in a one-horse chair. Jupiter, who had been his companion for more than ten years, accompanied him. Tom trusted him with everything. Jupiter carried his luggage, paid the saddler and the ferryman, bought bread and candles, and even lent his master some money when he ran out. On court days, when farmers came to the various county seats to buy and sell lands and slaves, Tom had an opportunity to get to know "ordinary citizens" and so gained an invaluable insight into their thoughts.

As a lawyer, Tom was very different from Patrick Henry. Henry, all fire, was more advocate than lawyer, seeking to win his case by passionate oratory. Tom was cool, unemotional, and always prepared. He had all the facts carefully and systematically written down before he began. He knew the law thoroughly, and he stated the issues clearly and concisely. He spoke softly, with ease and elegance. It was impossible for him to shout. If he raised his voice, it soon grew husky. But he was an impressive speaker who held the attention of his listeners.

Tom was aware of his own limitations. He didn't attempt what he knew he could not do. Rather, he used the talents he possessed to become a legal counselor and office lawyer. He was liked and trusted. When there was a case to be tried before a jury, he sometimes asked Dabney Carr or Patrick Henry to argue it for him. His own joy derived from digging into the case and discovering evidence for them to present.

VI
An imaginative leap

Just a few months after he was admitted to the bar, on August 3, 1767, Tom entered in his *Garden Book:* "inoculated common cherry buds into stocks of large kind at Monticello."[1] He had planted an orchard and had begun to graft cherry trees on the hillside just below the site he had chosen for his home.

He had long ago resolved to someday build a house atop "his" mountain and had confided his dream to his sister Jane and to his friend Dabney Carr. He knew when he and Dabney had studied together under the old oak tree there that this was where he would live. In those days, when he contemplated life as a bachelor, he had thought he might name his house *The Hermitage,* but now he decided to call it *Monticello,* from the Italian for "little mountain," pronouncing it the Italian way, *Montichel'lo*. It had a more romantic sound to him.

There was no precedent in America or England then for the romantic, impractical spot on which Tom chose to build. It took an imaginative leap to plan a house high on a hilltop, on the edge of a wilderness. But the site commanded a majestic panorama of the surrounding countryside, and the misty Blue Ridge Mountains that he loved were visible in the distance. His eye, like his mind, seemed to be searching for this broad view, this view of beauty, and for a new horizon beyond the mountains.

In order for him to build on his mountain, timber would have to be cleared from the summit and the stubborn soil leveled. Long, steep roadways would have to be built up the mountain and maintained. He knew there was a severe water shortage at Monticello, and water would have to be carried from a great distance. But Tom had found the one spot on his land that he loved and where he might study and enjoy nature, and he had made up his mind to build there.

The study of architecture as a profession did not exist in the colonies at that time, so when Tom decided that he wanted to build his own house, he did what was most characteristic of him. He turned to books to learn how. It was an example of his intellectual curiosity, of his willingness to say, "I don't know," and then to try to find out. It was consistent with everything he did throughout his life.

He decided, too, that he would not only design his home but also be one of its builders. He would engage in actual construction whenever he could. In this way he would learn even more.

Tom taught himself mechanical drawing also and became a competent, although limited, draftsman. He never simply sketched to convey an idea but always solved a problem by first working out the proportions mathematically. He was a designer whose architectural drawings revealed a patient beauty.

It was during his student days at William and Mary that Tom had bought his first book on architecture from an old cabinetmaker who lived near the college gate. He probably acquired additional books on the subject from Richard Taliaferro,* George Wythe's father-in-law, who had studied architecture in England and with whom Tom often discussed the subject. These books were the beginning of a collection that would ultimately be considered among the most important of its kind in America.

Now Tom turned to the writing of an Italian architect named Andrea Palladio. Palladio, next to Michelangelo considered the most important architect of the sixteenth century, believed that architecture must be governed by reason and by certain universal rules that he recognized in some of the ancient Roman ruins.

Tom felt himself being drawn to the mathematically correct classical proportions of the buildings Palladio had designed. When he began to think about the shape Monticello should take, he knew that he wanted a simple, classic design with clean lines and carefully planned symmetry. He thought about the Georgian manor houses that he was familiar with, such as Tuckahoe, Carter Hall, and Rosewell,

* pronounced *Tolliver*

but this was not what he wanted. He liked their grand scale but not their style. Nor did the buildings in Williamsburg appeal to him any longer. Now he called them a "rude, misshapen pile."

As Tom was beginning to feel the stirrings of political revolution, he was unconsciously searching for an architectural style that represented a break with the English architecture of the day, one that incorporated the principles of Roman design into a "new creation" that reflected America.

One month after his twenty-fifth birthday, on May 15, 1768, Tom made an agreement "with Mr. Moore that he shall level 250 f. square at the top of the mountain at the N.E. end by Christmas, for which I am to give 180 bushels of wheat, and 24 bushels of corn, 12 of which are not to be paid till corn comes in. If there should be any solid rock to dig we will leave to indifferent men to settle that part between us."[2]

Then, on Friday, July 14, Mr. George Dudley began making bricks for him. Tom had decided to use brick despite the fact that most houses then were built of wood. Frame houses, he felt, were too susceptible to fire. He wanted a durable material. He determined that the bricks would be seven and a half inches by two and a half inches and that they would be made in kilns at the top of the mountain. In this way he would not have to purchase the bricks, nor would they have to be hauled up the mountain. But he did note in his book that it required six hogsheads (barrels) of water to make two thousand bricks. Nails and woodwork were made on the mountain also, but the windows and "a small parcel of spare glass to mend breaks" were ordered from England.

The design Tom decided upon was a practical one that called for a two-story central house with two one-story cottages, or wings, on either side of the mountain, spread over a vast area and situated so as to take full advantage of all the spectacular views. Two L-shaped terraces would run from the main house to the cottages. The house would be simple yet dignified, solid but beautiful.

He decided, also, that instead of the ordinary rectangular rooms found in most colonial Virginia houses, his rooms would be polygonal—or many-sided. Once again, he was moving away from traditional ideas and using his imagination to develop an architectural style that was uniquely his own.

And he would take advantage of his hillside site. He would put all the outbuildings beneath the terraces behind the house. In this way the kitchen, laundry, smokehouse, meal room, pantry, and dairy would be hidden from view. They would be reached by an underground passageway.

This was the beginning. Monticello would be shaped and reshaped over a period of forty years, almost the rest of his life, for in his mind it would never be finished. He was making a home, and a home would have to change to accommodate changing family needs. It would become, too, a laboratory in which he could experiment with new and fresh architectural ideas. Tom was always willing to tamper; his genius is reflected in his ability to unite the old with the new.

For the rest of his life, no matter where in the world he was, Tom's heart would be on his mountaintop.

Jefferson's ink sketch of his first plan for Monticello, *c.* 1769.

VII
First assignment:
first failure

During the two years following the Stamp Act the people appeared to Tom to have fallen "into a state of insensibility and inaction."[1] The seething excitement over the Stamp Act had subsided. Yet the colonies were moving quietly but steadily toward a crisis.

They were, in fact, being pulled by two powerful, opposing tides—one toward the stability represented by the Old World, the other toward the opportunity and openness of the New.

In England, King George III, who had ascended the throne in 1760 at the age of only twenty-two, had learned from his failure to enforce the Stamp Act that he could not raise revenues that way. So he decided, at the suggestion of Charles Townshend, his flamboyant chancellor of the exchequer, to raise revenue from the colonies in a different manner, one he hoped they wouldn't notice.

In the summer of 1767, at just about the time that Tom was beginning to plant his orchard at Monticello, Townshend convinced Parliament to pass the famous acts that bear his name, the Townshend Acts of Trade and Revenue.

The most important of these imposed a small import duty on glass, white lead, paper, and tea. Unlike the Stamp Act, this tax was an *indirect* customs duty payable at American ports. Since the colonists had objected to *internal* taxes, Townshend thought he could accomplish his purpose by imposing *external* taxes. He considered the colonial uproar over taxes "perfect nonsense."

But the Virginians were not pleased. In their eyes the Townshend Acts threatened the authority and even the very existence of the colonial governments. This new tax on tea was particularly annoying because it affected so many. About one million people drank tea twice a day. Some even drank it when alcohol was not available. To add further insult to injury, the revenues from the tax would be used to pay the salaries of the royal governors and judges in America as well as the British expenses of colonial defense.

Once more a wave of protest swept through the colonies.

Then, in March 1768, a seemingly unrelated event gave impetus to the growing dissatisfaction over the Townshend Acts. After a long and difficult illness, Governor Fauquier died. Fauquier had done much to cultivate Tom's tastes and to expand his horizons. ". . . at [the governor's table] I have heard more good sense, more rational and philosophical conversations, than in all my life besides," Tom would comment later.[2] He would miss Fauquier.

Now, in the absence of a royal governor, the colonists could give free expression to their feelings. "No power on earth has a right to impose taxes on the people, or take the smallest portion of their property, without their consent given by their representatives," they said.

At a House of Burgesses meeting Patrick Henry vehemently denounced the acts: "Parliament has enslaved us," he shouted. "Oppose them with steadfastness and they will be repealed. . . . We shall not yield our God-given right to tax ourselves."[3]

That spring a messenger rode into Williamsburg, carrying a letter from Massachusetts to the House of Burgesses that announced Massachusetts's intention to resist the Townshend duties by all constitutional means and asking Virginia to do the same. The messenger then continued south to deliver copies of the letter to the Carolinas and to Georgia. A network was beginning that would make communication among all the colonies possible.

Some months later, on October 21, 1768, Tom and a group of his friends joined the throngs lining Duke of Gloucester Street when, just at sunset, the Right Honorable Norborne Berkeley, baron de Botetourt, arrived in Williamsburg from England to become the new governor of Virginia. Botetourt came with all the pomp of royalty: a large retinue of servants and baggage; a magnificent stagecoach; and six white horses to draw it. Botetourt was loyal to his king, but he was honorable and friendly, and the people soon grew to love him.

As when a new king comes to the throne Parliament is dissolved, so, on the arrival of a new governor, the House of Burgesses was dismissed and writs issued for the election of a new assembly. Thomas Jefferson was named a candidate for the county of Albemarle.

The House of Burgesses was composed of gentlemen, men of talent, training, and experience, but only gentlemen who were acceptable to ordinary citizens. Every eligible voter was *required* to vote at every election, under penalty of one hundred pounds of tobacco. So Tom spent the winter months at Shadwell, canvassing his county—visiting each voter and asking for his vote.

But it was not an easy task for him. He was a shy aristocrat. "His manners could never be harsh, but they were reserved towards the world at large," his second cousin Edmund Randolph wrote of him. "To his intimate friends he shewed [sic] a peculiar sweetness of temper, and by them was admired and beloved."[4] He was *not* a backslapper or a hand-shaker. But Mr. Jefferson, as he was called now, was well liked by all the people. They knew him to be kind and fair. They knew he was a fine lawyer who understood the farmers' needs as well as those of the aristocracy.

The custom of the time required candidates to entertain the voters on election day. And on this early spring day in 1769 Shadwell was the perfect spot. The locust trees were in full bloom, and the plantation was lovely. His mother held open house for him, serving punch and cakes throughout the day.

The details of the election are not clear. It is not known whether the incumbent burgess, Edward Carter, retired voluntarily or ran against Tom in the election. But Tom won the election easily.

Tom and his trusty Jupiter left Shadwell for Williamsburg in early April. They had a leisurely journey to the Tidewater, then spent a month settling in and enjoying the lovely Williamsburg spring.

Shortly before ten o'clock on the morning of May 8, 1769, Tom and Patrick Henry, who was beginning to dress a little more carefully now, left their lodgings and made their way together through the large crowds lining Duke of Gloucester Street. It was a bright, sunny day, and the people had come to watch Lord Botetourt, splendid in his red coat trimmed with gold, ride in his magnificent coach from the palace to the capitol, to open the provincial parliament.

At ten o'clock, when the House bell sounded to summon the members of the House of Burgesses, Tom was no longer obliged to stand in the lobby door.

Inside the House chamber all the etiquette of legislation was scrupulously observed. This Virginia parliament was noted for its dignity. In fact, members were fined for any breach of decorum. To interrupt a member cost the offender a thousand pounds of tobacco; to speak of a member with disrespect, five hundred. As the members were paid only one hundred and fifty pounds of tobacco per day, these fines were severe.

Now, at the governor's command, eight members of the council administered the oath of office to the assembled burgesses, who stood with their hats in their hands. There were nearly one hundred burgesses being sworn in that day, one of whom was a young colonel named George Washington. George Wythe, as clerk of the House of Burgesses, was present to see his young friend Thomas Jefferson sworn in.

The burgesses then replaced their hats on their heads and walked to their own chamber.

Then, at the governor's command, they filed out of the House of Burgesses, mounted the flight of stairs to the second floor, and proceeded to the Council Chamber.

There the governor, seated on a throne, instructed them: "Gentlemen of the House of Burgesses, you must return to your House and immediately proceed to the choice of a speaker."

The burgesses retraced their steps. Once back in their House, they unanimously elected Peyton Randolph as speaker of the house. As Randolph took his seat in the speaker's chair, the mace, the traditional seal of authority—still in use in our Congress—was laid upon the table.

Again the burgesses trooped up the steps and through the halls, this time with a speaker to lead them. The governor approved their choice, and the speaker, on behalf of the House, laid claim to all its ancient rights and privileges. In reply, the governor, with great solemnity, read a short speech.

A copy of the governor's speech was given to Mr. Randolph in order "to prevent mistakes." The members made their final trek back to their own chambers and there resolved to prepare a response to the governor's "very affectionate"[5] words.

It was the custom to assign some formal duty to new members in order to introduce them to public business and to give them an opportunity to display their talents. Accordingly, the task of drafting this response, in the form of resolutions, was assigned to the freshman member from Albemarle, Mr. Jefferson.

Tom completed his task in the courtly style of the day, combining loyalty with firmness, and stating that he hoped that any question affecting Great Britain that might arise would be resolved in light of the principle that "her interests, and ours, are inseparably the same." He prayed that "Providence, and the royal pleasure, may long continue his Lordship the happy ruler of a free and happy people."[6]

When Tom was then asked to prepare the address to the governor based on these resolutions, he wrote it simply and concisely. Some of the elder members, Robert Carter Nicholas, treasurer of the colony, chief among them, were not satisfied. They wanted a fuller discussion. Mr. Nicholas rewrote it.

Tom was devastated. He was certain that he had begun his political career with a failure.

Tom was appointed to other committees during the session, but he remained a silent member, expressing his own views quietly to just one or a few people at a time. He was learning a great deal.

England had reacted angrily to the Massachusetts circular that had been sent to all the colonies earlier that spring requesting united action against the Townshend duties. In spite of this, Peyton Randolph had sent word to the speaker of the Massachusetts House that the Virginia representatives "could not but applaud them for their attention to American liberty." He went on to say that they were in full agreement with Massachusetts and would support them.[7]

England ordered Massachusetts to rescind the circular. Massachusetts refused. Lord Hillsborough, secretary of state for the colonies, then instructed the provincial governors to dissolve any assembly that approved the circular. Parliament further recommended the revival of an old statute dating back to Henry VIII that allowed the government to call to England for trial persons accused of treason outside of the kingdom. The threat was specifically directed against the "traitors" in Massachusetts, but the law could have applied to Patrick Henry and Peyton Randolph as well.

Now groups of burgesses began to meet in each other's homes. In hushed voices they pledged themselves to stand by Massachusetts. Tom listened intently as they denounced Britain's right to impose taxes on any colony and to destroy their jury system, as Parliament's proposals threatened to do.

Nine days later the burgesses responded. In a "humble address" they declared that they and not Parliament had the right to levy taxes on the colony, that it was their privilege to petition the crown for a redress of grievances and to join with other colonies in doing so, and that all trials for treason should be held within the colony, and not removed to British courts.

They further resolved that the last of these points should be incorporated into a petition to the crown, and that the resolutions themselves should be circulated to the assemblies of the other colonies. They had openly defied the British government.

At the same time, though, they assured the king that they were "ready at any time to sacrifice our lives and fortunes in defense of your Majesty's sacred person and government."[8]

The result was inevitable.

At noon on May 17, a messenger entered the burgesses' chamber and announced: "The governor commands this House to attend His Excellency in the Council Chamber." The members marched to the other end of the building. They were probably not surprised to see the governor, dressed in a suit of plain scarlet, waiting for them. He addressed them sternly.

"Mr. Speaker and Gentlemen of the House of Burgesses, I have heard of your resolves, and augur ill of their effect. You have made it my duty to dissolve you; and you are dissolved accordingly."[9]

The governor might dissolve them, but he could not dampen their spirit. They conferred hurriedly, then "with the greatest order and decorum," went immediately to the home of Mr. Anthony Hay. There, they elected Peyton Randolph moderator and decided to continue to meet as an unofficial body in the Apollo Room of the Raleigh Tavern, where so many of them had only recently danced the minuet.

* * *

Shortly after ten o'clock the next morning Thomas Jefferson signed his first significant public paper. Published as the *Virginia Association,* the document was drafted by George Mason and signed, among others, by George Washington, Patrick Henry, Richard Henry Lee, and Thomas Jefferson. Essentially, it was a nonimportation, nonconsumption agreement: The colonists would not import or purchase any manner of goods that were taxed by act of parliament for the purpose of raising revenue in America.

The list of contraband goods was enormous. Designed to stop all trade with the mother country, it included such items as meat, butter, cheese, sugar, oil, fruit, wine, paper, clothing material, and leather. Members of the association agreed to inform their correspondents in England not to send them anything until parliament had repealed the acts to which they objected. This was the first time a colonial legislature had engaged in an act of rebellion.

The women, accustomed at that time to remaining in the background, became ardent supporters also. They dressed in "Virginia cloth," or homespun, instead of the beautiful silks and laces that they had imported from England for their ball gowns. Many even gave up drinking tea.

The British government, in an attempt at reconciliation, soon agreed to new elections to the House of Burgesses. It is interesting to note that every member of the dissolved House who had signed the *Association* was reelected. Those burgesses who had not signed were not returned.

The House convened on November 7, 1769, and the members learned that, except for the tax on tea, the Townshend duties would be removed. No further taxes would be levied against the Americans for the purpose of raising revenues.

Tom felt vaguely dissatisfied. In his opinion nothing had been settled. He considered the tax on tea an affront to the American principle and the main issue with Parliament no closer to resolution than at the start of the controversy. He considered himself a loyal subject of the king, but he was firm in his belief in colonial "rights."

He was not particularly active, but he did introduce a bill giving owners the right, which the law then did not, to manumit (free) their slaves. It was defeated. Again he endured failure.

At this point he began to realize that almost overnight his interests had shifted. He was more concerned with the many problems that were developing between the colonies and the mother country than with those associated with the law. Yet in that same year, 1769, he tried 198 cases before the General Court, the largest number he had ever tried in one year.

The session lasted until December 21, when the House adjourned until the twenty-first of the following May. Tom set out for home, visiting friends in York on the way, then stopping at Monticello. It was there, on a cold, snowy day late in 1769, that, with a mixture of pride and pleasure, he watched "four good fellows, a lad, and two girls of abt. 16," begin to dig a cellar in the stiff mountain clay.[10] His dream was becoming a reality.

He returned to Shadwell on New Year's Day.

On February 1, 1770, something happened that made Tom realize how fortunate it was that he had started building at Monticello. On that day he had dinner with his family at Shadwell at about 2 P.M., then left for Charlottesville on business. Shortly after he arrived there a servant arrived and breathlessly told him that Shadwell had burned to the ground. His fears about frame houses had, tragically, been realized.

After ascertaining that no one had been injured, Tom immediately asked if anyone had saved his books. "No, master" was the reply, "but we saved the fiddle!"[11] The fiddle had cost five pounds in Williamsburg the year before.

Tom was distraught. He had lost all that he valued most in the world: his books and his papers, both private and legal.

On February 21 he wrote to John Page:

> My late loss may perhaps have reached you by this time; I mean the loss of my mother's house by fire, and in it of every paper I had in the world, and almost every book. On a reasonable estimate I calculated the cost of the books burned to have been 200 pounds sterling. Would to God it had been the money, *then* it had never cost me a sigh! To make the loss more sensible it fell principally on my books of common law, of which I have

but one left, at that time lent out. Of papers too of every kind I am utterly destitute. All of these, whether public or private, of business or amusement, have perished in the flames. I had made some progress in preparing for the succeeding General Court, and having, as was my custom, thrown my thoughts into the form of notes, I troubled my head no more with them. These are gone, and like the baseless fabric of a vision, leave not a trace behind. The records also, and other papers which furnished me with states of several cases, having shared the same fate, I have no foundation whereon to set out anew.[12]

While he did indeed lose all his papers and all his books except the few that he had lent to friends, his *Account Books,* his *Garden Book,* and his *Commonplace Books* were all at Monticello and so escaped the fire.

His friends reacted as though there had been a death in the family. When Tom sent a letter to his friend Thomas Nelson, Jr., enclosing a list of the books he needed most, Nelson immediately replied that he had forwarded a *copy* of the list ("for fear the original should miscarry") to his book dealer. Nelson went on to assure his friend that his father, who was secretary of the Colonial Council of Virginia, would ask the courts to "indulge you with a continuance of your causes* . . . as the court has frequently done it where there have been good reasons for it."[13]

Thomas Nelson himself wrote: "I was extremely concerned to hear of your loss. . . . As I have a pretty good collection of books, it will give me pleasure to have it in my power to furnish you with any you may want."[14]

John Page also sent condolences, and George Wythe sent his young friend some grafts of nectarines and apricots and some grape vines. He wrote: "You bear your misfortune so becomingly that, as I am convinced you will surmount the difficulties it has plunged you into, so I foresee you will hereafter reap advantage from it several ways."[15]

The family moved into temporary quarters in the overseer's house, a building that had survived the fire, and Tom immediately began

* postponement of cases

to rebuild his library. He sent to Philadelphia for books and frequented the bookstores in Williamsburg whenever he was there. He also found constant stimulation in the college library at William and Mary. But he knew that the majority of books would have to be ordered from England.

As he began to draw up lists of the titles that he wanted, he realized that many were books that dealt with theories of government.

Some of the important ones that he had purchased in 1769 and now had to reorder were Locke's *On Government* and Montesquieu's *Esprit des Lois*. The more he read of Montesquieu, the more excited he became, for he realized that this French philosopher was expressing many of the ideas that he had been pondering himself these last months. Montesquieu's freshness and originality, his theory of liberty, his desire for reform and for the betterment of the human condition, were qualities that spoke to this young idealist.

He borrowed one hundred pounds from Dabney Carr to buy books. Within three years he owned more volumes than he had lost. By 1773 he had 1,256 volumes in his library. He may have spent as much as one quarter of his income annually on books. But he did more than simply collect them. He read and reread them, his mind eagerly absorbing the information and new ideas he encountered. He would be well prepared for the difficult tasks that lay ahead.

Even as he pondered the problems of government, Tom was fighting against the injustices of slavery.

In 1705 a white woman had given birth to a baby girl by a Negro father. The existing law condemned the mulatto (mixed-race) girl to slavery until she reached the age of thirty-one. During the years of her servitude she gave birth to a daughter who, in turn, gave birth to a son. The son was sold into slavery by the slave owner to whom the grandmother was bound, and the new owner claimed his service until he reached the age of thirty-one.

Tom acknowledged the legality of the grandmother's servitude. He further recognized that the Act of 1723 extended the sentence to her children. But, he pleaded in court, there was no law that reached to the grandson. "It remains for some future generation, if any should be found wicked enough, to extend [slavery] to the grandchildren and other issue more remote," he argued. "Under the law of nature all men are born free, everyone comes into the world with a right to his own person, which includes the liberty of moving and using it at his own will. This is what is called personal liberty, and is given him by the author of nature."[16]

The court was shocked. Never before had they heard opinions such as these expressed publicly. What did he mean by "all men are born free," "the law of nature," "personal liberty"? Even George Wythe, who was the attorney for the owner, was aghast at the ideas. Such was the sentiment in the courtroom that when Mr. Wythe rose to reply to Mr. Jefferson's argument, the Court interrupted, motioned him to his seat, and gave judgment in favor of Mr. Wythe's client. The boy went into slavery.

Tom had lost the case, but his deep feelings about human rights had come to the surface. He was finally expressing orally ideas that had been silently taking shape in his mind as he continued to read and reread the works of John Locke. Locke had written that all men are "naturally in" the state of nature—a state of perfect freedom and equality, "within the bounds of the law of nature."[17]

Most of the members of the Court had not yet begun to think this way.

VIII
"Worthy . . . of the lady"

By the fall of 1770, the first structure to be erected at Monticello was completed, and Tom was able to move into his mountaintop "laboratory" on November 26. A simple eighteen-by-eighteen-foot building, it was one of the wings and came to be known as the "South Pavilion." This little cottage would survive all the changes and remodelings of Monticello over the next forty years, demonstrating the careful planning that Tom gave to the overall scheme from the beginning.

By now, work had begun on the main house, and as Tom watched it taking shape, his hopes were high that he would soon be living there—perhaps with a wife.

Recently he had stopped copying into his *Commonplace Book* passages from the poets that disparaged women. Now he was copying, instead, lines from Milton's "Paradise Lost" celebrating the joy of marriage.

By this time most of his friends were already married, and Tom was beginning to feel that he was missing something as a bachelor. Certainly he was beginning to muse about the joys of married life.

Suddenly Jupiter found himself kept very busy buying hair powder and buckles as well as theater tickets for his master to go courting. It was the fall of 1770, the social season in Williamsburg had just begun, and Thomas Jefferson had met Martha Wayles Skelton.

Martha was a bright and beautiful young woman, at just twenty-two a mother and a widow. Tom, seven years older than she, fell quickly, and deeply, in love.

Martha had been married to Bathurst Skelton (whom Tom had known at William and Mary College) at the age of eighteen. She became a mother at nineteen and a widow before she turned twenty. Distraught, she took her baby, John, and returned to The Forest, her father's home in Charles City County, west of Williamsburg.

When the prescribed period of mourning was over, Martha found she had many suitors. Among those paying court to her was an eager Thomas Jefferson. While many were more handsome than he, Martha seemed to delight in Tom's intelligence and in their shared love of music. In Williamsburg, Tom had taken violin lessons from Francis Alberti, an Italian resident. Martha had been taught by the same man to play the harpsichord. Often, when Tom visited her in her father's home, the two played music together. Sometimes, he sang to her accompaniment.

One day when Tom was visiting Martha, two of his rivals happened to meet on Martha's doorstep. They were shown into a room from which they heard her harpsichord and her voice, accompanied by Tom's voice and violin, in the passages of a love song. They listened for a stanza or two. Whether it was something in the words or in the tones of the singers is not known, but the two men took their hats and left and never again pursued their suits.

Tom was very different now from the young boy who had danced with Belinda in the Apollo Room seven years before. He seems to have grown better-looking as he grew older. And he had now matured from a shy, bashful student to a successful lawyer and member of the House of Burgesses.

He made regular visits to The Forest, riding his horse from Williamsburg with his violin tucked under his arm. Jupiter always went with him. Tom courted Martha in the formal style of the times, but it was a real romance, and it would usher in the happiest period of his life.

Martha was the daughter of John Wayles, a successful lawyer, and Martha Eppes. She had been born in October 1748. Her mother died soon after her birth.

About two years later John Wayles remarried. Three girls were born of this union, Elizabeth, Tabitha, and Anne. Martha was close to all of them, but Elizabeth, three and a half years younger than she, became her special friend.

Martha was petite (an old slave called her "low") and lovely.

Her complexion was radiant, her hazel eyes large and expressive. Her thick hair was a beautiful shade of auburn. She was lively and impulsive and, at times, may have had a fiery temper. But she was gentle and warm-hearted as well.

Martha had a fine mind and was better educated than the average Virginia belle of the day. She read more widely than most and could discuss books with intelligence. But nothing appealed more to Tom than her love of music. They seemed to be unusually well matched. For the first time since his sister Jane had died, Tom had found a woman who could play music, sing, and talk on topics that interested him. Her gay spirit offset his characteristic seriousness. In her presence he could unbend, and he found himself drawn to her.

Tom spent much time visiting Martha at her father's home. He was there every ten days or two weeks. And he was always welcome. Even the servants looked forward to his coming and to his generous and regular tips. He enjoyed conversations with Martha's father, and he loved to play with little John. He looked forward to having him as a stepson and set up an account for him, with himself as guardian.

But this was not to be. The little boy died suddenly on June 10, 1771, not quite four years old. He had probably developed one of the infections common at that time that the doctors were helpless to diagnose or to treat. This was an era when two out of every three children failed to survive childhood diseases.

Tom was even more anxious now to make Martha his wife—to take her away from the environment in which she had known so much personal sorrow. But he had no home to take her to. Perhaps this was the reason, he thought, that her father was reluctant to give his consent to the marriage. The tiny house on the side of the mountain was hardly appropriate for the wealthy young widow he hoped to make his wife.

Suddenly, the little one-room cottage that had provided him with the solitude he often needed to write letters or read, away from the distractions and pressures of daily life—"the business of society," as he called it—was no longer adequate. Now it became necessary to step up the work on the main house and to engage a builder to expedite its completion.

Martha, too, was eager to begin over again—to attempt to build a new life with Tom—after a proper period of mourning for her little son.

John Wayles finally gave his consent to the marriage on November 11, 1771, and the wedding was set for the first day of the new year, 1772. A jubilant Tom tipped the servants at The Forest with abandon, then bounded off on his horse with Jupiter trailing behind. He would go to court in Williamsburg, then return home for his reelection to the House of Burgesses and to prepare for his marriage. The servants at The Forest offered toasts to Mr. Jefferson all week.

It was then that Tom wrote to his British agent once again, requesting that he send him "a Forte-piano . . . worthy of the acceptance of a lady for whom I intend it."[1]

On Christmas Eve, Tom set out for The Forest. As always, it was Jupiter whom Tom chose to accompany him. They did not arrive until after Christmas day.

Thomas and Martha were married at The Forest on New Year's Day 1772. On January 2 the *Virginia Gazette* announced: "Thomas Jefferson, Esqre married to Mrs. Martha Skelton, relict [widow] of Mr. Bathurst Skelton."[2]

The house was filled with guests, and the festivities lasted for days. It was not until January 18 that Tom set off with Martha in a phaeton for Monticello, more than a hundred miles away. Jupiter and some of the other servants had been sent on ahead.

The phaeton, a two-horse chaise that had been mended once before Tom and Martha began their journey, needed further repair after they left The Forest, so they stopped at Tuckahoe and spent a few days with the Randolph cousins. Tom and Martha did not reach Monticello until January 26. The trip had not been easy.

In Virginia there is often no serious winter until after the New Year, when all at once it comes rushing down from the north in a torrent of wind and snow. There was some snow on the ground when they left Tuckahoe, but it grew deeper as they neared the mountains. Finally it became too deep for their carriage. But they managed to push on through three feet of snow, the deepest Albemarle had ever known, until they reached their friend Edward Carter's Blenheim Plantation. Here they abandoned the phaeton. Then, just at sunset, they mounted their horses and rode the remaining eight miles over a rough mountain track.

When they finally arrived at the small clearing at the top of their mountain, Martha had her first view of her new home. Dark and deserted, the little brick house clung to the side of the steep slope. There was no light to greet them, no voice to welcome them, no fire to warm them. The house was bitterly cold, dark, and dismal.

The servants, who had waited until after dark for their master and their new mistress, had decided that the snow was too deep for travel and the hour too late for them to arrive. So they had put out the fires and returned to their own houses for the night.

Tom did not want to disturb them. He stabled the horses himself, then took his new bride into their home.

Southwest Pavilion. The first building to be completed at Monticello, this tiny (18′ × 18′) cottage began as a bachelor's retreat and became the home to which Jefferson brought his new bride.

As Martha shivered inside her long wool cloak, Tom lit a fire in the fireplace, then suddenly remembered a hidden treasure. With a shout of pleasure, he jubilantly pulled out from behind a shelf of books a half bottle of wine. It would serve them for warmth and for supper. Soon the snug little cottage, 580 feet above the world, with the village of Charlottesville, the blackened ruins of Shadwell, and the wild and romantic Rivanna River below them, but with three feet of snow to block out any intruders, was lit up with the laughter of sheer happiness and with song. As they stood before the fire, wrapped in each other's arms, the warmth of the fire, of the wine, and of their happiness and their love seemed to spread through the house.

The honeymoon lasted until April, for not until then did the Jeffersons come down from their mountain. Tom did not attend the meeting of the House of Burgesses in February, nor did he take care of any legal business in Williamsburg until the spring. Martha had her husband completely to herself.

Martha immediately set out to be a good housewife. She took Tom's leather-bound memorandum book in which he had recorded some cases that had come up in the General Court in 1768, gaily turned it upside down, and methodically listed the house linens in her new home and made "a list of our clothes."

For Mr. Jefferson:
9 ruffled shirts and 18 plain ditto, 20 old cambrick stocks,* 15 old rags of pocket handkerchiefs, 3 pr of English cordied breeches, 4 of Virginia ditto, 6 Virginia cordied dimity* waist-coats, 13 pr. white silk stockings, 5 red waistcoats, 2 buff, 1 white flannel ditto, 1 green coat, 1 black princes ditto.

For Mrs. Jefferson:
"16 old shifts, 4 new ditto, 6 old fine aprons, 4 Virginia petticoats, 9 pr. of silk stockings, 10 pr. of old cotton, 8 silk gowns, 6 washing ditto old and 2 new to make up, 2 suits of brussels lace, one suit of worked muslin."[3]

* fine white linen neckcloths
* fine cotton

At this point she seems to have hesitated, then drew two solemn little birds perched on a leafy twig. Then she continued her inventory: a goose was killed, and a beef, and on May 14 they began to eat cherries at Monticello. Six hams, four shoulders, two middlings were consumed in three weeks and two days, she tells us. At this point another bird appeared in the book. Perhaps keeping these records was more than Martha's lively spirit could bear.

The year 1772, the first year of his married life, was probably the happiest Tom was ever to know. It was then that he and Martha could enjoy each other and look forward with hope to a long and sunny life together.

A lull in the political storm gave Tom an interval of peace. The General Court did call him to Williamsburg in April and October, but for most of the year he remained on his mountain, with his ruler in his pocket and his case of instruments near at hand, watching every operation. As he rode or walked about his plantation, he could always be heard singing or humming to himself. He had a fine, clear voice and usually sang the minuets that were the popular music of the day. As he supervised the laying out of his grounds, the cutting of roads and paths through the woods, and as he planned parts of his house and watched his garden and ever-widening farms develop, he kept brief, exact records of whatever he did, saw, or learned.

When Tom brought Martha to live at Monticello, work on the main house was well under way. The foundations and the basement were finished, but the house itself was not livable. The northwest, or dining room wing, would be the first part completed, and it may have been enclosed if not finished that first winter.

In April Martha accompanied Tom to Williamsburg. They stayed for two months and were part of the spring social season there. They went to dances and to the theater. They rode out to Rosewell to visit the Pages. And they made visits to Dentist Baker and Dr. Brown, who confirmed their hopes that Martha was pregnant.

At the end of May they went to The Forest for a month, to visit Martha's father, then returned to Monticello at the end of June. Tom spent the summer overseeing the progress of the mansion. For Monticello continued to grow like a tree—slowly, steadily, gracefully.

* * *

On September 27, 1772, at one o'clock in the morning, Martha gave birth to their first child, a daughter whom they named Martha. She was a sickly child, and for six months they worried that she might not live. Then she "recovered almost instantaneously by a good breast of milk,"[4] probably given by a Negro wet nurse.

By the spring of 1773, Tom's peaceful, domestic interlude came to an abrupt end, and during that second year of married life he was often away from home. He was in Williamsburg when the Assembly met in March, and was among the burgesses who were disturbed about two recent incidents. A schooner called the *Gaspée* had been burned in Narragansett Bay in Rhode Island in June of 1772, and a special court of inquiry had been established there that had the power to send colonists to England for trial. The burgesses found this unacceptable. What happened in New England might happen to them.

Tom worried that the older, more conservative leaders might not be willing to take action. So he, Patrick Henry, Francis Lightfoot Lee and his brother Richard Henry Lee, and Dabney Carr met one evening in a private room of the Raleigh Tavern. They knew that they were already being branded by the older, more conservative members of the House as "young hot-heads."

These men were convinced that it was urgent to band together with the other colonies, to consider the British claims as a common cause to all, and to act as a united group.

Richard Henry Lee proposed the appointment of a "Standing Committee of Correspondence and Inquiry." At the direction of the Assembly, the committee would communicate to the assemblies of the other colonies the Virginians' anxieties about the reported threats to their ancient, legal, and constitutional rights and suggest that the other assemblies appoint similar committees. The men then drew up resolutions to be presented to the burgesses on the following day.

On the morning of March 12, when the burgesses took their seats, all Williamsburg was tense. Students at William and Mary had learned what was happening and crowded the Capitol.

Mr. Jefferson had been urged to move the resolutions but had declined in favor of Dabney Carr, "my friend and brother-in-law, then a new member, to whom I wished an opportunity should be given of making known to the House his great worth and talents."[5]

A hush of expectancy greeted Dabney Carr as he rose to address the House for the first time. He began:

> Whereas, the minds of His Majesty's faithful subjects in this colony have been much disturbed, by various rumours and reports of proceedings tending to deprive them of their ancient, legal, and constitutional rights. . . . Be it resolved, that a standing committee of correspondence and inquiry be appointed, to consist of eleven persons, to wit, the Honourable Peyton Randolph, Esquire, Robert Carter Nicholas, Richard Bland, Richard H. Lee, Benjamin Harrison, Edmund Pendleton, Patrick Henry, Dudley Digges, Dabney Carr, Archibald Cary, and Thomas Jefferson, Esquire . . . whose business it shall be to obtain . . . intelligence of all such acts and resolutions of the British Parliament . . . as may . . . affect the British Colonies in America, and . . . maintain a correspondence and communication with our sister colonies.[6]

Dabney's speech supporting these resolutions has been called "a happy blending of boldness, prudence and courtesy."[7] As he sat down, it was obvious that he had scored a triumph. The resolutions were carried, and the colonies were now working together through correspondence. And Dabney was on his way to becoming a rival to Patrick Henry for excellence in public debate.

The Virginia measure was the first that recommended colony-wide committees in a system of collective action. Within a few months every colony except Pennsylvania had a Committee of Correspondence. The chief function of these committees was to spread ideas and information by exchanging letters and, in this way, keep alive opposition to British policy.

These Committees of Correspondence were instrumental in stimulating sentiment in favor of united action and evolved directly into the first American Congress.

Tom was exhilarated by what he and Dabney had accomplished. And he was proud of Dabney. He was certain that his friend was destined for a brilliant career in politics.

The two young men rode home together at the close of the session. Then, early in April, Tom had to leave again for Williamsburg to attend the April term of the General Court. Dabney had cases to plead in the county court in Charlottesville.

Dabney had been happily married for eight years now, and he and his Martha had six children. The youngest, Dabney, Jr., was an infant.

Soon after he reached Charlottesville, Dabney was stricken suddenly with a malignant type of typhoid fever. Its course was so rapid that he died before anything could be done for him. He was buried at Shadwell before Tom even knew of his death, for Tom was still in Williamsburg. When he returned, remembering their boyhood pledge that whoever should die first would be buried beneath their favorite oak tree on the southwestern slope of Monticello, Tom had his friend's body moved to this spot.

The inscription he wrote for Dabney's tombstone and nailed temporarily on their tree attests to his strong feeling for this very special friend. It ends: "To his virtue, good sense, learning, and friendship, this stone is dedicated by Thomas Jefferson, who, of all men living, loved him most."[8]

Yet Tom was able to note with cool precision in his *Garden Book,* under the date May 22, 1773, that the graveyard he had planned years before was on this day begun as a resting place for his friend. He noted that "2 hands grubbed the graveyard 80 feet square = 1.7 of an acre in 3½ hours, so that one would have done it in 7 hours, and would grub an acre in 49 hours = 4 days," and that the first peas had come to the table.[9]

Never one to give outward expression to his private emotions, he turned for relief to figures, to garden peas and the weather, to the ordinary affairs of every day.

Tom and Martha immediately invited the entire Carr family to live with them at Monticello, although there was hardly room for them at the house then. They probably came to live there permanently in 1781. The baby Martha would grow up with "Aunty Carr" as a more or less permanent fixture.

Tom cared for his sister, took charge of Dabney's legal affairs, and raised and educated their children, particularly Peter, the eldest, as though they were his own.

Just days after Dabney's funeral, word reached Monticello that John Wayles had died suddenly on May 28, 1773. He was fifty-eight years old. Martha had been very close to her father and was, unquestionably, his favorite daughter. This loss, coming as it did on the heels of Dabney's death, was doubly difficult for both Tom and Martha to sustain.

From a practical point of view, though, Martha's inheritance, even after her father's considerable debts were paid, was substantial. It "was about equal to my own patrimony, and consequently doubled the ease of our circumstances," Tom would write later.[10]

Among the slaves who came to Monticello from the Wayles estate were the mulatto family of Hemings, as well as Ursula (known as Queenie), who would rule in the kitchen and care for little Martha and the other babies, and her husband, "King" George. They were as devoted to their mistress as she to them.

The Hemings family would provide much heartache for Tom. Half-white Betty Hemings had become John Wayles's mistress after the death of his third wife, and her children, fathered by Wayles, were Martha's half-sisters and brothers.

All the Hemings were brought to Monticello, and Tom saw to it that his home became their home. They were always treated with exceptional kindness and were given very little work to do. Tom himself saw to their education, making certain that the boys learned a trade so that they could support themselves when they reached maturity and so be given their freedom.

Tom was always kind and indulgent to all his slaves, and within the framework of an institution he disliked, he provided well for them. His "people," in turn, were devoted to him.

IX
Aristocrat turned rebel

Work was moving forward on Monticello. Bricks were still being molded on the mountaintop, and construction on the mansion was in progress.

Tom was constantly experimenting in his garden. He planted an extraordinary variety of trees, shrubs, grasses, grains, vegetables, bulbs, fruits, and nuts. He tried chestnuts from France, alpine strawberries, and melons and grapes from Italy. He was helped in these endeavors by a new friend and neighbor, Philip Mazzei, who had come to Virginia from Italy to plant vineyards. Tom was interested in Mazzei's desire to introduce the cultivation of the grape and the olive into the colony, so he invited Mazzei to remain as a guest at Monticello until his own house was built. When a dozen workmen arrived from Tuscany to assist Mazzei, they were delighted that their tall, friendly host spoke to them in Tuscan, which he had picked up by himself.

At two o'clock in the afternoon of February 21, 1774, all the buildings at Monticello suddenly began to shake. Startled, everyone ran outside. Family members and servants huddled together—frightened and perplexed. Soon the shaking subsided, and they realized that they had just experienced an earthquake. The next day, at about the same time, the mountain began to tremble once again.

Sometime during the confusion Tom's sister Elizabeth, who was referred to then as "deficient in intellect," wandered off by herself. She was found dead three days later. She was twenty-nine years old.

In the spring of 1774, soon after the peaches had come into full bloom, Tom laid out a permanent vegetable garden. He gave some of the vegetables Italian names, in honor of his friend Philip Mazzei.

His tobacco fields continued to earn him a good living. This was important because tobacco was the *only* crop that could be marketed for cash or sent to London to be exchanged for books, furniture, fine clothes, musical instruments, and choice wines. Tom was always adding to his library and his wine cellar.

He spent most of his time on his mountain, in part to work on his farm, and partly because Martha was expecting their second child in April. Pregnancy for Martha was an emotional as well as a physical crisis. Her own mother had died in childbirth, and that knowledge hung over her as a constant threat. And childbearing seemed to be, for her, particularly difficult physically as well.

But her fragility seemed to make her all the more special to her husband. He loved her even more, fussed over her, cared for her, stayed close to her, and considered himself the happiest of men.

Jane Randolph Jefferson, named for her grandmother, arrived at eleven o'clock in the morning on April 3, 1774. Her older sister, Martha, whom their parents called Patsy, was an eighteen-month-old toddler. Tom was delighted with his second little girl and relieved that Martha had come through the ordeal so well.

Tom would willingly have spent the rest of his life in the idyllic setting on his mountain, reluctantly going to Williamsburg to sit in the House of Burgesses twice a year. But this could not be.

Three and a half months before Jane was born, on December 16, 1773, the Boston Tea Party had occurred as a protest against the hated tax on tea that had been imposed by the Tea Act of 1773. A group of white townspeople, disguised as Indians, boarded three tea ships of the British East India Company in Boston harbor. They smashed 342 chests of tea and dumped the "cursed weed" into the harbor. A silent crowd watched approvingly from the darkness of the shore as salty tea was brewed for the fish.

Outraged, Parliament retaliated with measures that would brew a revolution. The most drastic of these, the Boston Port Act, threatened to close the tea-stained harbor.

Tom, in Williamsburg for the spring session of the Assembly, heard of these happenings on May 22, 1774, when dust-covered express riders from the Boston Committee of Correspondence came pounding into the Capitol with news of this retaliation and a plea for help from Virginia.

Tom was incensed at this British threat against Boston. He feared it would cause the "utter ruin" of a prosperous commercial city. His peaceful period on Monticello was coming to an end. The aristocratic young lawyer was becoming a revolutionary.

There was much excitement and heated debate in the Assembly as members argued over which side to take. They were split into two groups: the Tories, sympathetic to the British, and the Whigs, who were committed to the precept that people have the right to have a say in choosing those who will govern. The older and more cautious among both the Tories and the Whigs sought to resolve the issue without resorting to war. They still hoped to preserve their allegiance to the king. The younger Whigs were more aggressive and defiant. Tom, among them, was frustrated as he heard his friend George Wythe try to quiet the tumult. Tom knew that Mr. Wythe had the best interests of the colony at heart, but he felt that Wythe and most of the older members of the Virginia Assembly were clinging to the futile hope that they could gain colonial rights by more petitions to the king and that they would not have to break their tie to England. He began to realize that, much as he respected these men, leadership could no longer be left in their hands. They moved too slowly, he thought. They were fearful of change.

So Tom and Patrick Henry, Richard Henry Lee and Francis Lightfoot Lee began to meet quietly in the library every evening with a small group of men.

"We must boldly take an unequivocal stand in the line with Massachusetts," Tom said.

"An attack on any one colony should be considered an attack on the whole," they agreed.[1]

But how could they accomplish this? A plan had to be devised that could be presented and passed in the House.

For days Tom pored over journals and books, searching (as he had seen his uncle Peter Randolph do nine years before in the journals of the House of Burgesses) for some precedent, some idea to apply to this situation. Finally, he found what he was looking for: In 1746 the Puritans in Massachusetts had resorted to fasting and prayer for deliverance from the French.

Now Tom proposed a day of fasting, humiliation, and prayer to signal the closing of the port of Boston. It would focus attention on this affront to colonial liberty. It will "inspire us with firmness in support of our rights, and . . . turn the hearts of the king and parliament to moderation and justice," he said.[2]

Who could object to their praying for the people of Boston? he reasoned. And, too, gentlemen who kneel together side by side in prayer might suddenly find themselves on the same side in the controversy.

The plot that Tom "cooked up" (as he described it later) did not spring from a deep religious feeling. But these young men recognized the power of the church over the people and knew how strong its influence could be. They would give a religious appearance to a political maneuver.

The plan was to congregate in Bruton Parish Church on June 1, the day the port of Boston was scheduled to be closed. There they would pray to Heaven to avert the evils of civil war.

The men knew that Tom could draft an inspired resolution. But Tom knew that he could not be the one to introduce it in the House. Nor could any of the other young "radicals." It must be done by someone of stature, someone grave and religious and respected by both factions, Tories and Whigs. He suggested Robert Carter Nicholas, chairman of the committee on religion and one of the most conservative of the burgesses. His word would carry the needed authority.

Mr. Nicholas agreed, and on Tuesday, May 24, he offered the resolution to the burgesses. It passed without opposition and was printed in the *Virginia Gazette* two days later. An infuriated Lord Dunmore, who had arrived in October 1771 to become the new governor of Virginia, read it there and dissolved the House "as usual."

Once again, the members assembled in the Apollo Room in the Raleigh Tavern. There they agreed that an attack on the rights of one colony was an affront to all. Perhaps this statement, even more than the declaration that was to come from Tom's pen two years later, was the catalyst that sealed the fate of the colonies.

The men proceeded to form another association and instructed the Committee of Correspondence to "propose to the corresponding committees of the other colonies to appoint representatives to meet on September 5, 1774, in Philadelphia."*[3] This association would be known as the Continental Congress. The men recommended, also, that deputies of the various counties of Virginia meet in Williamsburg on August 1 to appoint delegates to this general congress.

In Williamsburg on the first day of June in 1774 the air was warm and thick, heavy with the scent of the linden tree, as the townspeople began to emerge from their houses and gather together for the short walk to Bruton Parish Church. Humble townspeople and elegantly clad ladies and gentlemen mingled together as they followed behind the speaker and the mace, along Duke of Gloucester Street.

But Williamsburg was not the only place where a fast day was being observed. All across the colony people answered the call to prayer. They thronged to their parish churches, anxiety and alarm evident on their faces.

Tom, at home with his family, attended a service at his parish in Albemarle. "The effect of the day was like a shock of electricity, arousing every man, and placing him erect and solidly on his center," he described it.[4] Virginians were moved deeply by compassion for the people of Boston and were fearful that they might be next to feel the wrath of the king. They understood full well what George Wythe meant when he said, "The tea that was thrown into the sea in Boston may yet wash ashore in Virginia."

On July 26, in all the counties throughout Virginia, the freeholders reelected every member of the original assembly to act as deputies at the Virginia Convention in Williamsburg on August 1 as an indication of approval of what they had done. Fairfax County reelected George Washington, and Louisa County returned Patrick Henry. Thomas Jefferson and John Walker were reelected in Albemarle, and resolutions that Tom had already drawn were adopted.

Tom had realized that the delegates to the Continental Congress

* Travel and communication difficulties made that much time necessary.

would require formal and exact instructions and had been thinking about this for the past two months. As he pondered the problem, he thought back to the reading he had done when he first began to practice law. He had gone back to the early British sources and traced the origin of the Common Law of England to the Angles and the Saxons. Now, as he reread the notes he had taken as a young law student, his great respect for King Alfred's Laws was renewed. He looked on Alfred as the establisher of the Common Law.

He came to the conclusion that, more than a thousand years before, the Anglo-Saxons had lived under customs and unwritten laws based on the natural rights of man, permitting the individual to develop freely, normally, and happily. He had found a *historical* precedent for the freedom he was so certain was right.

Now these carefully copied notes, filed away in his characteristically thorough and orderly way, became the basis for the resolutions he was drafting. These resolutions would be moved as instructions to the Virginia delegates to Congress and, he hoped, would then be incorporated into an address to the king. But, he cautioned, Congress should address the king so that he understood that the colonists were asking not for favors but for rights.

> our ancestors, before their emmigration [sic] to America, were the free inhabitants of the British dominions in Europe, and possessed a right, which nature has given to all men, of departing from the country in which chance, not choice has placed them.

He went on to say that the wilds of the American continent were settled at great sacrifice of the colonists. "Their own blood was spilt. . . . For themselves they fought, for themselves they conquered, and for themselves alone they have right to hold." The fierce determination of the pioneer spirit was surfacing. No longer was he the shy and timid new member of the House of Burgesses whose first assignment was rejected.

Kings, he informed George III (in an age when kings were approached with reverence), are the servants, not the proprietors of the people. "Open your breast, Sire, to liberal and expanded thought. Let not the name of George the third be a blot on the page of history," he lectured him.

Men were born to freedom, not to slavery, he asserted. This, he recalled, he had said publicly in 1770 when he had tried, unsuccessfully, to win freedom for the slave Samuel Howell. Now he was saying that the colonists were independent of the British constitution and subject to no laws except those they had freely adopted when they had consented to a new compact and formed a new society. Self-government, he knew, was right. "The God who gave us life, gave us liberty at the same time."[5]

He had studied, he had thought carefully, and he had come to the conclusion that the only solution was rebellion. His words would set aflame the imagination of the people and become their battle cry.

Two days before the scheduled meeting of the Virginia Convention on August 1, on an unusually hot and muggy day, Tom and his old friend John Walker, each accompanied by a servant, set out together for Williamsburg, one hundred and fifty miles away. Two carefully written copies of the resolutions Tom had drafted were in his saddlebag. He expected to be in Williamsburg early enough to be able to speak to Patrick Henry before the meeting. He would tell him some of the ideas that he had expressed in his paper. Patrick, he was certain, could sway the members at the meeting.

Often Mr. Henry's eloquent speech to the burgesses one morning reflected a private conversation with his friend Mr. Jefferson the night before.

But as Tom and John rode through the woods that comprised the first part of their journey, they were enveloped in the red dust of the dirt road that was kicked up by the horses' hooves, and besieged by swarms of flies. Suddenly, Tom was stricken with a severe case of dysentery. He knew he couldn't go on. He had to turn back. He insisted to Jupiter that he could get home alone—his horse knew the way and would get him there. Jupiter must continue on to Williamsburg to deliver his resolutions. One copy, he instructed him, must go to Peyton Randolph who, he was certain, would be elected chairman. The other must be delivered to Patrick Henry. Then, with barely enough strength to stay astride, he turned his horse around and rode home.

This was the *only* time in his life that he was unable to fulfill a public duty because of illness. It took Martha several weeks to nurse him back to health.

In Williamsburg, Peyton Randolph was elected to preside over the convention, just as Tom had anticipated. At the meeting members agreed that delegates would attend a congress of all the colonies to be held in Philadelphia on the first Monday of the following month, September 5, 1774. They elected Peyton Randolph, Richard Henry Lee, George Washington, Patrick Henry, Richard Bland, Benjamin Harrison, and Edmund Randolph to represent them there. Members agreed, also, not to import British goods or slaves and not to export tobacco. Mr. Jefferson's paper was "laid on the table" for the members' perusal. Jupiter had accomplished his mission.

That evening Peyton Randolph invited a large group of leaders to his home to hear him read Jefferson's resolutions. When he had finished, his parlor rang with enthusiastic applause from the younger members for their idealistic friend. The older, more conservative members, though, shifted uncomfortably in their chairs as they pondered the bold statements. This was the first time anyone, even among the most sympathetic Whigs, had categorically denied Parliament's authority over the colonial legislatures.

They "required time for consideration, before they could tread this lofty ground," Edmund Randolph wrote, describing the scene. His young cousin was "marching far beyond the politicks [sic] of the day,"[6] he said, and the conservative sentiment prevailed. The resolutions were not adopted.

"The leap I proposed was too long,"[7] Jefferson recalled later. And Patrick Henry, whose help Tom had counted on, said nothing. He had either lost his copy or, more likely, Tom thought, had been too lazy to read it.

But several of Tom's other friends, inspired by his daring ideas, had the resolutions, titled "A Summary View of the Rights of British America," printed without asking his permission. Then, hoping to protect Tom by not indicating that he was the author, they signed it simply, "By a Native and Member of the House of Burgesses." It was read by many people in the colonies, and while it did not bear Tom's name, many suspected who had written it. Eventually "A Summary View of the Rights of British America" found its way to England.

When it was read in Parliament by Edmund Burke, who was pleading the cause of the colonies, the name of Thomas Jefferson was placed on the rapidly growing list of "outlaws" to be brought to England for trial.

While the resolutions in the "Summary View" were not adopted and their author was not present at the Congress in Philadelphia, the bold spirit of his ideas seemed to echo in the minds of the Virginia delegates who were there. Tom may not have been elected a delegate to Congress because he had not been at the Williamsburg convention at which the delegates were chosen. Or perhaps, as Edmund Randolph said later, "he had not yet attained a marked grade in politics."[8]

Peyton Randolph was elected president, and Patrick Henry quickly gained the spotlight when he leaped to his feet and declared:

Where are your landmarks, your boundaries of Colonies? We are in a state of Nature, Sir. . . . The distinction between Virginians, Pennsylvanians, New Yorkers and New Englanders are no more. I am not a Virginian, but an American.[9]

The members were aghast. Until now, when a Virginian said "my country" he meant Virginia. Suddenly they were thinking of all the colonies as *one*.

But the tall young colonel named George Washington could still rise with the stately bearing of a soldier and say, "I am well satisfied that no such thing as independence is desired by any thinking man in all North America."[10]

Congress remained in session until October 26. A declaration of rights was agreed upon, and an association imposed on all the colonies. It was agreed not to import any British goods after December 1 and to export nothing after September 10, 1775.

In Virginia, a committee called the Committee of Safety was appointed to enforce this. Among its members were such conservatives as Robert Carter Nicholas, Richard Bland, Edmund Pendleton, Peyton Randolph, and George Wythe. They were certain that their firm actions would help to restore friendly relations with England. It never occurred to them that they might be fostering a revolution.

X
"The ball of revolution"

Tom spent the end of 1774 and early 1775 on his mountaintop, watching his house take shape, working on his grounds, entertaining friends, and enjoying the time he had with his wife and the two little daughters he adored. His sister Martha Carr and her children were not yet living at Monticello, but they were frequent visitors.

He continued to read and to ponder the problems still facing the colonies. He saw that he was devoting less and less time to his law practice, and politics was claiming his energies. Tom had been trained from boyhood to assume responsibility for many people, and he found now that to serve the people was what he really loved best to do.

He was a rich man, he reasoned, and he didn't need the income from his law practice. He could earn enough as a farmer. He decided to turn his law practice over to his handsome young cousin, Edmund Randolph, son of John Randolph, attorney general of Virginia. Edmund was fast becoming one of the outstanding lawyers in the colony.

Tom was a fine and successful lawyer. But he had never thought highly of lawyers as a group. "The lawyers' trade is to question everything, yield nothing, and talk by the hour," he said.[1] Years later he would write to a friend: "I was bred to the law, and that gave me a view of the dark side of humanity. Then I read poetry to qualify it with a gaze upon its bright side."[2]

Tom never returned to the practice of law, but he never regretted his training. ". . . he who knows nothing of [the laws of the land] will always be perplexed, and often foiled by adversaries having the advantage of that knowledge over him," he wrote to Thomas Mann Randolph, Jr., many years later.[3] It was the *power* of knowledge that was important to him.

* * *

Things moved very slowly in the eighteenth century, and because of this, as Tom continued to supervise the building of Monticello, he found himself with problems that he had not anticipated. Martha, with two small children to look after, had to contend with all the hazards and inconveniences of construction. Bricks that had been molded and fired on the mountaintop were stacked alongside lumber and building rubble, and scaffolding was left in place on unfinished walls from one season to the next. Fifty thousand bricks were fired in 1774 alone, and by the end of the year what Tom called "the middle building" was completed. It contained the parlor, library, and drawing room, with a bedroom above.

In May of 1774 he had ordered from England fourteen pairs of sash windows for his house. Now glass was among those items on which Congress had placed a boycott. Tom was in a quandary. His only solution was to write a letter to the Committee of Safety at Norfolk, explaining his situation. The committee decided to release the shipment to Tom when it arrived, and on August 11, 1775, fifteen months after he had ordered them, the windows arrived at Monticello. Only then was the "middle building" completely enclosed from the weather.

By now Committees of Safety had been formed throughout the colony to serve as governing bodies. Mr. Jefferson, who had become the most prominent citizen of Albemarle, was elected to head the Committee of Safety of Albemarle, and early in 1775 he and John Walker were elected to represent their county at the second Virginia Convention. This one would be held in Richmond on March 20. He took Martha and the children to stay at The Forest, Martha's childhood home, while he was gone.

In Richmond, the delegates met at St. John's Church, a simple white wooden building with about fifty to sixty pews, the only place in that city large enough to hold them.

Tom sat quietly, thoughtfully listening to the conciliatory resolutions being read. But these soon became too much for his friend Patrick Henry. Jumping to his feet, Mr. Henry called for a militia for the defense of the country.

Pandemonium broke loose. The members were not prepared for such a radical step. Revolution had an ominous sound. The conservative members opposed the resolution. They cautioned against armed resistance, fearing that military threats might hinder their progress.

Then Patrick Henry, with his perfect sense of timing, rose solemnly and majestically from his seat. "We have done everything that could be done to avert the storm which is now coming on," he cried. "There is no longer room for hope. If we wish to be free . . . we must fight! I repeat, Sir, we must fight!"

His voice fell to a whisper as he continued. Then, eyes blazing, it rose to a thundering challenge and rang like an anvil through the timbers in the little church:

> Is life so dear, or peace so sweet, as to be purchased at the price of chains and slavery? Forbid it, Almighty God! I know not what course others may take; but as for me . . . give me liberty or give me death![4]

Not a sound was heard as he finished and sank into his seat. The men sat stunned and silent. Then, with his "usual elegance," Richard Henry Lee rose and supported Mr. Henry. Everyone started to talk at once and above the din of voices could be heard such words as "liberty" and "freedom."

The fiery Patrick Henry, whose impassioned speeches often reflected the views he had discussed with his younger friend, Mr. Jefferson, the night before.

Suddenly, Thomas Jefferson asked to be heard. His friends were amazed. Never before had he participated in public debate. Now, overcoming his shyness, he argued "closely, profoundly, and warmly" in support of Henry and Lee.[5]

Captivated by Patrick Henry's charm, his ability to speak, and "the exact conformity of our political opinions,"[6] Jefferson and his radical friends vehemently supported Henry. But George Washington remained silent, deep in thought.

The resolutions passed with a vote of sixty-five to sixty, an example of "the inequality of pace with which we moved, and the prudence required to keep front and rear together," Jefferson said. "We often wished to have gone faster, but we slackened our pace, that our less ardent colleagues might keep up with us; and they, on their part, differing nothing from us in principle, quickened their gait somewhat."[7]

Mr. Jefferson was among the committee of twelve men appointed to prepare a plan for arming and training soldiers. He continued, as was his practice, to work behind the scenes, talking and planning in small groups. Good-natured, mild mannered, never aggressive, he managed to instill his ideas into others so subtly that they came to believe that it was they who had originated the ideas. He had a genius for friendship and a shy warmth that always attracted people to him. It proved extremely helpful now.

But he continued to wish that war could be avoided. It was not what he wanted.

Before the members adjourned, they decided that in the event that Lord Dunmore should call a meeting of the House of Burgesses, Peyton Randolph might not be able to attend the second Continental Congress, scheduled to be held in Philadelphia in May. So Thomas Jefferson was elected an alternate, to take his place.

But when the burgesses were, in fact, summoned by Lord Dunmore to consider a conciliatory proposition of Lord North, prime minister of Great Britain, Peyton Randolph prevailed upon Tom to postpone his journey to Philadelphia and come to Williamsburg to prepare the reply. By this time the name of Thomas Jefferson was frequently on the lips of the people of Virginia. And Peyton Randolph was convinced that there was no more effective writer in America. He chose him over all the older and respected veterans of the House of Burgesses. He was only thirty-two.

He wrote the reply with his characteristic simplicity and forthrightness. It concluded:

> These, my Lord, are our sentiments on this important subject. . . . For ourselves, we have exhausted every mode of application which our invention could suggest as proper and promising. We have decently remonstrated with Parliament, they have added new injuries to the old: we have wearied our King with supplications, he has not deigned to answer us; we have appealed to the native honour and justice of the British nation, their efforts in our favor have hitherto been ineffectual. What then remains to be done? That we commit our injuries to the even-handed justice of that Being who doth no wrong; earnestly beseeching him to illuminate the councils, and prosper the endeavors of those to whom America hath confided her hopes; that, through their wise direction, we may again see, reunited, the blessing of liberty and property, and the most permanent harmony with Great Britain.[8]

By this time "the shot heard round the world"* had been fired in Massachusetts. On April 29, Virginians learned that British soldiers had marched to Lexington, Massachusetts, where they fired without provocation, killing six militiamen and wounding four others. Then they moved on to Concord. This encounter, Jefferson wrote, "has cut off our last hopes of reconciliation and a phrenzy [sic] of revenge seems to have seized all ranks of people."[9]

As another show of strength, Lord Dunmore had secretly removed fifteen barrels of gunpowder from the magazine at Williamsburg and had them taken to a man-of-war lying in the York River. The colonists were infuriated.

"The . . . bloodshed at Lexington . . . ," Edmund Randolph said, "had in Virginia changed the figure of Great Britain from an unrelenting parent into that of a merciless enemy."[10] The Revolutionary War had begun.

The men who gathered in Williamsburg on June 1, 1775, for

---

* Ralph Waldo Emerson, "Concord Hymn"

the meeting of the Virginia Assembly were a far different group in appearance from the usual elegantly dressed, proper gentlemen who constituted the august House of Burgesses. Now they attended the meeting wearing hunting shirts, the "official" uniform of the militia, and carrying muskets. Even George Wythe was dressed in this fashion.

The following week, on June 8, the governor and his family fled the palace in the middle of the night. British rule in Virginia had come to an end.

Richard Henry Lee, smiling to himself at this turn of events, and probably thinking of his friends Mr. Henry and Mr. Jefferson, scratched into one of the white pillars of the Capitol the witches' opening lines in Shakespeare's *Macbeth:*

When shall we three meet again?
In thunder, lightning, or in rain.
When the hurly-burly's done,
When the battle's lost and won.

The Battle of Lexington had made the Second Continental Congress suddenly very important, and Tom was anxious now to be there. Small groups of men had already converged on the city of Philadelphia, making their way through the woods on horseback or in carriages from all the colonies—from New England in the north to the Carolinas and Georgia in the south.

It was a hot and humid day when Tom finally arrived in Philadelphia on June 20. In all, the journey from Williamsburg had taken ten days. He had covered well over two hundred and fifty miles, mostly over roads that were little more than trails through the wilderness.

Philadelphia was a large city, teeming with life. It had a greater population (about 40,000) than any other city in the colonies. Tom saw people from all walks of life on its streets. Fashionably dressed ladies in elegant silks mingled with plain, gray-clad Quakers and militiamen in their rough uniforms. Messenger boys hurried through the streets, jostling each other as they ran to deliver letters and important documents. Lovely shops lined the streets. Tom's observant eye missed nothing.

He found rooms with a cabinetmaker named Benjamin Randolph,

whom he paid for "a fortnight's lodging for self and servant 3–15." His horses were more expensive. He paid 3 pounds 10 shillings a week for their care.[11]

Congress sat in the red brick colonial State House (which would later come to be known as Independence Hall) on Chestnut Street, and Tom headed there on the morning of June 22. The Pennsylvania Assembly had lent Congress its room on the ground floor, a large, beautiful white-paneled chamber with windows lining two sides. A lovely glass prism chandelier hung in the center.

Crowds had already gathered outside in the yard to watch the Philadelphia Associators drilling their newly formed battalions of soldiers when Tom arrived that morning. A feeling of war was in the air.

The red brick State House, which later came to be known as Independence Hall, where Thomas Jefferson first met John Adams and Benjamin Franklin. It was here that the delegates to the Second Continental Congress met to decide to fight for "independency."

Inside, to ensure secrecy, the delegates, wiping damp and dripping brows, locked the doors and opened the high windows just a crack from the top in spite of the sweltering heat. Insects buzzed and banged against the panes.

The tall, thin, sandy-haired new member from Virginia presented his credentials to Congress and was seated as a duly certified member. He was greeted warmly, and his concern about participating in this august group of men was soon allayed. The other Virginia delegates had boasted about him, and many were anxious to meet this young man who, they had heard, wrote such eloquent prose about liberty and freedom.

Mr. Jefferson was introduced immediately to many of the members, but he was particularly drawn to two men. He had eagerly looked forward to meeting Benjamin Franklin, at sixty-nine America's most experienced statesman and a philosopher and scientist of world renown. Dr. Franklin had just returned from England, where he had met many government leaders face to face and had come to understand the workings of the British Parliament. Tom thought how wonderful it was to see him, his chair at the end of the row pulled out a little, his legs crossed as he sat calm and composed in his brown Quaker suit, his long gray hair falling on his shoulders.

And Tom was happy to meet John Adams of Massachusetts, the brilliant lawyer and a leader of the radicals whose political opinions, Tom had heard, were exactly the same as his. Mr. Adams was talked of as the ablest debater for the revolutionary cause.

John Adams, in turn, was instantly drawn to Tom. "He soon seized upon my heart," John wrote to his wife, Abigail, and remarked to a friend that he had heard that Tom was "the greatest rubber-off-of-dust." Tom had not been in Congress more than a few weeks when his quick, decisive way in committee became evident to all who worked with him. "He was prompt, frank, explicit . . . ," Mr. Adams described his new young friend. "He will be given work at once."[12]

Tom met the other members, too: John Jay of New York; John and Edward Rutledge of South Carolina; John Langdon, who would become a staunch ally of Mr. Jefferson; the wealthy John Hancock of Boston, who was named president of the Congress to succeed

Benjamin Franklin, elder statesman, whose interests far transcended politics. He won international renown as a writer, printer, philosopher, scientist, inventor, and philanthropist.

Peyton Randolph; and Samuel Adams, also of Boston, cousin to John. Sam, Tom noticed, was shabbily dressed, but his eyes burned with a quiet zeal, and he often appeared to be deep in thought. It was Sam Adams, Tom knew, who had been the prime mover in organizing the Committees of Correspondence.

George Washington, whom the Congress had recently appointed commander-in-chief of the Continental Army, was there, too, in his new uniform—a blue and buff coat with rich gold epaulets, a small, elegant sword at his side, and a black cockade in his hat—a quiet reminder of where they might be heading.

Jefferson was quickly invited to join a group of the delegates who dined together at the City Tavern, a new and fashionable inn, at the conclusion of the session every day. And he was just as quickly given an assignment, as John Adams had predicted. He was appointed to a committee to draw up a Declaration of the Causes and Necessity

John Adams, one of the most persistent and convincing voices at the Continental Congress. Jefferson would always remember with gratitude Adams's strong defense of his Declaration of Independence. Their friendship withstood a break over politics and resumed after both had retired.

for Taking Up Arms. It would be presented by General Washington to his troops.

Washington was preparing to leave to join the army near Cambridge, Massachusetts. The delegates felt that the soldiers should understand recent political happenings to justify the steps that were being taken toward war.

John Dickinson, a conservative who still hoped for reconciliation with England, wrote the first part of the paper. Of Tom's paper, only the final four and a half paragraphs were included. But Tom's stirring words, read aloud by Washington to his men, echoed through the colonies and brought the people closer to the side of the radicals:

We fight not for glory or for conquest. We exhibit to mankind the remarkable spectacle of a people attacked by unprovoked enemies, without any imputation, or even suspicion of offence. . . . In our native land, in defence of the freedom that is our birthright, and which we ever enjoyed until the late violation of it; for the protection of our property, acquired solely by the honest industry of our forefathers and ourselves, against violence actually offered, we have taken up arms. . . .[13]

Tom recognized that the moderates still shied away from independence, so he understood that he must move slowly and quietly. The colonies must be united in taking the final step. He did not want to instigate civil war.

Near the end of July, Mr. Jefferson was asked to write the reply, on behalf of the Congress, to proposals for conciliation advanced by the British prime minister, Lord North, since Tom had done the same for Virginia. His paper was adopted on July 31, and on August 1 Congress adjourned. Tom headed home to Virginia. His saddlebags were filled with books and music that he had bought in Philadelphia and four butter prints,* a special gift for Martha.

The Virginia Convention had by now become the revolutionary government of Virginia, and on his way home Tom stopped in Richmond to attend the session then in progress there. He was appointed a regular delegate to the next Continental Congress, scheduled to meet in Philadelphia on September 5. The other delegates would be Peyton Randolph, George Wythe, Richard Henry Lee, Francis Lightfoot Lee, and Benjamin Harrison and Thomas Nelson, Jr., old friends from William and Mary. Patrick Henry, who had been named commander-in-chief of the Virginia militia, and George Washington were considered ineligible because of their military status.

It was at this time that Tom learned that his cousin John Randolph was planning to return "home" to England. "Tory John," as he was called, whose brother Peyton and son Edmund were both staunch Patriots, did not sympathize with the revolutionary movement and thought it best to leave Virginia. Tom was saddened that he was leaving. "We *are* home," he thought.

He took advantage of the situation, though, and prevailed upon

---

* stamps for marking pats of butter

his cousin to intercede for the colonists in England. He still hoped for a reconciliation, he told John, adding, "I am sincerely one of those who would rather be in dependence on Great Britain, properly limited, than on any other nation on earth, or than on no nation. But I am one of those, too, who, rather than submit to the rights of legislating for us, assumed by the British Parliament, and which late experience has shown they will so cruelly exercise, would lend my hand to sink the whole island in the ocean."[14]

Before he left for England, John Randolph was able to satisfy a longing of Tom's that the two had discussed years earlier. He sold to Tom, for thirteen pounds, the violin that Tom had craved for years, perhaps the finest violin in the colonies at that time. The violin was a Cremona, made in Italy by Nicola Amati in 1660. It would remain a precious possession of his for fifty-one years.

Tom still played the violin whenever he could and had become a fine musician. He carried with him, on journeys, a miniature violin, called a kit, chiefly used by dancing masters. He had designed and made for it a tiny case small enough to be carried in a large pocket. It came in very handy on mornings when, always an early riser, he waited for breakfast to be served. In the evenings he could play softly without disturbing anyone in an adjacent room. His music was, for him, an escape from the problems whirling around him, a "respite from the cares of the day." It brought him a sense of peace.

Now, as Tom turned his horse toward home, his thoughts turned away from political problems. He was anxious to be back on his hilltop with Martha and his little girls. He had missed them. And he had missed the quiet of Monticello in the tumult of the big city. He was determined to make the most of the short time he would have there until Congress reconvened.

Tom arrived at Monticello on August 19 to a joyous greeting from all his family and servants. But his brief stay there was not to be a happy one. Baby Jane, just seventeen months old, was ill, and the family was struggling to preserve her flickering life. She died early in September. Martha was inconsolable.

Tom remained at home beyond the opening of Congress, trying to offer some measure of comfort to his wife. Eventually, he took her and little Patsy, who was then three years old, to Eppington to stay with Martha's half-sister, Elizabeth Eppes. It was only when he saw them comfortably settled there, and was reassured that they would be well cared for, that he finally felt able to tear himself away. On the nineteenth of September he hastened back to Philadelphia, arriving there on the twenty-fifth. He had made the journey in only six days, an amazing feat for both horse and rider.

It was during this session of Congress, on October 22, 1775, that Peyton Randolph, dining with Tom at the home of a friend, died suddenly of a stroke (then called apoplexy). He was fifty-four years old. Over the years Tom's respect and affection for his older cousin had deepened, and Randolph's sudden death was a sharp blow.

During all the time Tom was in Congress, he set aside the better part of one day a week for writing letters. But he didn't receive the ones he wanted the most. Six weeks after he had left Monticello, he wrote a frantic letter to Francis Eppes, husband of Martha's sister. He had, he told him, "never received the script of pen from any mortal in Virginia since I left it, nor been able by any inquiries I could make to hear of my family. . . . The suspense under which I am is too terrible to be endured. If anything has happened for God's sake let me know."[15]

He was beginning to worry more and more about his wife's health. She seemed unusually frail to him. Both childbearing and the loss of her baby had worn her out physically and emotionally.

Francis Eppes immediately wrote back that Martha was not seriously ill. But she had sunk into a state of depression and was too weak even to write to her husband. Each successive post brought only silence.

In November word came that the "Olive Branch Petition" that John Dickinson had written in July had been refused by the king. The petition was a final plea to George III to choose the "olive branch" of peace over the sword of war. The members of Congress were frustrated. Except for a brief recess, they had been sitting for six months, and they were tired. The burden of making war fell on Congress. Raising money and soldiers, starting a navy, planning strategy, appeasing Indians, opening new channels of trade, seeking alliances—all these were matters that the members had to deal with for long hours every day.

While they would have liked to adjourn for a while, they knew this was not possible. The best they could do was to take a short break over the Christmas holiday, from December 23 to 26, not long enough for Tom to reach Virginia.

Individual members were able to move about freely, though. Since each colony had only one vote regardless of the number of its delegates, all of them did not have to be present all the time. So Tom requested, and was granted, a longer leave, and he set out for Monticello just a few days after Christmas. He remained there for four months.

The year 1776 began in Virginia with a senseless ravaging of a peaceful seaport town, and this gave the final impetus to the push for independence. Norfolk, Virginia, was burned to the ground by the British on the first day of the new year. The war had reached Virginia.

Tom heard this maddening news as he was riding homeward. He learned, also, that there was fighting in many places along the coast, and that Falmouth, Maine, had suffered a fate similar to that of Norfolk.

Tom found his family eagerly awaiting him when he arrived at Monticello. Martha, he saw, was extremely frail, and he was worried about her. His mother, too, was ill, and he feared she was dying. He stayed close to both of them for the next few months.

Whenever Tom was home, he never expected Martha to be burdened with the business of running the plantation. He took over every aspect of this—including decisions regarding the interior decoration of the house. This time he designed the curtains and selected the fabrics. He even chose the meat for the next day's dinner. He tried hard to make Martha smile as of old. He hoped she would be strong enough to accompany him to Philadelphia when he returned to Congress.

He also found civic duties to attend to. He collected money for the relief of the poor in Boston and for the purchase of powder for the Virginia militia.

Tom kept abreast of the political situation through letters from his friends in Williamsburg and Philadelphia and by reading the Virginia *Gazette*. He read a pamphlet entitled *Common Sense,* written by Thomas Paine, an Englishman who had recently immigrated to America. Tom's friend Thomas Nelson, still in Philadelphia, had sent him "a present of 2s.* worth of Common Sense."[16]

In his pamphlet, published on January 10, 1776, Paine pleaded the case of the colonies in simple language. He would present, he said, "nothing more than simple facts, plain arguments and common sense."[17] The people were ready to hear what he had to say.

Paine made people think, and his words were soon on everyone's tongue. Eventually over one hundred thousand copies of *Common Sense* were sold. "The period of debate is closed," the pamphlet said. ". . . Now is the seed time of continental union, faith and honour."[18]

Tom, reading and rereading *Common Sense* on his mountaintop, thought it contained sound doctrine and logical reasoning. When he rode through the area to sound out the people in the nearby local counties, he came to the conclusion that nine-tenths of them agreed with Paine and favored independence.

Early in the morning on the last day of March, Tom's mother suffered a stroke and died within an hour. She was fifty-seven. He recorded it tersely in his little pocket account book in a simple, unemotional statement that was consistent with his reticence on all personal matters.

We know very little about Tom's relationship with his mother, for nowhere is there any indication of how he felt about her. But immediately after her death, in spite of his seeming lack of emotion, Tom suddenly became ill himself. An intense pain throbbed through his entire head for weeks. He called it "the head ach" [sic]. He seems to have been suffering from what we would now refer to as a migraine headache, the result, no doubt, of the terrible personal strain under which he was living. It kept him on Monticello for an additional six weeks. It wasn't until early May that he felt able to leave for Philadelphia.

He had been hoping all the time that he was home that Martha would regain her strength sufficiently to be able to accompany him.

* two shillings

His friend Thomas Nelson had his wife with him there, and she had offered to look after Martha if Tom brought her. But Martha wasn't strong enough yet to travel that distance or to be exposed to the crowded city. Reluctantly, he decided that he had to go alone.

His only companion this time would be his servant Bob Hemings, the slim, fourteen-year-old son of John Wayles by his half-white slave, Betty Hemings.

As he took his leave of Martha on a lovely May morning, he tried hard to keep his own emotions in check and to hide his disappointment—and his uneasiness—at leaving her behind. He tried, too, to allay her fears for him and her fears of a revolution. He was torn by his desire to remain on his mountaintop with the woman he adored and who needed him, and with his cheerful little daughter, who was growing up so quickly and in whom he delighted. But he understood that his country was calling, and it was his duty to answer the call.

XI
Reclaiming a birthright

When Tom arrived in Philadelphia on May 14, he found waiting
for him a month-old letter from John Page. "For God's sake declare
the colonies independent and save us from ruin," Page had written.[1]
But Tom knew that he was only a delegate, and he had to wait for
instructions from the Virginia Convention, then meeting in Williamsburg.

He would have much preferred to be in Williamsburg to have
a part in helping to formulate "a plan of government,"* for Virginia.
He was already more concerned with what would follow a formal
separation from England than with the action itself. He was anxious
to see his ideas about human rights actually carried out.

But Tom was not recalled to Williamsburg, and, in fact, he didn't
know that on May 15 the Virginia Convention had unanimously
approved resolutions that his friend Thomas Nelson had offered in-
structing its delegates in the Continental Congress to move at once
for "independency." It would take twelve days for the instructions
to arrive in Philadelphia.

In the meantime, Tom obtained lodgings once again with Benjamin Randolph on Chestnut Street, then went to take his seat in
Congress. He found the atmosphere there extremely tense. John Adams
described the long hours of debate and the overwhelming sense of
responsibility as "drudgery of the most wasting, exhausting, consum-
ing kind," concerned with measures that will affect "the lives and
liberties of millions yet unborn."[2]

That evening, after taking his supper at the City Tavern with

* On May 15, at the suggestion of John Adams, Congress had recommended that the colonies
form new governments to meet their needs.

his friends, as he had in the past, Tom returned to his rooms early to speak to his landlord. Mr. Randolph, Tom knew, was a fine cabinet-maker, and Tom had a project for him.

Tom explained that what he wanted was a travel lap desk convenient for writing, as well as an adjustable book rest for reading. It should be equipped with a drawer that could be locked, and within which Tom could store paper stock and written papers. It was to be fitted to hold supplies of ink, nibs for his pens, and sand for blotting. Mr. Randolph was happy to oblige.

The multipurpose desk met all Tom's specifications and was a fine piece of furniture. Crafted of beautiful mahogany, it was as small as possible and lightweight, with a maximum utilization of space. Neither its designer nor its builder could have anticipated then that this little desk would be revered by posterity.

The desk on which Thomas Jefferson wrote the Declaration of Independence. "On that little desk was done a work greater than any battle, loftier than any poem, more enduring than any monument."

*   *   *

Soon after he was settled at Mr. Randolph's, and with his mind still on the Virginia Convention, Tom hastily drew up a plan for the kind of constitution he felt Virginia should have. He sent it off to Edmund Pendleton, then Speaker of the House, by George Wythe, who was returning to Williamsburg for a brief stay. After stating that the "Legislative, Executive and Judiciary Offices shall be kept forever separate," the document granted voting privileges to a far broader spectrum of the people than had heretofore been provided, guaranteed religious freedom and freedom of the press, and abolished the inheritance laws of primogeniture and entail that Virginians had brought from England. All the heirs should have equal rights—male and female alike.

But his plan arrived too late. A draft, called The Virginia Declaration of Rights and prepared chiefly by George Mason, a Fairfax County planter who was a close friend of Washington and the Lees, had already been accepted. Williamsburg was hot, the delegates were tired, and they were not anxious to reopen the debate. Perhaps, too, Tom's "plan of government" was too radical a proposal for the conservative members of the Virginia Assembly. But they did adopt his preamble, a recital of all the wrongs the king had committed against Virginia.

At this point, desperately worried about Martha and, again, receiving no mail from her, Tom wrote two letters to the Virginia Assembly requesting that it not reelect him to the Continental Congress, and that he be granted permission to return home. The requests were denied.

Philadelphia was becoming oppressively warm, and while Tom was comfortable at Mr. Randolph's, he began to think of moving to a cooler spot. He was hoping "to get lodgings in the skirts of town where I may have the benefit of a freely circulating air."[3] He missed his mountains.

One week later he did move, although not to the outskirts of town, as he had wished. He took lodging in a quieter section, in a new brick house owned by Mr. Graff (Tom spelled it Graaf), a newly married young bricklayer. The house, situated on the southwest corner of Market and Seventh streets, was three stories high, "five windows wide and four windows deep." Tom rented the second floor, which

The house on Market Street in which Thomas Jefferson wrote the Declaration of Independence.

consisted of a furnished parlor and bedroom. There were only a few other houses nearby.

Tom took with him the little desk that Mr. Randolph had made, along with a revolving Windsor chair that he had asked for also.

Before the end of the month the Virginia delegation received instructions from the convention at Williamsburg to propose a declaration of independence and to call for foreign alliances and the confederation of the colonies. Richard Henry Lee hastened to comply.

On June 7, he rose in the State House in Philadelphia and, in a three-part resolution, moved, "that these United Colonies are, and of right ought to be, free and independent States, that they are absolved from all allegiance to the British Crown, and that all political connection between them and the State of Great Britain is and ought to be, totally dissolved."

The fiery Lee, whose one hand had lost its fingers in a hunting accident, gestured for emphasis with the hand wrapped in a black silk handkerchief. He went on to propose that the colonies immedi-

The fiery Richard Henry Lee, who proposed "that these United Colonies are, and of right ought to be, free and independent States."

ately "take the most effectual measures for forming foreign alliances."

Finally, he urged that "a plan of confederation be prepared and transmitted to the respective Colonies for their consideration and approbation."[4] This would be known as Articles of Confederation and Perpetual Union.

John Adams jumped to his feet to second the motion.

Congress was in an uproar. It sat until 7 P.M., then adjourned until "punctually at ten o'clock" the next day, Saturday, June 8. Heated debates continued all that day.

Pennsylvania, New York, New Jersey, Delaware, Maryland, and South Carolina were still under instructions to vote against a declaration of independence. Their delegates, among them Robert Livingston, James Wilson, and Edward Rutledge, and led by John Dickinson, argued that the time was not right. The radicals, led by John Adams, Richard Henry Lee, and George Wythe, replied that the declaration of independence would simply "declare a fact which already exists."

As Dickinson continued his desperate plea for time, all of New

England, Virginia, and Georgia argued that the debate had ended when American blood was shed at Lexington. And through it all, Thomas Jefferson said not a word but sat quietly, taking notes.

Congress recessed on Sunday, then continued the struggle to reach an agreement on Monday. Finally, a compromise was effected. The resolution would be postponed for three weeks, until July 1. But a committee would be appointed at once to prepare the declaration. In this way, should Congress agree, no time would be lost in drafting it. It was clear, Tom would say later, that the moderates were "not yet matured for falling from the parent stem."[5]

Drafting a resolution was a necessary task because a mere assertion of independence by Congress was considered inadequate. It was essential, Congress felt, to clearly and simply define the reasons for the resolution in such a manner that the colonists would understand the need for the action and would be inspired to fight for independence.

The facts must also be explained to the rest of the world. Congress understood that it must promote the American cause and justify the severing of ties with Great Britain and the establishment of America's own government. The support of other nations might be critical to the new nation's success.

At this point, the tide was running strongly toward independence, but there was still much to be done. Canvassing, intriguing, caucusing, persuading and would be needed behind the scenes. Here Tom did not simply take notes. Here was where he could shine. Never one to allow himself to be drawn into the battles waging among the delegates, Tom was always on good terms with the older, more conservative leaders and retained their confidence. He and Sam Adams, with that man's great skill in political organization and management, met regularly to devise plans and assign individual tasks to other members.

It is interesting to note that Mr. Dickinson, while he led the opposition and refused to change his mind, never lost the respect of the radicals. It was he who, for the most part, worked out the plan for the Articles of Confederation. The document proposed that the confederacy be officially designated "The United States of America," reflecting a desire to organize the thirteen colonies under a united national government that would assume the authority previously held by London.

*   *   *

On Wednesday, June 13, Richard Henry Lee did what Tom wanted so desperately to do himself: He left Philadelphia to return home to Virginia and to take part in the formation of their new government.

But Congress had other plans for Mr. Jefferson. He was chosen to head the committee to draft the declaration. He had already won for himself a reputation for his "masterly pen" and for his "peculiar felicity of expression." Benjamin Franklin, John Adams, Roger Sherman of Connecticut, and Robert R. Livingston of New York were also appointed to the committee. But the highest vote for any of the five went to the quiet young man from Virginia.

All of the men elected were distinguished. Franklin, at seventy, was one of the most commanding figures of his time. His name was known throughout the colonies and in Europe. Adams, at forty-one one of the most famous Patriots in New England, had a fine reputation as a political thinker and speaker. His name, too, was known in London. Sherman, fifty-five, was the most distinguished Patriot in Connecticut, and Livingston, the only one younger than Tom (he was thirty), while relatively new in public office, was destined for a brilliant career.

But Thomas Jefferson was the one chosen to write the declaration. All the members recognized that he could disagree politically yet still remain on friendly terms socially. He was unyielding in his principles, they knew, but he "bore the olive branch." He was the one man who knew the history, the law, and the principles of government thoroughly, who had an unshakable faith in the ability of men to govern themselves, and who wrote graceful, elegant prose.

Accordingly, when the committee first met at the stone farmhouse several miles outside the city where Dr. Franklin was recuperating from the gout, they unanimously insisted that Mr. Jefferson should write the declaration. The committee members discussed the general content, or "articles" of the document, then nominated Jefferson "to draw them up in form and cloath [sic] them in proper dress."[6]

He accepted the assignment, later saying of it simply, "The committee for drawing the declaration of Independence desired me to do it. It was accordingly done."[7]

Forty-six years later John Adams would give a somewhat different version. He *and* Jefferson were asked to "make the draught," he said. Then, "Jefferson proposed to me to make the draught."

I said, "I will not."
"You should do it!"
"I will not."
"Why?"
"Reasons enough."
"What can be your reasons?"
"Reason first—You are a Virginian, and a Virginian ought to appear at the head of this business. Reason second—I am obnoxious, suspected, and unpopular. You are very much otherwise. Reason third—You can write ten times better than I can."
"Well, if you are decided, I will do as well as I can."
"Very well. When you have drawn it up, we will have a meeting."[8]

Tom returned to his lodgings in Mr. Graff's house and isolated himself for the next seventeen days. He was glad, now, that he had moved there, for the house, remote from the center of the bustling city, provided him with the quiet that he needed.

His routine followed a pattern that varied only slightly. He arose each day at dawn, when there was just enough light in the sky by which to read, soaked his feet in a basin of cold water which, he believed, helped to ward off colds, played his violin softly for a while, then sat in his chair in the sunny second-floor parlor, propped his new desk on his lap, took his quill pen in hand, and began to write.

He had no books in front of him as he composed, but his encyclopedic memory recalled much that he had read over the past years. As he pondered the task facing him, he knew that the time had come to express the conclusions that he had reached slowly, gradually, as he had read the historians, the philosophers, the old lawyers, and had copied some of their ideas into his *Commonplace Book*.

He would call now on all this earlier reading, on his writing, and on his legal experience, and he would distill all the ideas already in his mind from these many sources into one short document. He would adapt some of the ideas he had put forth only last month in his Preamble to the Virginia Constitution. He would try to write simply, clearly, logically.

He had read John Locke's *Second Treatise of Government,* as had many of his compatriots, again and again, and it was strongly impressed on his mind. Locke had written that no one ought to harm another in his life, health, liberty, or possessions. Tom would amend that. He would speak of life, liberty, and the pursuit of happiness, for he believed that happiness of the people was one of the objects for which governments existed. It was this concept, he felt, that could lay the foundation for a commonwealth of freedom and justice.

He would address this declaration to the American people, he decided, and he would express in it the principles that had directed his Saxon forefathers in their "settlement" of England. He would explain the rationale of their descendants who had brought with them to America the right to settle in a sparsely inhabited land and to live there freely and happily under their own chosen government. He would simply reclaim the colonists' Anglo-Saxon birthright.

He would include no new ideas, nor would he say things that had never been said before. To attempt to justify a revolution on principles that no one had heard before would be foolish, he knew. He would simply "place before mankind the common sense of the subject, in terms so plain and firm as to command their assent." He would express simply and concisely, in "language really used by men," the wishes and ideals of his country. He would say exactly what everyone was thinking. It would be "an expression of the American mind."[9]

Now, bending his head over his little writing box, sipping the tea that Bob had quietly placed in front of him, he began to put his thoughts on paper, adding, "interlining," and crossing out as he went along. As a page became too difficult to read because of all the changes, he copied it "fair," then repeated the process. He worked on it in sections, rather than as one continuous text, until he was almost finished. Only then did he put it all together.

As he wrote, he chose his phrases carefully until the sound and the sense were perfectly matched. He could hear the pitch and cadence and rhythm of what he wanted to say. He wrote quickly and easily, but he revised constantly, always searching for the better word, the happier phrase, the smoother transition. He aimed for the ease and simplicity of good conversation.

> we might have been a great & a happy people together, but communicated of happiness & of grandeur it seems is beneath their dignity. ~~we will climb then the roads to glory & happiness apart~~ be it so, since they will have it. the road to glory & to happiness is open to us we will climb it ~~in a separate state~~ and acquiesce in the necessity which ~~pronounces~~ our ~~everlasting Adieu!~~ eternal separation![10]

Tom had never before been much concerned with spelling or capitalization when he wrote, and he always avoided the initial capital letter when he began sentences. Now he took unusual pains to be consistent.

He knew that should the colonies win their independence, the declaration would become an extremely important public document. He knew, also, that the fate of the colonies might rest on his document. He had been given the mandate of convincing the world that the colonists had a legal and a moral right to separate from Great Britain.

> this is too much to be borne even by relations: enough then be it to say, we are now done with them.

No, he decided, this sentence was awkward. He struck it out altogether.

He had to convince the world that the colonists were *not* rebelling against established political authority, but were a free people maintaining long-established rights against a usurping king. Revolution, he knew, was not legal according to British law as stated by Blackstone. His task, then, was to plead his country's cause in terms of the rights of *men*. His appeal would be to a higher law, "the Law of Nature and of Nature's God."

No longer was he a lawyer writing a legal brief. He had become a deeply committed man, pouring his own emotions—his faith, his burning passion for his country and for the rights of man—into electrifying phrases.

A Declaration by the Representatives of the UNITED STATES OF AMERICA, in General Congress assembled.

When in the course of human events it becomes necessary for one people to dissolve the political bands which have connected them with another, and to assume among the powers of the earth the separate and equal station to which the laws of nature & of nature's god entitle them, a decent respect to the opinions of mankind requires that they should declare the causes which impel them to the separation.

We hold these truths to be self-evident; that all men are created equal, that they are endowed by their creator with inherent & inalienable rights; that among these are life, & liberty, & the pursuit of happiness; that to secure these rights, governments are instituted among men, deriving their just powers from the consent of the governed; that whenever any form of government becomes destructive of these ends, it is the right of the people to alter or to abolish it, & to institute new government, laying it's foundation on such principles & organising it's powers in such form, as to them shall seem most likely to effect their safety & happiness. prudence indeed will dictate that governments long established should not be changed for light & transient causes: and accordingly all experience hath shewn that mankind are more disposed to suffer while evils are sufferable, than to right themselves by abolishing the forms to which they are accustomed. but when a long train of abuses & usurpations [begun at a distinguished period &] pursuing invariably the same object, evinces a design to reduce them under absolute Despotism, it is their right, it is their duty, to throw off such government & to provide new guards for their future security. such has been the patient sufferance of these colonies; & such is now the necessity which constrains them to expunge their former systems of government. the history of the present king of Great Britain is a history of unremitting injuries and usurpations, [among which appears no solitary fact to contradict the uniform tenor of the rest all of which have] in direct object the establishment of an absolute tyranny over these states. to prove this, let facts be submitted to a candid world, [for the truth of which we pledge a faith yet unsullied by falsehood]

Rough draft of the Declaration of Independence. Jefferson aimed for the ease and simplicity of good conversation as he wrote and rewrote the document, always searching for the best word, the best phrase, the smoothest transition.

But all the while that he was writing, Tom never for a moment forgot his own personal anguish. He was all too aware of the precarious state of his wife's health and longed to be back on Monticello with her. Was he sacrificing her to this cause? he brooded. "Every letter brings me such an account of her health, that it is with great pain I can stay here," he wrote to John Page.[11]

But he did stay, and he produced what has come to be considered one of the greatest documents ever written—a monument of literature, a manifesto of freedom, a bulwark of Western civilization.

When Tom was satisfied that he had done the best he could, he made one more fair copy. This he gave first to John Adams, then sent it by messenger to Dr. Franklin, still confined to his rooms with the gout. They changed only two or three words, "interlined in their own handwritings."[12] Tom made a few more changes of his own, then showed it to the whole committee, which made no additional changes.

On Friday, June 28, he presented it to Congress. As the delegates sat in their high-backed cushioned chairs, shuffling papers on the tables in front of them or whispering behind cupped hands, it was read aloud, then left on the table for their perusal. There was no discussion.

Numerous other matters of ordinary business were dealt with, and then Congress adjourned until "nine o'clock Monday next."

Such was the reception of the Declaration of Independence.

Tom was left to wait until after the weekend for any word of approval. But his job was done, and he would try not to brood on it. On Saturday he bought a straw hat for ten shillings, a map, and spurs, and paid his wine merchant and his barber.

Monday morning, July 1, dawned bright and cloudless. By eight-thirty, as Tom walked from his lodgings toward the State House, the bricks and cobbles were already giving off heat. As he walked up the three steps and through the wide double doors of the building, he was grateful for the cool of the hallway inside.

The tension mounted as the members began to assemble. Today they would vote on Lee's resolutions that the colonies were free and independent states.

John Dickinson, his face pale against his plum-colored coat, rose to defend for the last time the conservative point of view. He spoke for nearly an hour. John Adams answered him in what Jefferson would describe years later as "a power of thought and expression that moved us from our seats."[13] As Mr. Adams spoke, pounding his hickory walking stick on the floor for emphasis, a storm broke outside and he had to raise his voice against the roll of the thunder. It grew dark. Candles were brought in. Still the debate raged on. It continued for nine hours, with no break for dinner. Even John's cousin, Sam Adams, who rarely spoke in Congress, spoke today, quietly and convincingly, rising on his toes in his characteristic manner as he ended a sentence.

Finally the delegates from South Carolina requested that the decision be postponed until the next morning so that they might have time to reconsider.

Everyone understood that voting for independence was voting for war, and a unanimous vote was essential. Colonies that voted against independence would not be included in the confederation and so would become, in effect, enemy states. No one wanted this to happen.

The delegates understood, too, that voting for independence meant jeopardizing their fortunes as well as their lives. They knew that English law provided that traitors could be partly strangled, their bowels torn out and burned before their eyes, their heads then cut off and their bodies quartered.

They recognized, also, that once Congress voted formally, its decision was final. A vote on independence taken too soon could destroy Congress. In order to prevent this, they had the day before turned themselves into a Committee of the Whole, in which both debate and vote were unofficial, a trial balloon, so to speak. Therefore, no colony need leave Congress because of a recommendation.

When Congress became a Committee of the Whole, President John Hancock had stepped down and Benjamin Harrison had taken the chair as head of the Committee. Everyone else remained where he was.

During the past weeks more and more of the delegates had come over to the side of the Patriots. Their faith was proving greater than their fear. When they met this Tuesday morning, South Carolina had made the decision to join their ranks. John Dickinson, who could never bring himself to vote for independence, and Robert Morris, both of Pennsylvania, had stayed away, allowing their state to vote "aye" without them. And Caesar Rodney, who had ridden eighty miles in darkness and heavy rain, arrived from Delaware drenched and covered with mud just in time to cast the deciding vote in favor of independence. Only the New York delegates, still waiting for instructions from home, did not vote. But their vote was promised and, within a few days, they, too, sent approval. Independence was established.

John Adams, writing to his wife, Abigail, the next day, expressed the momentous significance of the decision:

> Yesterday, the greatest question was decided, which ever was debated in America, and a greater, perhaps, never was nor will be decided among men. . . . The second day of July, 1776, will be the most memorable epoch in the history of America. I am apt to believe that it will be celebrated by succeeding generations as the great anniversary festival. It ought to be commemorated, as the day of deleverance, by solemn acts of devotion to God Almighty. It ought to be solemnized with pomp and parade, with shows, games, sports, guns, bells, bonfires, and illuminations, from one end of this continent to the other, from this time forward, forevermore."[14]

But the momentous "epoch" that so excited Adams would be reduced to a historical footnote by the event that was to follow two days hence.

Now the delegates turned their attention to the paper that Mr. Jefferson had placed before them the preceding Friday. Once again, the white-paneled chamber in the State House resounded with long and heated debate. It would last for the greater part of the second, third, and fourth days of July. It was not a happy time for Tom. Word by word, sentence by sentence, page by page, his document was criticized, ripped apart, changed by men whose talents were certainly not literary.

As he listened to the often rude criticism, he sat silently squirming in his seat. He did not speak on behalf of his "instrument." It would be better, he felt, to listen to the opinions of others who could be more impartial judges than he. But feisty John Adams, angered at the evident distress of his friend and at the mutilation of what he considered to be a brilliant document, kept jumping to his feet to defend it, fighting for every line as Tom had written it as though he were fighting for his life. Tom would remember him for this always with gratitude and affection.

The pragmatic Ben Franklin, too, in his own way tried to comfort his young colleague and to soften the blows. Sitting beside him, he leaned over and whispered a story:

When I was a journeyman printer, one of my companions, an apprentice Hatter, having served out his time, was about to open shop for himself. His first concern was to have a handsome signboard, with a proper inscription. He composed it in these words: "John Thompson, Hatter, makes and sells hats for ready money," with a figure of a hat subjoined. But he thought he would submit it to his friends for their amendments. The first he shewed it to thought the word "hatter" tautologous, because followed by the words "makes hats" which shew he was a hatter. It was struck out. The next observed that the word "makes" might well be omitted, because his customers would not care who made the hats. If good and to their mind, they would buy, by whomsoever made. He struck it out. A third said he thought the words "for ready money" were useless as it was not the custom of the place to sell on credit. Every one who purchased expected to pay. They were parted with, and the inscription now stood "John Thompson sells hats." "*Sells* hats," says his next friend? Why nobody will expect you to give them away. What then is the use of that word? It was stricken out, and "hats" followed it, the rather, as there was one painted on the board. So his inscription was reduced ultimately to "John Thompson" with the figure of a hat subjoined.[15]

* * *

But it was not until years later that Tom could appreciate the humor of Dr. Franklin's story.

Tom was saddened as he heard a passage deleted that exposed his own feelings:

> We must endeavor to forget our former love for them [the English], and hold them as we hold the rest of mankind, enemies in war, in peace friends. We might have been a free and a great people together.[16]

And he was particularly upset when Congress struck out the clause condemning slavery and slave trade and denouncing the king's determination "to keep open a market where men should be bought and sold."

> He [the king] has waged cruel war against human nature itself, violating its most sacred rights of life and liberty in the persons of a distant people who never offended him, captivating and carrying them into slavery in another hemisphere, or to incur miserable death in their transportation thither.[17]

In deference to South Carolina and Georgia, which wished to continue slave traffic, this paragraph was struck out. "Our northern brethren also I believe felt a little tender over those censures; for though their people had very few slaves themselves, yet they had been pretty considerable carriers of them to others," Tom wrote of it later.[18]

Congress continued to question, edit, harden the phrases, but much of Tom's simple, direct, precise prose was left intact. Congress speedily approved the preamble. His final words—"we mutually pledge to each other our lives, our fortunes and our sacred honour"—they agreed, could not be improved. In spite of what Tom might have thought at the time, his colleagues were not as ruthless as the friends of John Thompson, the hatter, and the declaration emerged a stronger document.

A severe thunderstorm on the night of July 3, such as Philadelphia had not experienced in a long time, brought a cold and dreary morning with a bracing north wind on July 4. When Tom arose at dawn, as was his custom, he noted in his little *Account Book* that the temperature was sixty-eight degrees Fahrenheit at 6 A.M. From this time on he continued to keep a record of the temperature wherever he happened to be. As the day progressed, the sun came out and the temperature rose to a pleasant seventy-six degrees at one o'clock. Later, it became oppressively hot and humid in the crowded chamber, even with the windows open.

The delegates continued their debate, but they were becoming increasingly uncomfortable and irritable. Next door to the State House was a livery stable from which swarms of flies emerged. They entered the delegates' room through the open windows, alighting on the legs of the delegates and biting hard through their silk stockings. The men, in turn, lashed furiously at the flies with their handkerchiefs, but to no avail. Years later Tom would say that the debate that day finally came to an end and a vote was taken merely to get away from the flies. Treason was preferable to discomfort.

Late in the afternoon Benjamin Harrison, chairman of the Committee of the Whole, announced that the delegates had agreed to the document that had been presented. The situation that afternoon was essentially the same as that which had existed on July 2. Twelve colonies voted in the affirmative, while New York kept silent. To someone listening at the door, it might have sounded unanimous, for there was no dissenting vote heard.*

Now Mr. Harrison read aloud the title, "A Declaration by the Representatives of the United States of America in General Congress Assembled," paused, overcome by the magnitude of the occasion, then continued,

> WHEN in the Course of human events, it becomes necessary for one people to dissolve the political bands which have connected them with another, and to assume among the powers of the earth, the separate and equal station to which the Laws of Nature and of Nature's God entitle them, a decent respect

---

* New York adopted a resolution approving and supporting the Declaration on July 9. It was laid before Congress on July 15. It then became "The Unanimous Declaration of the Thirteen United States of America."

to the opinions of mankind requires that they should declare the causes which impel them to the separation.

The delegates sat in complete silence as the haunting cadence of the words of the preamble echoed through the hall.

He continued with Tom's revolutionary philosophy of democracy:

> We hold these truths to be self-evident, that all men are created equal, that they are endowed by their Creator with certain unalicnable Rights; that among these are Life, Liberty and the pursuit of Happiness.—That to secure these rights Governments are instituted among Men, deriving their just powers from the consent of the governed.—That whenever any Form of Government becomes destructive of these ends, it is the Right of the People to alter or abolish it, and to institute new Government, laying its foundation on such principles and organizing its powers in such form, as to them shall seem most likely to effect their Safety and Happiness.

The body of the document is a stinging indictment of the king who caused the crisis. Relentlessly repeating "He has . . ." nineteen times, Tom listed all the specific grievances against George III. Read aloud, this steady piling up of offenses became a mournful bell tolling the death of American allegiance to the king.

The fourth and final section asserts that for men accustomed to freedom, there is only one choice:

> WE, THEREFORE, the Representatives of the UNITED STATES OF AMERICA, in General Congress, Assembled, appealing to the Supreme Judge of the world for the rectitude of our intentions, do, in the Name, and by the Authority of the good People of these Colonies, solemnly publish and declare, That these United Colonies are, and of Right ought to be FREE AND INDEPENDENT STATES; that they are Absolved from all Allegiance to the British Crown, and that all political connection between them and the State of Great Britain is and ought to be totally dissolved; and

that as Free and Independent States they have full Power to levy War, conclude Peace, contract Alliances, establish Commerce, and to do all other Acts and Things, which Independent States may of right do.—And for the support of this Declaration, with a firm reliance on the protection of divine Providence, we mutually pledge to each other our Lives, our Fortunes and our sacred Honor.[19]

Nowhere is Mr. Jefferson's "peculiar felicity of expression" more evident than in the closing sentence of his declaration. The members of Congress had chosen well.

When Mr. Harrison finished reading, he ordered the document signed.

Members hurried to the table to witness the signing and to toast the Declaration with Madeira wine. Spirits were high now, as the tension of the past weeks was relieved. As John Hancock, president of the Continental Congress, signed his name boldly, he said, "There, John Bull may read *my* name without spectacles and may now double his reward 500 pounds on my head. That is my defiance."[20] Congressional Secretary Charles Thomson then signed his name to authenticate Mr. Hancock's signature.

As the men gathered around the table, John Hancock urged the necessity for all the members to hang together. To this the wise and witty Ben Franklin replied, "Yes, we must indeed all hang together, or else, most assuredly, we shall all hang separately."[21]

Suddenly, time was of the essence. It was urgent that the Declaration be printed for immediate distribution to the states for proclamation. There was no time even for Charles Thomson to make a copy of the draft with its amendments or to transcribe it into the Secret Journal. He simply left space in the volume for the attachment of a printed copy.

Tom, as the author and head of the Committee of Five, personally delivered the document to the Market Street shop of John Dunlop, printer to Congress. Later in the evening Thomson joined him at the shop to help in the task of proofreading. In an effort to get the job done as quickly as possible, Mr. Dunlop cut the manuscript into sections and assigned each to a different compositor. The manuscript got so cut up and dirtied in the process of printing that it was discarded. Consequently, the historic copy actually approved by Congress did not survive.

Mr. Dunlop was able to publish the entire text of the Declaration in his *Pennsylvania Packet,* and before sunset that night the *Pennsylvania Evening Post* came streaming off the press with the terse announcement:

This day the
CONTINENTAL CONGRESS
declared the
UNITED COLONIES FREE
and
INDEPENDENT STATES.

But it had been inserted just at press time on a back page.

"The original Rough draft," from which Tom had made the copy that he had presented to Congress on June 28, he kept for his own files. From this he made additional copies to send to his friends who were anxious to know what was happening. He wanted them to see the way the document read before it was "mangled" by Congress. His friend Richard Henry Lee assured him by return post that "the thing is in its nature so good that no cookery can spoil the dish for the palates of free men."[22] His old friend John Page, addressing him as "My dear Jefferson," said simply, "I am highly pleased with your declaration. . . . God preserve the United States."[23]

XII
"Public service
and private misery"

Late on the morning of July 8, 1776, crowds began to gather in the State House yard. Precisely at twelve noon, under the authority of the Continental Congress and by order of the Committee of Safety of Pennsylvania, the Declaration of Independence was proclaimed by the sheriff of Philadelphia and read aloud by his deputy. Immediately following the reading there were three cheers, and then the crowd, led by the mayor of Philadelphia and other city officials, marched down the street to hear it read once again at the Court House.

That evening, under a star-filled sky, bonfires were lit throughout the city, battalions paraded on the common, and church bells tolled. The coat of arms of King George III was removed from the State House and brought to the commons, where, as the great crowd of spectators cheered, it was placed on a pile of casks and burned. The lead would be used to mold bullets for Washington's army.

Jefferson was there, watching from the sidelines. No one except the members of Congress knew that he was the author, since his name had not been attached to the Declaration. Cheers and celebrations continued all night. But they were not for him.

Within a few days the Declaration reached General Washington and was read at the head of each brigade of the Continental Army in and near New York City amidst "demonstrations of joy." Similar scenes were enacted throughout the colonies as the news arrived.

It was not until August 2 that the Declaration was finally hand lettered on parchment and laid on the table to be signed by the members. Tom signed his name simply, Th Jefferson. He was one of many. He knew, as did all the members gathered round the table, that if the war with England were to be lost, all those who signed could be hanged for treason. Consequently, the signed parchment copy was kept in a secret place until January 18, 1777.

John Dickinson was not among the signers. He still hoped fervently for an eventual reconciliation with England. But he was patriot enough to ride off to join his regiment and fight to defend the Declaration.

Tom had done his job, and now his thoughts were all with Martha. In an anguished letter to Francis Eppes, he wrote: "I wish I could be better satisfied on the point of Patty's* recovery. I had not heard from her at all for the two posts before, and no letter from herself now."[1]

It seems likely that Martha had suffered a miscarriage and was experiencing great difficulty recuperating from it both physically and emotionally. In the eighteenth century childbearing exacted a harsh toll on both mother and baby. In Martha's case, the circumstances were always particularly complicated. Recent medical opinion speculates that Martha may also have been suffering from diabetes, a condition probably not readily diagnosed, or treated, in eighteenth-century Virginia, and one that is often aggravated by pregnancy. But there is little doubt that she was seriously ill.

Soon, though, a letter did arrive from her, begging Tom to come home. Impulsively, he wrote back immediately saying that he would be there by the middle of August. Then he set about trying to arrange his leave from Congress. He sent a letter to Edmund Pendleton that must have been a very difficult one for him to write:

"I am sorry the situation of my domestic affairs renders it indispensably necessary that I should solicit the substitution of some other person here, in my room. The delicacy of the House will not require me to enter minutely in to the private causes which render this necessary."[2]

Then, to his extreme distress, he realized that, one by one, the older members had all gone, leaving him the sole guardian of Virginia's vote in Congress.

Desperately, he wrote to Richard Henry Lee, imploring him to return to Philadelphia and relieve him: "For God's sake, for your

* the intimate name Tom used for Martha within the Wayles family only

country's sake and for my sake, come. I receive by every post such accounts of the state of Mrs. Jefferson's health that it will be impossible for me to disappoint her expectation of seeing me at the time I have promised. . . . I pray you to come. I am under a sacred obligation to go home."[3]

But Lee would not be hurried.

Tom remained in Philadelphia through a sweltering August, attending to the business of Congress. He served on committees and wrote reports. And he collaborated with Adams and Franklin once more, this time on the design for a seal of the United States. The motto *"E Pluribus Unum"** was the result. Franklin's suggestion, *"Rebellion to tyrants is obedience to God,"* was adopted for the "other side." Tom liked Franklin's motto so much that he used it himself, stamping it on the wax with which he sealed his own letters.

Finally, he could wait no longer. He bought some hats and guitar strings, settled his accounts for his lodgings and his horses, and packed his belongings. On Tuesday, September 3, the sandy-haired aristocrat, sitting straight and tall in the saddle, and the slender dark-haired slave, each riding one horse and leading another with their packs, set out for Monticello. On the way they stopped at The Forest to collect Martha and little Patsy. Tom and his family would have eighteen days together on their mountaintop.

By October Martha seemed to have recovered some of her strength, and she agreed to accompany her husband to Williamsburg for the meeting of the Virginia Convention. Tom was overjoyed. George Wythe had graciously made his Williamsburg house available to them. As they were preparing for the trip, Tom felt a sense of well-being, a jubilance at the thought of returning to his familiar haunts in Williamsburg, of once again taking his seat in the legislature there and having a hand in preparing the laws of Virginia—so dear to his heart. And he would have his wife at his side. Never again would he be far from her, he vowed. He would concentrate his efforts on the local scene.

Autumn in Williamsburg with her husband seemed to make Martha blossom again. She visited the doctor several times and was growing steadily stronger.

* "Out of Many, One"

They had been in Williamsburg just a few weeks when Tom was faced with a wrenching decision. A letter arrived by messenger from John Hancock, offering Tom the post of commissioner to France. He would serve with Benjamin Franklin and Silas Deane, who was already in France. The war was not going well, and French aid was sorely needed. Jefferson's ability with words, his fluency in French, his intelligence, and his diplomatic skill were well known in Congress.

"If it is your pleasure, one of our armed vessels will meet you in any river in Virginia that you choose,"[4] Richard Henry Lee had written by way of added inducement.

For three days Tom kept the messenger waiting as he agonized over the decision. But he knew he couldn't go. Martha was in the very early stages of another pregnancy and certainly could not be expected to endure the rigors of a trip across the sea—a voyage that might take up to two months in cramped quarters with poor food and in possibly rough weather. And he couldn't leave her home without him.

The letter that he sent to John Hancock declining the post serves as just another example of his unusual reserve and shyness. He could not expose his personal life to public view.

"It would argue great insensibility in me could I receive with indifference so confidential an appointment from your body. My thanks are a poor return for the partiality they have been pleased to entertain for me. No cares for my own person, nor yet for my private affairs would have induced one moment's hesitation to accept the charge. But circumstances very peculiar to the situation of my family, such as neither permit me to leave nor to carry it, compel me to ask leave to decline a service so honorable and at the same time so important to the American cause. The necessity under which I labor, and the conflict I have undergone for three days, during which I could not determine to dismiss your messenger, will I hope plead my pardon with Congress."[5]

Tom was unable to tell the president of Congress, in simple and direct words, that his wife was ill and expecting another baby.

When Richard Henry Lee, in a stinging letter, accused him of putting "private enjoyment" before his duty to his country, Tom was devastated. But he could not bring himself to reply.

*   *   *

When Tom took his seat in the newly formed House of Delegates in October of 1776, most of the faces there were familiar ones. Edmund Pendleton was the new Speaker, and Robert Carter Nicholas, Thomas Nelson, and Benjamin Harrison were among some of Tom's old friends. Patrick Henry had been elected the first governor of the Commonwealth of Virginia, and John Page was president of the Council of State.

Henry's elevation to the governorship had left a vacuum of leadership in the assembly, and Tom was quick to fill it. He became a leader in day-to-day legislative procedure, but his effectiveness was primarily the result of his tact, his enduring friendships, his genuine feeling for his country, and the forcefulness of his ideas.

When, on October 12, the House called for a general revision of the laws of Virginia, the opportunity was granted Tom once again to utilize his special talents for his country. He was appointed chairman of a committee of five men who were instructed to repeal, amend, or revise the laws in force to make them clear and intelligible, to introduce others, and finally to report the whole for the action of the legislature.

The members of the committee were Edmund Pendleton, George Wythe (who resigned his seat in Congress in order to accept what he considered a more important assignment), George Mason, and Thomas Ludwell Lee, another liberal assemblyman. But the bulk of the work fell to Tom and George Wythe, leaving them free to express their own ideas. How rewarding it must have been for Tom to be able to work closely with the man who had been his mentor and whom he esteemed above all others. The task would occupy them for the next three years.

The men divided the work between them, and to Tom fell the revision of the criminal code as well as proposals for bills on religion and education. These ultimately resulted in humane criminal laws, which eliminated the brutality that had accompanied the ancient concepts, complete religious freedom, and public education.

But it was his bill against entails, introduced on October 14, 1776, and passed just one month later, that Tom would describe as the first blow against the aristocracy. By eliminating entail, whereby estates were passed down from one generation to another through a particular line of descent, Tom was changing the base of the existing system from inherited privilege to merit.

Primogeniture, by which property descends to the eldest son, neglecting other sons and all daughters, was also unacceptable to him. The eldest son, Tom believed, should not be preferred simply because of his earlier birth, with no consideration of ability or character. Furthermore, as the father of daughters, and having a great respect for the intelligence of women, he saw no justice in disinheriting women.

He was exhibiting here his basic belief in human beings, his intolerance of artificial privilege of any sort. But he was also earning for himself the bitter hatred of some of the members of the landed gentry.

The revisors were working separately, with plans to meet periodically, so much of the time Tom worked at home, in his own library. In fact, he could not have accomplished the job anywhere else.

In the meantime, the war was going badly and, in mid-December of 1776, Tom received a letter at Monticello from Governor Patrick Henry appointing him county collector of blankets and rugs for the freezing soldiers in New Jersey. The winter of 1776–1777 was the coldest in anyone's memory. The wells at Monticello went dry, and water had to be dragged up the winding road to the mountaintop. And there was worry about Martha, too, who was expecting a baby in the spring.

In the middle of May, Tom was granted a leave of absence from the spring session of the legislature to be with his wife when their child was born, and he went home to Monticello with high hopes. These were realized when, on May 28, his friend Dr. George Gilmer delivered Martha of a son. There was much rejoicing among the family, friends, and servants, for a son was very special to Virginians with their deep sense of family pride.

But their joy turned quickly to sorrow: "Our son died 10 H, 20 M. P.M.," Tom wrote seventeen days later.

Tom stayed close to Martha and couldn't answer John Adams's letter until August. Unaware of the tragedy, Adams had written, "We want your Industry and Abilities here extreamly [sic]. . . . Your Country is not yet, quite Secure enough, to excuse your Retreat to the Delights of domestic Life."[6]

Work on the mansion continued very slowly, and Monticello's wells remained dry for the rest of the year. Tom, as always, buried his grief in work and continued his revision of the laws of Virginia. In October he forced himself to leave Martha to take his seat at the fall meeting of the House of Delegates, but he was ten days late.

The year 1778 found Tom busy once again on his mountaintop, interspersing work on the laws with the supervision of the plantation that he loved. And he was staying close to Martha, who was once again expecting a baby. Ninety thousand bricks were made that year, and in one month during the summer, more than fourteen thousand were laid. In the spring Tom added many grafted trees to his orchard—cherry, apple, pear, quince, plum, apricot, and bitter almond—and in the fall he got from Philip Mazzei's neighboring place the shoot of an Italian olive tree. As he planted it, he reflected that it would take ten years to bear fruit.

"Our third daughter born," Tom recorded in his precise manner on August 1, 1778, at 1:30 A.M. They named her Mary. She would come to be known as Maria and, by the family, as Polly. Her sister Patsy was now almost six.

There had been much anxiety over this birth, particularly in light of the babies they had lost and of Martha's fragility, and Tom did not take his seat in the Assembly until he was certain that both Martha and the baby were out of danger. The session was almost over when he arrived in Williamsburg.

As the year 1779 dawned, the children appeared to be thriving, Martha seemed well, and Tom was nearing completion of the laws. He was pleased with what he saw emerging from his years of effort. What he had been attempting was to create a more favorable climate for the freedom and happiness of his countrymen.

His proudest success of the three years of work on the revisions was, for Tom, his Bill for Establishing Religious Freedom in Virginia. In fact, he always believed that it was, with the possible exception of the Declaration of Independence, the most important document he ever wrote. Nothing else he ever accomplished gave him greater satisfaction.

In Virginia, both believers and dissenters were forced to pay taxes for the support of the Anglican Church. While most Virginians were tolerant of dissenting sects, Tom, in "the severest contests in which I have ever been engaged,"[7] demanded much more than tolerance. The state, he insisted, had no business restricting or supporting *any* religious belief or practice. The mind must be free from authority of any kind. There must be a "wall of separation between Church and State."

> Well aware that . . . Almighty God hath created the mind free, and manifested his supreme will that free it shall remain by making it altogether insusceptible of restraint; . . .
>
> We the General Assembly of Virginia do enact that no man shall be compelled to frequent or support any religious worship, place or ministry whatsoever, nor shall be enforced, restrained, molested, or burthened in his body or goods, or shall otherwise suffer, on account of his religious opinions or belief; but that all men shall be free to profess, and by argument to maintain, their opinions in matters of religion, and that the same shall in no wise diminish, enlarge or affect their civil capacities.[8]

These were strong words in eighteenth-century Virginia.

Tom described his Bill for the More General Diffusion of Knowledge, along with his bills for Amending the Constitution of William and Mary College, and for Establishing a Public Library as "a systematical plan of general education."[9] These bills were accompanied by a detailed plan for a public school system. He looked on intelligence as the most precious gift of nature, and he wanted to see it nurtured and developed in all children. Once again, he was fighting against the privilege of wealth and station, providing for an informed, educated electorate—an aristocracy of learning and intelligence.

As he rewrote the laws of Virginia, he was dealing with one state, but he was, in effect, proposing a model for a nation. Virginia was his laboratory of democracy.

As Tom neared completion of the laws, the war suddenly came closer to him. General John Burgoyne was defeated at Saratoga by the American General Horatio Gates on October 17, 1777, and forced to surrender his entire command, which included more than 4,000 English and Hessian soldiers. In September 1775, King George had hired thousands of German troops (called Hessians) to help crush his rebellious subjects. Now Gates stipulated that the captured soldiers should be returned to England. Accordingly, arrangements were made and, in January 1779, the British troops were marched nearly seven hundred miles from Boston, where they had been held for a year, to Albemarle. When they arrived, Congress decided the men should stay.

But the barracks weren't finished, the weather was bad, and the meat provided for the men had spoiled. Soon the farmers in Albemarle were complaining that with four thousand more mouths to feed there wasn't enough food to go around. Now there was talk of a plan to move the troops and separate the officers and men.

Tom was outraged at what he considered the cruelty and injustice of disrupting the prisoners. "But is an enemy so execrable, that, though in captivity, his wishes and comforts are to be disregarded and even crossed? I think not. It is for the benefit of mankind to mitigate the horrors of war as much as possible," he wrote to Governor Patrick Henry in March. This would be a violation of the surrender terms signed at Saratoga, he told him, and "a breach of public faith." Such a measure "would suppose a possibility that humanity was kicked out of doors in America, and interest only attended to."[10]

The plan was dropped, the men went to work and completed the barracks themselves, and soon planted gardens to provide the necessary produce for their own subsistence. The gay appearance of the stocky, red-faced Baron Von Riedesel and his German officers in their blue regimentals with bright red facings and silver frogs, broad lace upon their hats and coats, became a familiar sight in the neighborhood.

Tom and Martha invited the British and the German officers to dinner at Monticello, had musical evenings with them, playing duets on the violin, and discussed philosophy and science with those who were interested. But what they most enjoyed was the music the soldiers brought to Albemarle, "an enjoyment the deprivation of which with us cannot be calculated," Tom said.[11] Mme. Von Riedesel had a beautiful voice, and she, too, participated in the musical evenings.

* * *

During the years 1776 to 1779 Tom had been active on every important committee in the Virginia House of Delegates. At each session he served on anywhere from twelve to twenty-four committees, drawing innumerable reports and bills. Over the course of these years he easily assumed leadership of this group and soon attained the power and popularity that had belonged to Patrick Henry. He became the symbol of the rising tide of democracy.

It was not surprising, then, that as Henry's term as governor neared expiration, Tom's friends nominated him for that office. His instincts told him to decline. Just the month before he had talked of retirement from politics altogether. Martha's health was steadily worsening, and he knew that he would not be able to take her to Williamsburg with him. The governorship, then, would mean another separation from her and from his children.

But his friends were adamant, and Tom understood that it was his duty to accept. He wrote to Richard Henry Lee: "In a virtuous government, and more especially in times like these, public offices are, what they should be, burdens to those appointed to them, which it would be wrong to decline, though foreseen to bring with them intense labour, and a great private loss."[12]

That he accepted the nomination and was elected governor of Virginia has been called the great misfortune of his life. No period of his career laid him open to more abuse.

By the beginning of 1779 most Americans were sure the Revolutionary War was coming to an end. France had entered on the American side, and the people thought that England, unable to gain victory, would give up the struggle. But suddenly, at just the time that Tom was elected governor, the war entered a new and ominous phase. Unable to destroy Washington's army in the North, the British determined to "unravel the thread of rebellion from the southward."[13]

Virginia was virtually defenseless. She was open to attack along her long exposed coastline as well as from hostile Indians spurred on by the British in the Blue Ridge Mountains and on the frontiers beyond. She had no regular army for her defense, since all the regular soldiers were in the Continental Army in the North. Even these were often ragged and hungry, for Congress had no money to pay them. Inflation was making paper money worthless.

All able-bodied freemen still at home were enrolled in the militia, but they were untrained, undisciplined, and often unarmed. They were called to action only at the sound of an alarm. And they had to fight against English soldiers, the best-trained troops in the world, who were being supplied by the world's greatest navy.

Smallpox, also, was causing a great loss of lives. Extremely contagious, often fatal, and with no known cure, it had felled thousands of soldiers. "The smallpox is ten times more terrible than Britons, Canadians and Indians together,"[14] John Adams wrote. The colonies had already suffered more than fifty epidemics.

Such was the state of affairs when Thomas Jefferson became governor of Virginia on June 1, 1779. He had just turned thirty-six. It was the next day when he stood, in powdered wig and fashionable dress of the period, in the great hall of the House of Delegates, where he had served as a burgess for so many years, to express his thanks to the General Assembly. Martha was not there to hear him or to share with him all the warm wishes and letters of congratulation that poured in from all over the colonies. "I will not congratulate you, but my country," his old friend William Fleming wrote.[15]

Tom had seen Martha and the two little girls comfortably settled in the cool, familiar shade of The Forest before he himself had set out for Williamsburg. The town in midsummer was far too hot for her delicate constitution. He feared for her health as well as her comfort. He visited her as often as possible, then brought her to the Governor's Palace to live in the fall, when the city was cooler and she had regained some strength.

But Tom didn't have very much time to spend with Martha. The responsibilities of the governor involved many details, and he devoted long hours to his work. This included executing laws, maintaining relations with Congress, dealing with Indian affairs, prisoners of war, public works, trade and taxes, raising troops, ordering militia, overseeing naval affairs and fortifications, and arranging for support of the army, among countless other tasks.

He found now that the British advance on the South was controlling all his thinking and his actions. But there was little he could do except watch the lengthening shadow of war move steadily closer. As governor, Tom found himself playing an entirely different role from that of reformer and political leader in the legislature. Remembering all too well the power of the royal governors, the framers of the Virginia Constitution had stripped the governor of the state of virtually all power. The state was, in effect, ruled by a Council of State, which consisted of eight members chosen by joint ballot by both houses of the assembly. The governor simply carried out its decisions.

Nor was executive leadership a strong quality of Tom's. Nothing in his background had prepared him for it. Accustomed to following his father's maxim, "Never ask another to do for you what you can do for yourself," he was not in the habit of delegating authority. While his attention to detail was legendary, it is ironic to note that he was bitterly criticized for his lack of efficiency. His strength lay in legislation. This student of the law, this classical scholar, had not been trained to be a war chief. He was not the military leader that the moment called for.

War in Colonial America was very different from the way we know it today. The belief prevailed that those who wanted to fight, and could, should be soldiers, politicians should remain in the legislature or Congress, and businessmen should continue to conduct business and trade. The Revolutionary War itself was not a swift-moving conflict. It was a slow, tedious struggle that demanded infinite patience from the small group of leaders who were guiding it.

Throughout, Tom complied with General Washington's wishes that the needs of Virginia be subordinated to the needs of the main armies, the "grand army," as he called it, and that the best-trained troops be sent to support them. So Tom sent men, money, and arms both north and south, although they were desperately needed at home. He continued to rely only on a poorly armed and unwilling militia. He was faced with a further calamity when a blight hit Virginia's crops in the fall of 1779. Food became even scarcer. Yet through it all, Tom never ceased to put the needs of the Union before those of his state.

Tom remained in the Governor's Palace in Williamsburg until April 1780, when the capital was moved inland to Richmond for security. Richmond, then, was a sleepy, commercial town, and Tom quickly set about drawing elaborate plans for the new capital. Once again, he had an opportunity to indulge his delight in architecture.

He rented a beautiful house from a relative and, on a cold day in April, he brought Martha, the girls, his servants, and assorted household goods to live there.

One month later, just after Tom had begun his second term as governor, Charleston, South Carolina, fell to the British. Tom had rushed the best of Virginia's militia to aid General Gates, the hero of Saratoga whom Congress had just placed in command. Gates was marching south to challenge the British hold on Georgia and South Carolina. But the men, ragged and almost totally inexperienced, many without arms, were completely wiped out in the worst disaster of the war when they encountered the British troops under General Charles Cornwallis at Camden.

As he continued to grapple with the seemingly insoluble problems of war and with the devastating loss of lives, coupled with the knowledge that the British were moving steadily closer, Tom's mind was also on his family. Martha was expecting another baby. As always, the family lived in a state of terrible apprehension until the end of November when, at 10:45 P.M. on November 30, amid the all-too-familiar atmosphere of crisis, Lucy Elizabeth was born. The little girl seemed to thrive very quickly, and, within a month after the delivery, Martha, too, had regained her strength and worry abated.

During these troubling months Tom managed once again to demonstrate his capacity for friendship. He found the time to befriend a young colonel in the Continental Army whom George Washington had sent to him.

James Monroe was a twenty-two-year-old Virginian who had served with distinction in the North but had become bewildered and discouraged and was at a loss now as to what to do. Tom kindly took him under his wing, recommended a legal career, and offered to guide him in his studies. Then he helped him solve his military problems as well. He sent the young soldier to the South to establish a line of communication between the capital of Virginia and the Carolinas. Monroe's letter to Tom a short time later is a tribute to the compassion and understanding that Tom exhibited and to the friendship that was formed—one that would never be broken:

A variety of disappointments . . . nearly destroyed me. . . . had I not formed a connection with you I should most certainly have retir'd from society. . . . In this situation you became acquainted with me and undertook the direction of my studies and believed in me. . . . I feel that whatever I am at present in the opinion of others or whatever I may be in future has greatly arose from your friendship.[16]

The year 1781 began ominously. Brigadier General Benedict Arnold, who had demonstrated daring and skill in a gallant fight for the American cause from Ticonderoga to Saratoga (1775–1777), had, in the spring of 1779, suddenly turned traitor and transmitted military intelligence about the American Army to the British. Now he was in command of a British Army that would invade Virginia from the coast and wreak untold havoc.

Tom first heard of the invasion on a mild Sunday morning, the last day of the year 1780. A messenger arrived to tell him simply that a fleet had been sighted in Chesapeake Bay. Neither the flag the vessels bore nor their destination was known. News such as this had become commonplace and often turned out to be no more than rumor. So it was not unusual that Tom, in his unruffled manner, decided not to disturb the country by calling out the militia until he had more precise information. That information did not arrive for fifty hours.

It was Tuesday morning before Tom learned that the fleet was British, not French, as had been suspected, and that it was not in the Chesapeake, but had entered the James River and was heading toward Richmond. Arnold's fleet, favored by good winds and a strong tide, had swept up the broad river rapidly and had landed troops at Westover, twenty-five miles from Richmond.

Only then did the governor swing into action. He called out 4,600 militia, issued orders for the removal of official papers and military stores from Richmond, and sent his family to Tuckahoe for safety. House servants Bob Hemings and Jim went with them. Jupiter, married now to Sukey, the cook, was left behind in Richmond with some of the other servants to look after the house.

But not until the British fired three rounds of cannon, announcing their arrival in Richmond, did Tom instruct his servant John to saddle a horse and bring it round for him. Years later, one of Tom's slaves recalled that within ten minutes of the firing of the cannons, there was not a white man to be seen in Richmond. Not a member of the Council remained to help the governor. But the governor had stayed to do what he could to safeguard public property before he left the city.

It was one o'clock in the morning when Tom finally arrived at Tuckahoe to check on his family and rest for a few hours. Then, deciding that Tuckahoe was too close to Richmond for safety, Tom took Martha and the three little girls across the river in the early dawn and sent them on to Fine Creek, a plantation eight miles farther inland.

Martha had barely recovered from her pregnancy and delivery, and little Lucy was only two months old. But Tom's worry for their immediate safety from the British had to take precedence over his fears for their ability to withstand the trip in the dead of winter. And he had to force himself to turn away from his anxiety for them to the task at hand. Resolutely, he headed his mare toward Manchester, a small village just across the river from Richmond, and for the next two days he rode furiously through the countryside in snow and drenching rains, looking after records, arms, and stores, and doing what he could to organize resistance. But before he could reach Manchester, his horse, unfed and exhausted, sank under him and died. There was nothing Tom could do but leave the animal on the road. He put his saddle and bridle on his back, then walked until he came to a farmhouse, where he borrowed the only horse that was left—an unbroken colt. He reached Manchester just in time to watch helplessly as Arnold set fire to strategic parts of the city across the river.

Arnold couldn't hold Richmond against the militia, but his raid had a different effect. It destroyed stores and crippled morale. It damaged arms and ammunition, clothing, food, and most of the papers of the auditor and the Council of State. These last had been left in Richmond despite Tom's orders to remove them.

After only twenty-three hours Benedict Arnold escaped by the same timely shift in wind that had brought him up the river. The breeze took him swiftly down the James and away from the militia that was in hot pursuit. The governor was mortified. He had been caught off guard.

Overnight, the man who had written the Declaration of Independence, reformed ancient laws, served on important committees, championed the rights of the people, and who had steadily supplied General Washington with all the troops, arms, and horses the state had, was condemned because he couldn't keep the British out of Virginia.

Jefferson promptly wrote a frank letter to General Washington, acknowledging his failure. That man replied with gentle words of comfort, and finally recognizing the seriousness of the situation, sent 1,200 regulars under the Marquis de Lafayette to Virginia. Lafayette was a wealthy young French nobleman who had volunteered in the Continental Army at the age of nineteen. Now at twenty-three, he was a major general, highly regarded by Washington. But he came too late to capture Benedict Arnold. His arrival, though, marked the beginning of a long friendship between him and Jefferson.

The war continued to rage on Virginia's soil and in her waters. Jefferson did what he could. All that Virginia had of men and resources were enlisted in the cause. In fact, so many men were in service during the planting season that Tom feared that there wouldn't be enough food raised to feed the people. Finally, he begged his friend Benjamin Harrison, now Speaker of the assembly, to go to Philadelphia to plead for arms in person. If they could not provide a supply, he said, at least they might repay Virginia the arms she had lent for the protection of the Carolinas.

And there seemed to be no end to Tom's misery. On a raw, rainy day in April, at ten o'clock in the morning, little Lucy Elizabeth, only five months old, died. Public service was taking a terrible toll.

Martha was so distraught that Tom didn't know what to do for her. Nor did he dare leave her alone. Although his Council met just a few yards from his house in Richmond, he sent a note to one of the members, saying, "The day is so very bad that I hardly expect a Council, and there being nothing that I know of pressing, and Mrs. Jefferson in a situation in which I would not wish to leave her, I shall not attend today."[17]

Tom was more certain now that he would retire from office at the conclusion of his second term—June 2, 1781. "I think public service and private misery inseparably linked together,"[18] he would later write to James Monroe.

By May the legislature, fearful of another attack on Richmond, made plans to meet in Charlottesville instead on May 24. Tom's second term of office would expire on the first of June, but the Assembly had not yet found time to arrange for a new election. Some of the members were beginning to talk of appointing Patrick Henry a temporary dictator. Tom was horrified. What Virginia needed most, he felt, was a strong, able general, in whom the people could have confidence. He believed that in such a crisis civil and military power should be in the same hands. He suggested to his friends in the legislature that Thomas Nelson, commander-in-chief of the Virginia Militia, be elected governor.

He even wrote to General Washington on May 28, asking if it were possible for "Your Excellency" to come to Virginia because "the presence of their [Virginians'] beloved countryman . . . would restore full confidence."[19]

Washington replied, "Give me leave . . . to Express the obligations I am under for the readiness and zeal with which you have always forwarded and supported every measure which I have had occasion to recommend thro' you, and to assure you that I shall esteem myself honored by a continuance of your friendship."[20]

But Washington couldn't come. May ended, and Virginia had no governor.

During this time Lord Cornwallis was pushing up the coast from the Carolinas into Virginia, and General Banastre Tarleton and his cavalry were galloping toward Charlottesville under instructions to capture Thomas Jefferson and the members of the legislature.

John Jouette, a captain in the militia and a citizen of Charlottesville, was in the Cuckoo Tavern in Louisa County late in the evening of June 3, when Tarleton's legion swept by on the main road. Suspecting their destination, "Jouette quickly mounted his fine horse and rode furiously toward Monticello by a less used and shorter route.

Galloping over rocks and fallen trees, his face lashed by branches, he covered the forty miles to the top of the mountain several hours ahead of the enemy, arriving shortly before daybreak.

As he came pounding up Monticello's winding road, the clatter of the horse's hoofs awakened Tom and the members of the legislature who were his guests at the time. They were startled to hear this outlandish-looking figure in scarlet coat, military hat and plume, his face streaked with blood, tell them that Tarleton was on his way with 180 green-coated dragoons and 70 red-coated infantry, also on horseback.

Only Tom took the news calmly. He quietly ordered that a carriage be brought round, and that Caractacus, his favorite horse, be taken to Monticello's blacksmith to be shod. Then he awakened Martha and the children and insisted that they and their guests have a leisurely breakfast. He insisted also that Jack Jouette stop long enough to refresh himself with a glass of Madeira wine. Years later, in his old age, Jouette, who had come to be called Virginia's Paul Revere, would laugh and say that he would "do it again for another glass of Mr. Jefferson's Madeira."[21]

They were all certain that Tarleton's heavily armed men could not possibly equal Jouette's pace, and that there was time to spare. Besides, Tom reasoned, he was no longer governor, and the British were not interested in capturing him. He was simply a private citizen with a family to look after. But he was wrong. As the author of the Declaration of Independence, he had become one of the most wanted men in America.

Soon Jouette turned his horse back down the hill to warn the other members of the Assembly in Charlottesville, all of whom fled immediately.

After breakfast, Tom's guests left also, but Tom, Martha, and the children remained in the house. Suddenly, a young officer came rushing up to the door to tell Mr. Jefferson that the British were almost to the foot of the mountain. Only then did Tom bundle his family and a few servants into the waiting carriage and send them off to his friend Colonel Carter's nearby Blenheim plantation. Once again, as on their honeymoon, Blenheim would be for them a lee port in a storm.

Tom tried to allay Martha's fears and to reassure her that they would all be safe. He would meet them at Blenheim in time for dinner, he promised her.

As soon as the carriage pulled out, Tom told two trusted servants, Martin and Caesar, to hide the silver plate and other valuables, and ordered his horse brought to a point in the road between Monticello and neighboring Carter's Mountain. Then he walked through the woods, cutting across his land to the valley between the two mountains. When he reached his horse, he began walking it up the mountain, pausing to look back at Charlottesville through a telescope he had brought along. The city was quiet.

Deciding that there was still time to remove some of his papers from the house, he started back down the mountain. He was fearful that when the British reached Monticello they would set fire to it. Suddenly he noticed that the little dress sword he had been wearing at his waist was gone. It had slipped out of its scabbard, he guessed, as he had knelt down to sight his telescope. He went back to retrieve it.

Before leaving again, Tom decided to have another look at the city below. This time Charlottesville was swarming with Tarleton's dragoons. Tom mounted his horse and galloped into the woods on Carter's Mountain. The sword had saved his life.

As Tarleton's troops, under Captain McLeod, arrived at Monticello, Martin was handing down the last of the silver to Caesar, who was under the wooden floor of the front portico. A glimpse of white through the trees warned Martin, and he quickly slammed down the plank, leaving his comrade imprisoned below. There Caesar would remain, cramped and silent, without food or light, for the next eighteen hours.

Martin, standing on the plank, received McLeod with dignified politeness. The captain returned the courtesy. He was under orders from Tarleton to capture Governor Jefferson, but he was not to disturb anything in the house. He even locked the door to Tom's study and gave the key to Martin. But the soldiers plundered the wine cellar. They broke the necks off the bottles with their swords, drank some of the wine, and spilled the rest out.

One of the dragoons, anxious to locate Tom, put a pistol to Martin's chest, cocked it, and threatened to fire unless the slave revealed his master's whereabouts.

"Fire away, then!" Martin retorted.

Tom's faith in his servants was well founded. The family never forgot their devotion.

Meanwhile, Tom had joined his family at Blenheim, as he had promised. Later, he took them further away, and, finally, another seventy miles to Poplar Forest in Bedford County, where he felt certain they would be safe.

At the same time that Tarleton's men were pursuing the governor and the members of the legislature in Charlottesville, Cornwallis had advanced up the James River to Tom's plantation at Elk Hill, probably the most valuable of all his farmlands. Here Tom was not so lucky. Describing the devastation a few years later, Tom said that the ruthless Cornwallis had "destroyed all my growing crops of corn and tobacco; he burned all my barns, containing the same articles of the last year; having first taken what corn he wanted; he used, as was to be expected, all my stock of cattle, sheep and hogs for the sustenance of his army, and carried off all the horses capable of service; of those too young for service he cut the throat; and he burned all the fences on the plantation, so as to leave it an absolute waste. He carried off also about 30 slaves. Had this been to give them freedom he would have done right, but it was to consign them to inevitable death from the small pox and putrid fever then raging in his camp."[22] But his special "people," such as Jupiter and John, Sukey, "King" George and his wife, Ursula, and the Heming family, were safe at Monticello.

Tom's friends in the legislature finally realized that he had been serious when he said he would not seek a third term. Now they heeded his advice and elected Thomas Nelson as governor. It was then that the military tide turned. In the South the British were pushed back on Charleston and Savannah. In the North George Washington and a French Admiral named de Grasse began a fortunate union that forced the British commander Cornwallis on to the defensive. Cornwallis surrendered his entire force of 7,000 men at Yorktown on October 19, 1781.

Thomas Nelson proved to be an unpopular governor, and he resigned his office after only six months. Benjamin Harrison succeeded him.

Although Tom had hated the job of governor, he had worked

tirelessly to solve what were essentially insoluble problems. His fear of overstepping the strict legal rights of the office even in an emergency; his wise allocation of Virginia's resources to the common cause rather than to her own defense; and his fleeing to safety from Tarleton's dragoons, just as Samuel Adams and John Hancock had fled from Lexington at Paul Revere's warning, all served to brand him a coward. Tom was industrious, he was attentive to details, and he was careful to abide by all the measures taken by the legislature. Yet a legend grew up about his inefficiency. His faithful dedication to public duty served, in the end, to brand his administration a failure.

XIII
"That eternal separation"

As Tom was riding his horse Caractacus from Monticello to Poplar Forest one day, the high-spirited animal suddenly reared up and pitched its master out of the saddle, leaving him crumpled in the dust with a broken left wrist. Tom was so badly shaken up that he was confined to the house at Poplar Forest for the next six weeks.

Soon after, he learned that Mr. George Nicholas, a new young member of the Virginia legislature, had instituted an inquiry into his conduct as governor, accusing Jefferson of having neglected to take proper measures of defense. His friends in the legislature, believing that an inquiry would actually do honor to him, seconded the motion, then elected him a member so he could vindicate himself on the floor of the House. Tom was mortified.

He immediately requested a list of the charges. Mr. Nicholas, who would be caricatured later as a plum pudding with legs because of his excessive weight, provided them; then, apparently deciding that he had made a mistake, and embarrassed, he did not attend the hearing when the legislature met in December. Tom, though, rose in the silent hall, read off the list, then proceeded to answer each charge.

At the conclusion the House unanimously passed a resolution declaring "Mr. Jefferson's ability, rectitude and integrity as Chief Magistrate of this Commonwealth."[1] In fact, such was the esteem in which he was held that he had already been appointed a delegate to Congress. But on the very day that he was exonerated by the Virginia legislature, he declined the national appointment, and several days later he took his family to Tuckahoe to spend the Christmas holidays with their Randolph cousins. The damage had been done, and the pain was deep. The charges were "a shock on which I had not calculated."

They "inflicted a wound on my spirit which only will be cured by the all-healing grave."[2]

Tom was never able to handle public criticism, and he brooded over these accusations for many months. The rebuke had come at an extremely bad time. His family had been driven from their home, his baby daughter had died, his farms had been ravaged, many of his servants had been abducted or had died, and his private affairs were in ruin, all because of his faithful dedication to public duty. He was overworked, exhausted, and severely shaken by his accident. He described his condition in a letter to George Washington as a "state of perpetual decrepitude."[3] What he neglected to add, though, was that he was alarmed at the state of Martha's health. She was pregnant again, and Tom knew all too well the toll that pregnancy took on her. He resolved to withdraw from public life completely.

While all his friends could exult in the attainment of victory over England, Tom felt only an overwhelming sense of personal defeat.

"I have retired to my farm, my family and books, from which I think nothing will ever more separate me," he wrote to Edmund Randolph.[4]

"If you can justify this resolution to yourself, I am confident that you cannot to the world," Randolph replied.[5]

But Tom was adamant, and out of this determination to remain in retirement came his *Notes on Virginia*.

From childhood, when he had first wandered in the woods with his sister Jane looking for wildflowers, or hunted and fished with his father, Tom's love of nature had been so intense that his eye observed everything and forgot nothing. As he matured, he had continued to observe, to ask questions, to study, to collect. And he had kept careful notes on everything.

His *Garden Book*, which he had started to keep in 1766 with the poetic entry, "Purple hyacinth begins to bloom," began simply as a diary of his garden. But it became, over the years, a written repository for many varied interests.

His incredible attention to detail went even beyond his *Garden Book*. Tom kept many memorandum books—even notes jotted on loose sheets of paper—teeming with facts and opinions on every branch of learning.

Now a letter arrived from Marquis Francois de Barbe-Marbois, the French consul in Philadelphia, requesting answers to a list of twenty-three questions about Virginia. Tom, in his characteristic manner, seized on this opportunity to organize his notes, to think about them, and to compile them into what would later become his only book, *Notes on Virginia*. A combination of hundreds of useful scientific facts with a proud description of the beauty of his "country," it was at once factual and lyrical.

Mingling reason and romance, Tom described Virginia's climate and crops, its resources for commerce and communication, its wilderness landscapes, its history, its archaeology, its native societies. Marbois would get much more than he had bargained for.

Tom didn't intend the work for publication. It would simply be his answer to the Frenchman's questions, a friendly sharing of scientific knowledge—in three hundred pages.

He catalogued facts, he described Virginia's natural beauty, he proved that American animals were larger than their European counterparts, and he defended the American Indian. Tom's pride in America shone throughout.

And his indictment of slavery is nowhere better stated:

The whole commerce between master and slave is a perpetual exercise of the most boisterous passions, the most unremitting despotism on the one part, and degrading submissions on the other. Our children see this, and learn to imitate it; . . . the parent storms, the child looks on, catches the lineaments of wrath, puts on the same airs in the circle of smaller slaves, gives a loose to the worst of passions, and thus nursed, educated, and daily exercised in tyranny, cannot but be stamped by it with odious peculiarities. The man must be a prodigy who can retain his manners and morals undepraved by such circumstances. . . . And can the liberties of a nation be thought secure when we have removed their only firm basis, a conviction in the minds of the people that these liberties are the gift of God? Indeed I tremble for my country when I reflect that God is just: that his justice cannot sleep forever.[6]

*   *   *

The existence of slavery, he felt, was as degrading to the master as to the slave. Slavery was not only a moral wrong; it was a violation of the natural order of things. The very freedom that had just been won with such sacrifice could not, he was certain, survive as long as the institution of slavery remained.

As Tom continued his task, thinking that he was merely answering Marbois's questions, he was unwittingly setting down his own views on politics, religion, science, education, and philosophy—an index, as it were, to his own mind. *Notes on Virginia* became his view of how life in America should be, his vision of the possible, his dream for the future.

All the while that Tom was working on his *Notes,* he remained close to Martha, spending every free moment with her. During this time, a handsome young Frenchman, the Marquis de Chastellux, who had been one of the commanders of the French Army at Yorktown, came to visit Tom at Monticello. This meeting with Chastellux, and the friendship that developed, was the beginning of a fondness for the French people that would last for the rest of Tom's life.

"Let me describe to you," the marquis wrote, "a man, not yet forty, tall, with a mild and pleasing countenance, but whose mind and understanding are ample substitutes for every exterior grace. An American, who without ever having quitted his own country, is at once a musician, skilled in drawing, a geometrician, an astronomer, a natural philosopher, legislator, and statesman. . . . It seemed as if from his youth he had placed his mind, as he had done his house, on an elevated situation from which he might contemplate the universe."[7]

Monticello was not completed at the time that Chastellux visited, but enough had been done to convince the marquis that "Mr. Jefferson is the first American who has consulted the fine arts to know how he should shelter himself from the weather."[8]

Chastellux saw very little of Martha during his visit, so his description of her tells us only that she was "mild and amiable."[9] Martha was expecting another baby any day, and she was keeping to her room. Tom and Chastellux, though, stayed up far into the night, drinking punch and enthusiastically reading poetry aloud to one another by candlelight.

Just a few days after Chastellux departed, on May 8, 1782, Martha gave birth to an unusually large baby girl, whom they named Lucy Elizabeth, after the little girl they had lost. The baby seemed to thrive, but her mother couldn't regain her strength. Day by day she grew steadily weaker and seemed to be wasting away in front of them.

Half nurse, half companion, Tom sat with her for hours on end, holding her hand, reading to her, willing her to live. When she slept he wrote his *Notes* in a little room just off the bedroom, near enough to hear her stir. All other ordinary activities—even correspondence—were suspended. Martha lingered for four months. Tom was rarely out of calling.

Occasionally, he would take time out to stroll around the grounds hand in hand with Patsy and little Polly. By now, he had begun to stock his park with beautiful white-tailed deer, and father and daughters often stopped to feed them. And they always stopped to talk to Shadwell, Martha's parrot.

Two days before the birth of the baby Tom had abruptly declined the seat in the Virginia legislature to which he had just been elected. Now he learned that he was being accused of selfishness and threatened with arrest. Speaker John Tyler wrote to him: "I suppose your [reasons] are weighty, yet would I suggest that good and able men had better govern than be governed, since tis possible, indeed highly probable, that if the able and good withdraw themselves from society, the venal and ignorant will succeed. . . . I can not but think the House may insist upon you to give attendance without incurring the censure of being rigid."[10] At that time it was within the power of the House of Delegates to send a sergeant at arms to Monticello to drag Tom to Richmond under arrest.

Tom's only response, though, if it can be called that, was to write to his understanding friend James Monroe of the thirteen years he had devoted to public service and of his right to retire. But it was the final lines of the letter that revealed the real reason: "Mrs. Jefferson has added another daughter to our family. She has been ever since and still continues very dangerously ill."[11]

Martha grew steadily weaker.

One day, as Tom and Martha were reading together, Martha asked for a pen, and recognizing that she was slowly slipping away, she wrote from memory a stanza from *Tristram Shandy,* a favorite book of theirs:

> Time wastes too fast: every letter
> I trace tells me with what rapidity
> Life follows my pen. The days and hours
> Of it are flying over our heads
> Like clouds of windy day, never to return—
> More everything presses on—

Her strength ran out. She couldn't go on. But Tom, who knew the passage as well as Martha, and knew, too, that its author, Laurence Sterne, had written it to a loved one as he was dying, completed it:

> —and every
> Time I kiss thy hand to bid adieu,
> Every absence which follows it, are preludes to
>   that eternal separation
> Which we are shortly to make!

Just before she died, Martha made one last anguished plea of her husband. Some of the favorite house servants had been allowed to come in to see her, and they listened as she struggled to hold back the tears and to tell her husband some of the things she hoped he would do. Her greatest concern, she whispered, was for her three little girls, and her fervent wish was that the children should not be brought up by a stepmother, as she had been. Quietly, solemnly, Tom promised that he would never marry again. But he continued to reassure her—and himself—that she was not dying.

When she sank into a final coma, ". . . he was led from the room almost in a state of insensibility by his sister, Mrs. Carr, who with great difficulty, got him into the library, where he fainted, and remained so long insensible that they feared he never would revive," Patsy described it years later.[12]

Alarmed by her brother's reaction, fearful that he, too, was dying, Martha Carr frantically called out to Elizabeth Eppes, still bending over her lifeless sister, "Leave the dead and come and take care of the living!"[13]

But it was ten-year-old Patsy, patient, sensitive, understanding, who finally drew her father out of the stupor into which he had fallen:

*   *   *

He kept his room three weeks, and I was never a moment from his side. He walked almost incessantly night and day, only lying down occasionally, when nature was completely exhausted, on a pallet that had been brought in during his long fainting fit. My aunts remained constantly with him for some weeks—I do not remember how many. When at last he left his room, he rode out, and from that time he was incessantly on horseback, rambling about the mountain, in the least frequented roads, and just as often through the woods. In those melancholy rambles I was his constant companion—a solitary witness to many a burst of grief, the remembrance of which has consecrated particular scenes of that lost home beyond the power of time to obliterate.[14]

A bond was forming between father and daughter that would never be broken.

Martha was buried beneath the great oak tree on the side of their mountain, beside the bodies of their three tiny children and their dear friend Dabney Carr. The simple note in Tom's *Account Book* for September 6, 1782, reads, "My dear wife died this day at 11:45 AM."

The inscription he wrote for the simple slab of white marble that would mark her grave probably tells more about his love and devotion than other words could convey:

To the memory of
Martha Jefferson
Daughter of John Wayles;
Born October 19th, 1748, O.S.
Intermarried with
Thomas Jefferson
January 1st, 1772
Torn from him by death
September 6, 1782:
This monument of his love is inscribed

*   *   *

Then, in Greek:

> If in the house of Hades men forget their dead,
> Yet will I even there remember my dear companion.

And he went beyond the epitaph. He destroyed every letter that he and Martha had exchanged over the years. He would never be able to reread them, never reopen old wounds. He would ensure, also, that their letters to each other would not become public property, that they would never be open to prying eyes. Martha belonged not to the country but to him.

Forty-four years later, after Tom himself had died, a secret drawer was discovered in a private cabinet that contained locks of hair and other little mementos of his wife and each of the children, including those who had died, all labeled in his own handwriting. Although carefully arranged, everything gave evidence of having been frequently—and lovingly—handled.

Suddenly, life seemed meaningless for Tom. She who had been "the cherished companion of my life," and with whom he had lived "in unchequered happiness,"[15] had been snatched away from him. As he rode his horse through the Albemarle hills, or paced the floors of Monticello, there seemed little reason to go on living. What remained for him? Even filled as Monticello was with his children, his sister and her children, and the servants, the house became for Tom an empty shell, devoid of the spirit that had given it its beauty.

Redheaded, freckle-faced Martha, at ten already large boned and growing tall like her father, became his shadow, riding with him five or six miles a day and trying to lessen his grief simply by being there.

In anguish Tom wrote to his sister-in-law Elizabeth Eppes, "This miserable hand of existence is really too burthensome to be borne and were it not for the infidelity of deserting the sacred charge left me, I could not wish its continuance a moment. . . . The care and instruction of our children indeed affords some temporary abstractions from wretchedness. . . ."[16]

He did honor the sacred charges left to him, and in November took his own and all the Carr children to be inoculated against smallpox at Ampthill, the home of his friend Archibald Cary, who had lent it to him for that purpose. He remained with them as their "chief nurse,"[17] caring for them all until they recovered.

From Ampthill he wrote to the Marquis de Chastellux that he was just "a little emerging from the stupor of mind which had rendered me as dead to the world as was she whose loss occasioned it."[18]

By the time that Tom returned to Monticello, Congress had thrown him a lifeline. Once again they offered him the commission to negotiate peace in Paris. His friends in Congress, Madison foremost among them, guessed correctly that now he would welcome this opportunity. And they were right. This time Tom accepted.

Tom took Polly, now four years old, and Little Lu, as he called her, to the Eppes, where his sister-in-law had offered to care for them. Patsy, he decided, much to her delight, was old enough to accompany him. But the ship that was to carry them to France was caught in the ice at the entrance to the Chesapeake, and a provisional peace treaty was signed before they could sail.

By the middle of May he and the children were all back at Monticello. For Tom it was a quiet summer, filled with haunting memories of his Martha.

His unmarried sister, Anna Scott, came to stay with him. His brother Randolph, Anna's twin, lived simply on his own lands nearby. A well-liked and kindly man, Randolph had not inherited his older brother's keen intelligence, but he and Tom maintained an affectionate relationship. Tom handled Randolph's legal and financial affairs and was consulted by him on all matters of importance.

In June word came that Tom had been elected to Congress. His term would begin in November. Tom was glad that he could once again "lend a hand to the laboring oar."[19]

He tried hard to keep busy in the interim. He classified and catalogued his entire library, which by now had grown to 2,640 volumes. Working alone, he arranged the books according to Sir Francis Bacon's divisions of knowledge. He began an index of his correspondence, which he called an "Epistolary Record," and, from then on, for the rest of his life, he kept a careful record of all his letters. It is from these tens of thousands of letters that his thoughts and activities can be pieced together like a mosaic. He seemed always to be writing. The act of writing appeared to be for him the act of thinking. He clarified his own thoughts as he wrote them.

Tom used the summer, also, to instruct Martha, now nearing eleven, and the Carr children. He was concerned about their education because there were relatively few good schools in Virginia at that time. He worried particularly about Martha, and wrote to Marbois in Paris, "the chance that in marriage she will draw a blockhead I calculate at about 14 to 1."[20] This meant that the education of her own family would "rest on her own ideas and direction without assistance." Tom was taking no chances.

On October 16, accompanied by Martha in the phaeton and his servant James on horseback, Tom set out for Philadelphia. When they arrived there, they discovered that Congress had unexpectedly moved to Annapolis, Maryland. With a heavy heart, Tom decided that it was not wise to take his daughter with him to Annapolis and so prevailed upon Mrs. Thomas Hopkinson, widowed mother of Francis Hopkinson, a friend and fellow signer of the Declaration of Independence, to care for her. He then made arrangements for her to study under the guidance of several tutors.

Tom attended to his own affairs, and when he was confident that Martha would be happy with the kindly Mrs. Hopkinson, he hurried to catch up with Congress. As soon as he arrived in Annapolis, he wrote to this daughter the first of many letters to his children that would continue for the rest of their lives. Written during long periods of separation, these letters provide a glimpse into the soul of Thomas Jefferson and reveal a side of him not visible in any of the tangible memorials he left behind. Beautiful letters of advice, of love and tenderness, and often of wit, they show how deeply interested he was in every little detail of their young lives, and how difficult it was for him to be apart from them. He had become both father *and* mother.

* * *

Annapolis, Nov. 28th, 1783

My dear Patsy—After four days' journey, I arrived here without any accident, and in as good health as when I left Philadelphia. The conviction that you would be more improved in the situation I have placed you than if still with me, has solaced me on parting with you, which my love for you has rendered a difficult thing. The acquirements which I hope you will make under the tutors I have provided for you will render you more worthy of my love; and if they can not increase it, they will prevent its diminution. . . . With respect to the distribution of your time, the following is what I should approve:

From 8 to 10, practice music.

From 10 to 1, dance one day and draw another.

From 1 to 2, draw on the day you dance, and write a letter next day.

From 3 to 4 read French.

From 4 to 5, exercise yourself in music.

From 5 till bed-time, read English, write, etc.

Communicate this plan to Mrs. Hopkinson, and if she approves of it, pursue it. . . . I expect you will write me by every post. Inform me what books you read, what tunes you learn, and inclose me your best copy of every lesson in drawing. Write also one letter a week either to your Aunt Eppes, your Aunt Skipwith, your Aunt Carr, or the little lady[*] from whom I now inclose a letter, and always put the letter you so write under cover to me. Take care that you never spell a word wrong. Always before you write a word, consider how it is spelt, and, if you do not remember it, turn to a dictionary. It produces great praise to a lady to spell well. I have placed my happiness on seeing you good and accomplished; and no distress which this world can now bring on me would equal that of your disappointing my hopes. If you love me, then strive to be good under every situation and to all living creatures, and to acquire those accomplishments which I have put in your power, and which will go far towards ensuring you the warmest love of your affectionate father,

Th. Jefferson

[*] her little sister Polly

P.S.—Keep my letters and read them at times, that you
may always have present in your mind those things which will
endear you to me.[21]

Patsy strove to comply. Cheerful, loving, and enthusiastic, she
took to heart her father's advice and tried hard to pattern herself
after him. That he was consistently loving and kind softened for her
the effect of his moralizing. Secure in the knowledge that she would
always be dear to him, she didn't always follow his instructions. She
occasionally let as much as two months slide by without writing or
sending the copies of her lessons that he requested.

When Congress finally did assemble in Annapolis, Tom discovered
that many of his old friends were no longer there. They were occupied
elsewhere, and Congress was filled with new, younger members. In
this group, Tom stood out and quickly assumed leadership. His work
during the next five months would leave a permanent imprint on
American life.

One of the first orders of business for Congress was the acceptance
of George Washington's farewell. At that time Washington could
have become a king or a dictator, but he chose, instead, to relinquish
his command of the army and retire to his farm in Virginia.

Tom was chosen chairman of the committee to arrange the ceremonies, and he drew up a simple but dignified and impressive order
of proceedings scheduled to take place two days before Christmas.
Then, characteristically, he quietly stepped aside.

At the ceremony in the emotion-packed room, as Washington
read, with shaking hands, of his departure from "the great theatre
of action" and bid Congress "an affectionate farewell,"[22] spectators
and congressmen alike wept. Tom called it "an affecting scene."[23]

When the president of Congress rose to reply, there were very
few in the audience who did not realize that Thomas Jefferson had
written his speech. Yet that very evening, Tom could shift easily to
a different role. From a leader in Congress and a writer whose words
stirred the hearts and minds of his countrymen, he could become a
concerned father, anxious to instruct his daughter. He admonished
Patsy:

*   *   *

I omitted . . . to advise you on the subject of dress, which I know you are a little apt to neglect. . . . be you, from the moment you rise till you go to bed, as cleanly and as properly dressed as at the hour of dinner or tea. . . . Nothing is so disgusting to our sex as a want of cleanliness and delicacy in yours."[24]

Tom took no part in the gay social life swirling around him in Annapolis. As members of Congress attended lively balls and parties given by the wealthy socialites of the city, Tom remained at home, reading and writing. Still deeply depressed by Martha's death, he admitted his "gloom" to a new young friend, a Dutchman named G. K. von Hogendorp. In a rare show of his emotions, Tom told him, "I have been happy and cheerful. I have had many causes of gratitude to Heaven; but I have also experienced its rigors. I have known what it is to lose every species of connection which is dear to the human heart—friends, brethren, parents, children."[25] Yet he couldn't bring himself to include the word "wife."

Tom worked tirelessly in Congress and continued to put his unique stamp on the future of his country. During the next five months he was a member of nearly every important committee. He drafted thirty-one state papers.

One of these, his "Notes on the Establishment of a Money Unit and of a Coinage for the United States," established the dollar as the basic American currency. Tom had already simplified the laws of Virginia. Now he was attempting to simplify the arithmetic of money. Congress accepted Tom's plan, but not his equally simple system of weights and measures.

Perhaps his most important contribution during that period was his "Report" of March 22, 1784. A few months earlier Tom had been appointed chairman of a committee to deal with the question of the future government of the vast new territory called the Northwest. Virginia had ceded her claims to the lands north and west of the Ohio River to the country. She had, in effect, given away an empire. Now Tom's "Report" outlined simply and concisely a plan of government for this territory. It allowed for new territories to be admitted to the Union on equal status with the thirteen original states. It provided in detail for ten new states, stipulating that their governments be republican, with no hereditary titles, and that slavery not be permitted after the year 1800.

Although the section on slavery was voted down, Tom's desire to exclude it from the Northwest Territory helped limit its hold, and it never flourished there.

Here Tom showed himself to be a prophet once again—a major architect of American expansion. His "Report," although never put into effect, is ranked by historians as second in importance only to the Declaration of Independence and became the basis of the Northwest Ordinance of 1787. This law, which came to grips with how a nation should deal with its colonial peoples, also forbade slavery in the Old Northwest.

Tom had one more important duty to fulfill for Congress, and in this he was, without realizing it, to anticipate the next five years of his own life. Congress recognized that friendly commercial relations had to be established with foreign countries as quickly as possible if the United States were to survive as a nation. So Tom was asked to prepare the list of instructions for diplomatic agents to follow in negotiating treaties with these countries. Nothing like this had been done before. But, once again, Tom had already thought long and hard on the subject, and he was prepared.

Among his suggestions was one to send a mission to Europe to negotiate with those countries with which the United States still had no formal connection. Two representatives were already there: Benjamin Franklin had been minister to France since 1776; and John Adams, who had been in Europe since December 1779, was minister to the Hague, in Holland. Now Mr. Jefferson was nominated to be the third.

On May 7, 1784, Congress appointed Thomas Jefferson minister plenipotentiary to negotiate treaties of commerce with the maritime powers of Europe and those of Africa bordering on the Mediterranean. Suddenly his mind was filled with a thousand plans—for his family, for Monticello, for his forthcoming trip. He immediately sat down to write letters.

His first was to William Short, a young man of unusual ability and promise whose studies Tom had been guiding, asking him to accompany him to France as his private secretary. Next he made arrangements to take his servant James Hemings with him. He wrote to his good friend James Madison, asking that man to accept as a "tender legacy" Peter and Dabney Carr, sons of "the dearest friend I knew."[26] Madison, he hoped, would oversee their education while he was gone. He invited Martha Carr and her entire family to remain at Monticello and extended an invitation to pass the hot season there to Mr. and Mrs. Skipwith (his wife's sister Ann Wayles and her husband), and to his own sister Anna Scott Jefferson.

In the last letter Tom wrote, he asked his sister-in-law Elizabeth Eppes to continue to care for his two little girls. They were too young to risk the perils of an ocean voyage. He would take his Patsy with him to share the big adventure. At long last the door to Europe was open to him. Perhaps it would be the door to a new life as well.

XIV
"Behold me on
the vaunted scene of Europe"

Jefferson hurried to Philadelphia from Annapolis—the trip took four days—then celebrated his arrival there by attending "the playhouse." He spent the next two weeks dealing with the endless details of preparing for the trip.

He shopped in Philadelphia for many of the things that he and Patsy would need for their journey, furnishings and bedding for their cabin aboard ship among them. There was so much to be done that there was not enough time to make the long trip back to Virginia to see his two little children.

There were no papers for him to study, no precedents to guide him in his new role. He was a pioneer who would have to learn as he went along. To begin his education, he decided to tour the northern states before he departed for France and to see and absorb all that he could.

He collected Patsy, and together they set out for a trip through New England in the little time remaining. Patsy, sitting straight beside her father in the phaeton, and dressed in the best clothes he could purchase for her in the city of Philadelphia, was delighted with the pocket money her father had given her for souvenirs along the way.

Since he would be dealing with questions of commerce in Europe, Jefferson met with the governors of each of the states he and Patsy visited and discussed with them their commercial needs. Father and daughter went as far north as New Hampshire, then returned to Boston, where they boarded the *Ceres*. The date was July 4, 1784, the eighth anniversary of the Declaration of Independence. They set sail from Boston harbor at four o'clock the next morning.

There were only five other passengers, "all of whom Papa knew," Patsy wrote to their friend Mrs. Elizabeth Trist in Philadelphia, "and fine sunshine all the way, with a sea which was calm as a river."[1] The trip was remarkably short—only nineteen days from land to land—with favorable winds most of the way. When they were becalmed for three days off the coast of Newfoundland, they spent the time fishing.

Shadwell the parrot had come with them, and he often amused the crew and passengers with his caustic comments.

In contrast to his usual activity, Jefferson used the voyage to relax and enjoy his fellow passengers, sharing with them the fresh apples and oranges and the fine wines he had brought on board. He did take some time, though, to learn Spanish with the help of a grammar and a copy of *Don Quixote* that he had with him.

Jefferson looked forward to seeing the friends such as Chastellux and Lafayette who were waiting for him in France and to being able to add to his store of knowledge—to gather facts, to make comparisons. The "vaunted scene of Europe,"[2] as he would call it later, would offer new opportunities to satisfy his ever-curious mind. And he would be able to send home to America the useful information he gathered.

This tall, spare man in black, now forty-one years old, knew life and people, and he understood the workings of his government. No one else in America was better qualified to represent it than he. He may not have realized it at the time, but he had become, after George Washington and Benjamin Franklin, the most famous national figure.

As he paced the deck, thinking, he resolved to correct the impression in Europe that the United States was a loose confederation of states. He would convince the Europeans that his country was a nation worthy of their respect. Suddenly, he realized that when he said "my country," he was no longer thinking of Virginia alone.

They landed in Portsmouth, England, near the end of July, then crossed the English Channel to Havre in a tiny boat, in a violent rainstorm. The cabin on the vessel was so small that they had to crawl into it, and Patsy teased her distinguished father about his long legs. From Havre they followed the Seine to Paris. The harvest season was just beginning, and Tom's farmer's eye appreciated the fertile fields along the way. But they looked in vain for the sun.

Once settled in Paris, they saw very quickly that before Tom could begin to conduct official business, they would have to be dressed properly. Their simple American clothes looked strange there, and they were warned that to be out of fashion was more criminal than to be seen in a state of nature. So Tom summoned the staymaker, milliner, shoemaker, and dressmaker for Patsy, then ordered a suit, hat, shirts, kneebuckles, and shoebuckles, as well as a sword, belt, and lace ruffles for himself.

About a week after the Jeffersons arrived in Paris, John and Abigail Adams, their eighteen-year-old daughter, Nabby, and seventeen-year-old son, John Quincy, came to France. Abigail and Nabby had arrived in London from Massachusetts just three weeks before. John and John Quincy had been in the United Netherlands (Holland), where John Adams had been negotiating a financial loan for Congress. The Adams family was overjoyed to be reunited after a four-year separation and went to live in a lovely house just beyond Passy, the little village west of Paris where the aged Dr. Franklin was living. Tom and Patsy were frequent guests there and quickly came to love the house and its inhabitants.

Before Mr. Jefferson embarked on his official business in Paris, he located a school for Patsy and arranged to enroll her there. Shadwell went with her in a new French cage. The school, called the Abbaye Royale de Panthemont, was considered the finest in Paris. Mother Louise-Therese, the director of the school, was kind to Patsy, but the little girl couldn't bring herself to call her "Mother." She was lonely at first, but her father visited her for a while every day until her French improved. She knew very little of that language when she started, and the girls at the school knew no English, so communication was almost impossible. In spite of this, though, she made friends quickly and soon learned to chatter away in French. Her schoolmates began to call her "Jeffy," and she began to feel at home.

Immediately on his arrival in Paris, Mr. Jefferson had gone to pay his respects to Benjamin Franklin. Now that Patsy was comfortably settled in school, he felt free to begin the work for which he had come to France. He, Dr. Franklin, and John Adams, the triumvirate who had worked together in Philadelphia, reassembled and set to work to prepare the framework of new commercial relations between America and the Old World. Their objective was to negotiate as many treaties of friendship and commerce with various European countries as they could.

The first meeting of the American ministers plenipotentiary took place on August 30, 1784, amid a feeling of optimism. The three men were happy to be collaborators once again and confident that they would be successful in their negotiations.

Jefferson was a diligent and skillful diplomat, and he met many people through Franklin, but negotiating was a very slow process, and soon he was writing, "We do not find it easy to make commercial arrangements in Europe. There is a want of confidence in us."[3]

He still found himself depressed much of the time. Paris winters are far more severe than Virginia winters, and he was disappointed by the gray Paris sky. It was a year before he could report a completely cloudless sky—and he loved the sun. He longed for the red clay hills of Albemarle and the view of the Blue Ridge Mountains from Monticello. And he was still mourning his Martha.

December found him ill and confined to his house for six weeks. Even after that he was still "very weak and feeble," according to Abigail Adams.[4]

He looked forward eagerly to his friend Lafayette's anticipated return to France in January, but when Lafayette did come he brought devastating news: Little Lu had died in October.

Jefferson's anguish can only be guessed at. By now his adored wife was gone and four of their six children. Even Martha's little son John Skelton had died. All he had left were Patsy and Polly. "The sun of happiness [had] clouded over," he said, "never again to brighten."[5] His gloom seemed to echo the wind and the rain of Paris. He was ill for the rest of the winter.

He wrote to Francis Eppes as soon as he was able, ending the letter, "Present me affectionately to Mrs. Eppes, who will kiss my dear, dear Polly for me. Oh! could I do it myself!"[6] How he missed her! He knew, too, how Polly would suffer at the loss of her little sister, whom she called "my baby."

He didn't learn until May that the Eppes had lost their little Lucy at the same time. Both little girls had had whooping cough. Elizabeth Eppes had written to her brother-in-law immediately, but somehow it took almost seven months for her letter to arrive in Paris. "Life is scarcely supportable under such severe afflictions," she had written.[7]

When the sun finally began to shine again in March, and Jefferson could walk six to eight miles each day in the Bois de Boulogne, the largest park in Paris, he began to feel a little better. He loved the sights and sounds of the country. The sun was always medicine for him. Now he resolved to have Polly come to him in France. He must keep what was left of his family together. He began planning her voyage immediately, but it would take two years to accomplish.

On May 2, 1785, Thomas Jefferson was notified of his election by Congress to succeed Benjamin Franklin as minister to the French court. Dr. Franklin had finally received the permission he had been requesting for some time to retire and return home to America. At about the same time, John Adams was named minister to the court of St. James and began preparations to move to London.

Franklin's wit and learning, his wisdom and diplomacy, had won the hearts of the French people, and Jefferson had preferred to remain in the background during his first year in France. He deferred to the seniority and greater experience of his two colleagues, always asking their opinions first. Now he would be on his own.

He had always had the utmost respect for Franklin and considered him the greatest American. So Jefferson could say later, "On being presented to anyone as the minister of America, the common-place question used in such cases was, *'C'est vous, monsieur, qui remplace le Docteur Franklin?'* ('It is you, sir, who replace Dr. Franklin?') I generally answered, 'No one can replace him, sir: I am only his successor.' "[8]

Immediately upon becoming minister to France, Jefferson, according to protocol, informed the comte de Vergennes, the French foreign minister, of his appointment. It was Vergennes who had been the architect of the Franco-American alliance that had helped the colonies win the war with England.

Mr. Jefferson delivered a "letter of credence" to the king and, outfitted in full court dress, had his first official audience with Louis XVI, Marie Antoinette, and the royal family. But Thomas Jefferson was not impressed. And he didn't like the queen. He considered her unpredictable and devoted to pleasure and expense; and he knew that she was rumored to be unfaithful to the king.

Of Louis XVI he said, he "loves business, economy, order and justice, and wishes sincerely the good of his people, but he is irascible, rude, very limited in his understanding and religious bordering on bigotry. He has no mistress, loves his queen, and is too much governed by her."[9]

As was proper, Jefferson gave a dinner for about twenty people to celebrate his appointment. Among the guests were the marquis de Lafayette and his wife, several other notable members of the French court, Commodore John Paul Jones, the courageous and daring naval hero of the American Revolution, and the Adamses.

The outspoken Abigail Adams didn't like the etiquette of a French dinner party. The men, she complained, sat down only when they dined. When they were standing, they shut out all the fire from the ladies, leaving them very cold.

Abigail was the personification of New England pride and reserve, but she was captivated by Tom. This tall and engaging Virginian always had a funny story to tell or a witty observation to make. His fund of information on a multitude of topics was vast and stimulating. He was naturally courteous, his instinctive southern gallantry always evident. In a letter to her sister, Abigail described him as "one of the choice ones of the earth."[10]

While in France, Jefferson had been correcting and enlarging his *Notes on the State of Virginia*. Now he had two hundred copies printed privately, a few of which he gave to his friends in Europe. The rest he sent to friends in America: James Madison, James Monroe, and fellow members of the American Philosophical Society. Jefferson had been elected a member of the society in 1780. The oldest learned

The marquis de Lafayette, a Frenchman who volunteered to serve in the Continental Army. His friendship with Jefferson blossomed when Jefferson was in France.

society in America, it was founded in Philadelphia in 1743 (the year of Thomas Jefferson's birth) by Benjamin Franklin to promote useful knowledge.

Jefferson was not interested in a large printing of the *Notes* for the public. But he did hope that his book would be read by students at the College of William and Mary, in order to set them "into a useful train of thought."[11]

When a French bookseller got hold of a copy and took it upon himself to print a bad French translation, an English bookseller asked Jefferson for permission to print the English original.

Suddenly, Jefferson's standing in the circle of men whose approval he valued most was enhanced. They recognized him as a man of science and letters, a representative of a free and reasonable society. He was becoming a much-sought-after guest at the Paris salons. Here in France, in addition to his role as a negotiator, he could finally be the kind of person he wanted to be—a "detached philosopher," living a life of intellectual pursuits.

As a diplomat, Jefferson, in his own words, "practiced no subtleties, meddled in no intrigues, pursued no concealed objects."[12] His direct approach disarmed his adversaries.

He was settling in to his new routine, and through Lafayette, was expanding his circle of friends. A strong bond of affection grew between the two men. But by the end of August Jefferson was still nostalgic for America. Mail was exasperatingly slow—the packet from New York came only once a month—and letters were often opened. He begged his friends for details, bits of information to help him stay in touch.

To Elizabeth Eppes he wrote, "Pray write to me, and write me long letters. . . . You always know facts enough which would be interesting to me to fill sheets of paper. I pray you, then, to give yourself up to that kind of inspiration, and to scribble on as long as you recollect any thing unmentioned, without regarding whether your lines are straight or your letters even."[13]

Most of all, he missed his little daughter. Now he stepped up his plans to bring her to him.

Soon after his appointment as minister to France, Jefferson moved from the small house in which he had been staying to a much grander one on the Champs Elysées called the Hôtel de Langeac. One of the most beautiful houses in Paris, it was built in the latest fashion of Louis XV and boasted a flush toilet. He would remain there for the duration of his stay in France. William Short moved with him. Patsy came to spend every Sunday.

Jefferson immediately purchased "table furniture"—china, glass, table linen, silver, plated ware, lamps, and household utensils—and, captivated as he had become by French cuisine, found a good French cook named Adrien Petit to run his house.

As a foreign diplomat, Jefferson was obliged to entertain graciously and felt justified in these expenses. But he soon found himself employing many more servants than he had anticipated needing. "It is the policy of this country to oblige you to a certain number of servants, and one will not touch what belongs to the business of another," Abigail Adams explained it.[14]

The allowance paid to the minister by the American government was totally inadequate for this kind of living, and Jefferson found himself in an awkward position. He couldn't afford the expense himself, and Congress was not prepared to deal with the issue. Abigail sympathized with him: ". . . it would take two years of an American minister's salary to furnish the equipage of plate which you will find upon the tables of all the foreign ministers here," she wrote from England.[15]

Troubled by the situation, he wrote to his friend James Monroe in America and asked him to intercede for him in Congress. "All the ministers who came to Europe before me, came at a time when all expenses were paid and a sum allowed in addition for their time." Congress was no longer doing this, and he had spent almost a thousand guineas* of his own money, for which he was in debt. "I ask nothing for my time," he continued, "but I think my expenses should be paid."[16]

His role was developing into something quite different from what Congress had originally envisioned. The triumvirate who had set to work in the summer of 1784 were no longer together, and Jefferson's job was far more encompassing than had originally been expected. The outspoken defender of republican simplicity had become a member of a highly aristocratic and sophisticated society. The philosopher of the New World was now confronting the Old World.

In the midst of his many diplomatic duties, though, he still found time to indulge his interest in art. He had been commissioned by

* British coin worth one pound and one shilling

Congress to have a marble statue made of George Washington. Now he arranged to have Jean-Antoine Houdon, whose reputation as a sculptor, Jefferson assured his fellow Americans, was unrivaled in Europe, undertake the task. In order to ensure that he could execute an exact likeness, Houdon made the long voyage to America to see Washington for himself, rather than relying on a portrait that Jefferson had brought with him. Jefferson was involved in all the planning, until the sculpture was finally completed in France and was then sent home to be erected in Richmond, Virginia.

Jefferson rummaged in the bookstalls of Paris; he walked beside the Seine or strolled under the fragrant foliage of the Bois du Boulogne with newfound friends. He shopped for his family and friends in America.

To his little Polly he sent "sashes" and Parisian dolls. To Peter Carr, the most brilliant of Dabney's children, he sent books and offered advice and guidance in letters to him. He still felt, as he had in 1769, that "the only help a youth wants is to be directed what books to read, and in what order to read them."[17]

He sent books and wine to George Washington, James Monroe, and James Madison. For Madison, also, he purchased Diderot's new *Encyclopédie Methodique*. Madison reciprocated his friend's generosity by sending long, informative letters that kept him in touch with political developments in America.

Soon word came that Virginia had approved his Bill for Religious Freedom.* Madison, he felt certain, had worked hard to win the necessary votes to accomplish this. He wrote to his friend: "The Virginia act for religious freedom has been received with infinite approbation in Europe and propogated with enthusiasm. . . . It has been translated into French and Italian, has been sent to most of the courts of Europe. . . . It is inserted in the new *Encyclopedie*."[18] His pride was evident.

Early in March of 1786, Jefferson received a letter from John Adams, indicating that he thought that England might be ready to negotiate a commercial treaty with America. The wealth of the new nation depended on the growth of foreign commerce, and it was essential to widen American markets.

* January 22, 1786

James Madison, Jefferson's cherished friend and political ally in the Virginia legislature. He guided the Constitution through the convention and kept Jefferson—when in Paris—informed of developments in America.

Jefferson immediately rushed to England, only to realize after he arrived that his friend had been far too optimistic. The two men were kept waiting endlessly and were treated rudely. When they were finally introduced to George III at Buckingham Palace, the king, in full view of surrounding courtiers, abruptly turned his back on the author of the Declaration of Independence without saying a word. Jefferson would never forget this insolence, and a negative feeling toward England remained with him always.

He determined, though, not to waste this opportunity to see some of the country, so he and John Adams toured together. Jefferson was particularly smitten with English gardening, and he took careful notes to aid him later in planning and maintaining an English garden at Monticello.

While in England he had a model made of a polygraph, a portable copying machine that he had found in France. From that time on, he made copies of all his private letters and carefully and methodically preserved them as well as all his personal papers. Many years later, when he was an old man, a gentleman called on him to inquire about a lawsuit in which the gentleman's father had been involved— nearly a half-century before. Jefferson walked to a case, removed a batch of ancient papers from a cubbyhole, and in less than one minute produced the desired document.

This visit to London gave Jefferson an opportunity to strengthen his already deep ties to the Adams family. And it was here that he met a group of American artists who had moved to England, and he sat for his portrait for the first time. This was painted by Mather Brown, a member of the group that included Benjamin West and John Singleton Copley. While Mather's painting is the first portrait of Thomas Jefferson, it is also the most artificial, for it depicts him as a man of fashion. He never wore a wig, yet this portrait shows him in a powdered wig with hair rolled over his ears, completely out of character.

Among these American artists was the slender, black-eyed and black-haired John Trumbull, a dreamy young painter who had come to London to study under the well-known Benjamin West. It was John Trumbull who introduced Jefferson to a lovely young woman who would, quite literally, sweep him off his feet.

XV
"Dialogue between the head and the heart"

When Jefferson returned to Paris from London in May, he had just turned forty-three, and he was a very lonely man. Martha had been gone for four and a half years, Patsy was happily ensconced in school, and Polly was resisting her father's attempts to lure her to France. Until now there had been no hint of romance in his life. But at this time he was more vulnerable to an emotional attachment than he had been since Martha's death.

He always made friends slowly, and the pattern did not change in France. Gradually, though, he drew around himself a small circle of close friends, artistic men and women with whom he shared an enjoyment of all the arts that Paris had to offer—painting, architecture, plays, and concerts.

He explained his feelings about art in a letter to his friend James Madison: "But how is a taste in this beautiful art to be formed in our countrymen, unless we avail ourselves of every occasion when public buildings are to be erected of presenting to them models for their study and imitation? . . . You see I am an enthusiast in the subject of the arts. But it is an enthusiasm of which I am not ashamed. . . ."[1]

He particularly liked being part of the circle of friends and family of Lafayette and his lovely young wife, as well as Lafayette's aunt, Madame de Tessé, who was young enough for Lafayette to call her his cousin. Madame de Tessé loved architecture and gardening, and Jefferson enjoyed talking to her. He formed a number of friendships with women in Paris. These were long-lasting attachments based on mutual interests and respect. Three of these women were among the most beautiful of their time. All were married.

He spent much time with the very lovely Angelica Church, sister-in-law of Alexander Hamilton, and her friend Madame de Corny, young, witty, extremely pretty—and married to a man much older than she. Madame de Corny and Jefferson particularly enjoyed each other's company and often took tea together or walked in the Bois de Boulogne, but she complained that he was too polite and too respectful. When she left Paris for a visit to England with her husband, she wanted to smuggle her devoted admirer in her pocket.

This was a time when women were still regarded as ornaments of society, and gallantry was in order. This Jefferson could practice in the ultimate. He liked women who were gentle yet accomplished, and objected to the idleness and dissipation of many of the ladies of the French upper class. He was particularly disturbed because he saw France as a land where marital fidelity was "an ungentlemanly practice."

Before he had left London in May, Jefferson had invited John Trumbull to be his guest in Paris. Trumbull accepted, and he arrived in early August. He soon introduced Jefferson to some of the leading artists in France, artists with international reputations, who invited Jefferson to visit their studios. It was at this time that he became an enthusiastic supporter of Trumbull's project to paint some of the great scenes of the American Revolution. Soon after, Jefferson sat for his portrait in Trumbull's painting of the "Signing of the Declaration." It shows him with unpowdered hair and a strong face and is considered a far better likeness than Mather Brown's painting of him.

Among the artists in Paris when Trumbull arrived were Mr. and Mrs. Richard Cosway, who had recently arrived from London. Richard Cosway was about Jefferson's age and was the most popular miniature painter of his day—at a time when the miniature was a prized form of art. He was a very short, absurd little man who was said to have a face like a monkey. He was pompous and vain, and his elaborate dress—he wore a mulberry silk coat ornamented with strawberries—made him an easy target for caricature and satire. But the public liked his work, and he had amassed a fortune.

Cosway was married to the beautiful and talented Maria Hadfield, a twenty-seven-year-old artist in her own right. Maria was slim and graceful, with a mass of curly blond hair, deep blue eyes, fair skin, and "modesty, beauty, and that softness of disposition which is the ornament of her sex and the charm of ours," as Jefferson described her.[2] Maria spoke many languages, but liked Italian best. She had been born in Italy of English parents and spoke English with a beguiling accent. She was the essence of femininity.

Maria's marriage to Richard Cosway had been orchestrated by her mother as a "marriage of convenience." Maria was a devout Catholic and had wanted to become a nun, but her mother had prevented it. Now, after only five years of married life, Cosway was beginning to treat his wife callously. He flirted outrageously with the ladies who came to his salon and had had several flagrant affairs. Maria had tried hard in the first years of their marriage to please her husband, but she was aware that he was being unfaithful to her. She had come to fear and detest him. But she loved the world that Richard Cosway's success made possible for her and recognized her financial dependence on him.

The Cosways lived extravagantly and entertained lavishly. They numbered among their friends many of the English nobility. In fact, the Prince of Wales was rumored to have been intrigued by the lovely Maria.

Wishing to introduce the Cosways to Jefferson, Trumbull invited them and some friends to the Halle aux Bles, the big, new, noisy Paris grain market where Jefferson had hoped to get some architectural ideas for a public market to be built in Richmond, Virginia. The most notable feature of the Halle aux Bles was its giant dome.

This day, when Jefferson first saw it, he was impressed by the "noble dome," but he was far more impressed by Mrs. Cosway. In fact, he was so distracted by her that he sent a note making an excuse to miss his dinner appointment that evening.

Then this normally proper man went surreptitiously to the lovely park of St. Cloud, with its deep shaded lanes and its cascades tumbling from marble fountains toward the Seine, for dinner with his gay companions. When he learned that Maria was as accomplished in music as she was in painting (she sang, played the harp, and composed music), he arranged to end the memorable day with a visit to the renowned composer and teacher of the harp, Johann Baptiste Krumpholtz, whose wife Julie, a fine harpist herself, entertained them to a late hour. Reflecting on it later, Jefferson compared it to a long "Lapland summer day,"[3] filled to the brim with happiness.

For the next month Tom and Maria were together every day. She had captivated him completely.

It seems likely that Trumbull accompanied them some of the time, but he left Paris for Germany at the beginning of September, and Richard Cosway, having work to complete, was content to leave his pretty wife on her own. Alone or in a "charming coterie,"[4] as Jefferson later described it, he and Maria saw something beautiful in Paris every day. And each day they had either breakfast or dinner together.

There were unforgettable days in their favorite haunts, and they were incredibly happy together. He was playing with fire, he knew, but he was happy and he didn't care. It was a golden September, and Thomas Jefferson had fallen in love.

For Tom, Maria was art and music and the embodiment of loveliness. She was bright and sensitive, although somewhat immature. Some of their friends called her a flirt, spoiled and self-centered, but to Jefferson she was charming and talented, and he was in love with her. For the first time since his Martha had died, he felt carefree and gay. For a short while he was young again.

Then, on September 18, while strolling together along the Seine on one of their daily outings, Jefferson, in just such a joyous mood, jumped over a low fence, caught his foot, and crashed to the ground. Attempting to break his fall with his right hand, he succeeded only in breaking his wrist.

He tried to keep the results of his mishap from Maria, holding the injured arm in his left hand until he delivered her to her home. Returning to his own house, he summoned a surgeon, but the wrist was not set properly and was never to heal completely. Two years later the hand would still be withered, with swelled and crooked fingers. It stiffened seriously as he began to grow old and continued to cause him much pain, making it difficult for him to play his beloved violin. Now he remained in excruciating pain, confined to his house for several weeks.

The beautiful Maria Cosway. Jefferson's days with her were "filled to the brim with happiness."

When word of the accident finally reached Maria, she sent a note, with many little excuses:

"I meant to have seen you twice, . . . Though we were near your house, coming to see you, we were obliged to come back, the time being much past that we were to be at St. Cloud, to dine with the Duchess of Kingston." Then she added, "Oh I wish you was well enough to come to us tomorrow to dinner and stay the evening. . . . I would serve you, and help you at dinner, and divert your pain after with good musik [sic]."[5] But Jefferson was unable to venture out of the house. He was unable to be with Maria. And he was unable to write.

A few weeks later, on October 4, Jefferson learned that the Cosways were planning to leave Paris the next day. Richard Cosway had completed his commissions in London and was anxious to go

Jefferson as minister to France in 1789.

to Antwerp to visit the galleries there. Tom had to see Maria. So he attempted one last excursion together. But as their carriage rattled over the pavement, his shattered wrist, set badly in the first place, was shaken up even more.

"I have passed the night in so much pain that I have not closed my eyes,"[6] he wrote laboriously to Maria with his left hand the next morning. Plans to see her off that morning would have to be abandoned. He had summoned another surgeon.

This time Maria replied promptly, blaming herself for having been the cause of his pain. "Why would you go, and why was I not more friendly to you, and less so to myself by preventing your giving me the pleasure of your company? You repeatedly said it would do you no harm. I felt interested and did not resist."[7]

She went on to speak of him as "unusually obliging." She would remember with "exquisite pleasure" the charming days they had spent together and would long for the spring, when she hoped to return to Paris. Meanwhile, would he send her a line to Antwerp with news of his wrist?

The letter was more than he could bear. How could he wait for the spring to see her again? He canceled the surgeon, got out of bed, hired a carriage, and accompanied the Cosways to the posthouse at St. Denise. There he provided dinner for them; then, "having performed the last sad office of handing you into your carriage . . . and seen the wheels get actually into motion, I turned on my heel and walked, more dead than alive," to his own waiting carriage and was taken home.[8]

Three weeks later he wrote to a friend, "How the right hand became disabled would be a long story for the left to tell. It was by one of those follies from which good cannot come, but ill may."[9]

Soon reason began to triumph over passion. His head told him that it was folly for a man of forty-three, who had always before held himself in check, to give way now to amorous emotions. The way back could be hard to find.

So, seated at his fireside, solitary and sad, he wrote—painstakingly with his left hand—one of the most amazing love letters ever penned, "Dialogue Between the Head and Heart." He called it a "history of the evening I parted from you." One of his biographers has called it "one of the most unusual tributes ever paid a pretty woman by a distinguished man."[10] It is, in fact, a rare insight into the emotions of this otherwise very private man and reveals his need to convey to Maria some sense of his past, of his feelings, of himself. Perhaps, too, it was his way of sorting out his own turbulent emotions.

The letter, written in the form of a conversation between his head and his heart, the realist and the romantic, began with his heart telling his head, "I am indeed the most wretched of all earthly beings,"[11] and concluded by begging Maria to write to him: "If your letters are as long as the Bible, they will appear short to me. Only let them be brimful of affection." Then he tells her, "my health is good, except my wrist which mends slowly, and my mind which mends not at all, but broods constantly over your departure."[12]

Jefferson sent the twelve-page letter—along with a love song by Sacchini that he had promised her. "Bring me in return its subject,

Jours heureux!"[*][13] he pleaded. He entrusted the packet to John Trumbull, who was to meet the Cosways in Antwerp and could be counted on to deliver it personally to Maria. He would carry most of their correspondence back and forth between them in order to avoid the prying eyes of the London and Paris post offices and of Mr. Cosway.

It was at this time that Jefferson learned of Shays' Rebellion, the uprising in western Massachusetts of farmers and debtors against creditors that had taken place in November 1786. Impoverished backcountry farmers, many of them Revolutionary War veterans, were losing their farms through mortgage foreclosures and tax delinquencies. Under the leadership of Daniel Shays they took up their muskets and rebelled.

While Jefferson never condoned their use of force, the incident helped crystallize his feelings about government. He came to see insurrection as an example of the need for expressions of discontent in a free society. He articulated this in a letter to James Madison: "I hold it that a little rebellion now and then is a good thing, and as necessary in the political world as storms in the physical. . . . It is a medicine necessary for the sound health of government."[14]

There was less need to punish the insurgents, he felt, than to draw the proper lessons from the incident.

On Christmas Eve Tom sat by his fire and wrote another long letter to Maria. "If I cannot be with you in reality, I will be in imagination," he began. He wondered if she meant to disappoint him by not returning in the spring, as she had promised. But he could not live without hope. He ended, "Think of me much and warmly. Place me in your breast with those who love you most, and comfort me with your letters."[15]

But Maria wrote to him of her friends, of the gloomy London weather, of her own melancholy mood. She was painting all day, she told him, and playing music in the evenings. Her letters were *not* "brimful of affection," as he had requested. Certainly, they were not the letters of adoration he was writing to her. Gradually, the correspondence lessened, and he began to plan a trip to the south

[*] Happy days

of France to see firsthand the commercial seaport cities, inspect the agricultural regions of southern France and northern Italy, and try the healing effects of the mineral springs in Aix-en-Provence recommended for his wrist by his doctors. And, he hoped, he would forget the pain of his separation from Maria. His head would win over his heart.

Jefferson set out alone for the south of France on the last day of February, in 1787. After the wind and the rain of Paris, he was looking forward eagerly to the warm blue skies of southern France and Italy. He had left even his servants at home in the hope that he would have no distractions and would have time to reflect quietly on all that he saw.

He was enchanted with the French countryside. In Bordeaux, he made a thorough study of the wines and the vineyards. His experienced eye missed nothing. The rich, fat fields reminded him of his own Virginia. But when he saw fields planted with clover, flax, and grain, in contrast to the tobacco planted in Virginia, which wears out the soil, he took careful notes. He was impressed by the French plan of crop rotation. He was always the questioning tourist, anxious to learn what he could to bring back to his own country. He talked to all the farmers he encountered and recommended to Lafayette that he do the same. But, he wrote to him, "To do it most effectively you must be absolutely incognito. You must ferret the people out of their hovels, as I have done, look into their kettles, eat their bread, loll on their beds under pretense of resting yourself, but in fact to find out if they are soft." This knowledge could then be used to improve the lot of the common people by "the softening of their beds, or the throwing a morsel of meat into their kettle of vegetables."[16]

He reaffirmed his belief on this trip that those who labor in the earth are God's chosen people, and that tillers of the soil have an instinct for order and justice.

Before leaving Paris, Jefferson had spent time with Patsy, then fifteen, and had promised to write her long letters every week. But he used these to lecture her about the need for industry and activity. When Patsy wrote that she was having difficulty with her Latin, he replied, "We are always equal to what we undertake with resolution." He went on to tell her that, "Nobody in this world can make me so happy, or so miserable, as you. . . . Be industrious then, my dear child. Think nothing insurmountable by resolution and application, and you will be all that I wish you to be."[17]

Good-naturedly, Patsy responded by telling her father, "I am not so industrious as you or I would wish, but I hope that in taking pains I soon shall be. I have already began to study more . . . for what I hold most precious is your satisfaction, indeed I should be miserable without it. You wrote me a long letter, as I asked you, it would have been much more so without so wide a margin."[18]

In another letter Jefferson couldn't refrain from offering Patsy advice: "Determine never to be idle. No person will have occasion to complain of the want of time who never loses any. It is wonderful how much may be done if we are always doing."[19] Patsy well knew that her father practiced what he preached.

The Maison Carrée in Nîmes, France—considered "the most perfect and precious remain of antiquity in existence." Jefferson said of it: "I gaze at it for whole hours . . . like a lover at his mistress."

The Virginia state capitol at Richmond, designed by Thomas Jefferson and modeled on the Maison Carrée.

* * *

Jefferson had long dreamed of visiting "the classic ground" of Europe and experiencing with his own eyes the remains of antiquity in their "purest form," rather than simply seeing them in books. It was his hope that he might introduce a simple and pure style of architecture into American buildings. Roman buildings, he knew, were the supreme examples of this.

Soon he sent home to Virginia a plan for the new state capitol modeled on the Maison Carrée, a small Roman temple he had seen in Nîmes. The execution of this plan became the Virginia state capitol at Richmond and initiated a revival of classical architecture in America. Once again, in his architecture as well as his politics, Thomas Jefferson was changing the shape of his country.

From Nîmes he went on to Aix to try the waters there, noting carefully in his book that the temperature at the spout was ninety degrees Fahrenheit. The waters did not have the hoped-for healing results, and his wrist remained the same. But the sun was shining brightly, and his spirits were beginning to improve. After four days he left for Marseilles, to see firsthand this seaport city and to attempt to further the commercial interests of his country.

When he crossed into Italy and saw the machines used for cleaning rice there, he hired a muleteer to smuggle out* samples of rice seed to send to South Carolina and Georgia so that planters there might experiment with it. Everywhere he was concerned with what might benefit American agriculture.

He had originally gone to the south of France in part to forget Maria Cosway. But when he returned to Paris in early June and discovered that she had not come as planned, he wrote to her of his trip: "Why were you not with me? So many enchanting scenes that wanted only your pencil to consecrate them to fame. . . ." Then, if you are not coming, he cried out, "What did you ever come for? Only to make people miserable at losing you?"[20]

Maria did return to Paris in August—without her husband— but she stayed in a remote section of the city and surrounded herself with an entourage that made it impossible for Jefferson to spend time with her alone. Childlike and spoiled, she was probably never able to comprehend the depth of his feeling for her.

Early in December, on the eve of her planned departure for England, Maria invited Jefferson to have breakfast with her the next morning to say good-bye. When he arrived, Maria had already left. She had sent him a note the evening before, shortly after she had extended the invitation, which did not reach him in time.

"I cannot breakfast with you tomorrow," she wrote. "To bid you adieu once is sufficiently painful, for I leave you with very melancholy ideas."[21]

Jefferson replied: "I went to breakfast with you according to promise, and you had gone off at 5 o'clock in the morning. This spared me, indeed, the pain of parting, but it deprives me of the comfort of recollecting that pain."[22]

Two years later, when he was about to return home, he wrote to her, "I am going to America, and you to Italy. One of us is going the wrong way, for the way will ever be wrong which leads us farther apart."[23]

He never stopped hoping that she would someday come to Amer-

* a practice punishable by death

ica, where he could show her beautiful scenes of his country, "scenes worthy of your pencil."[24] She never came, and they never met again. The mood of gay abandon that he had initially captured with her did not return, and his letters to her eventually became more restrained. His head was now fully in control of his heart. His passion turned to tenderness. He busied himself with his work in France, and he never again embarked on a romantic adventure. But he loved her all the rest of his life.

XVI
"She must come"

By the summer of 1785 Jefferson had determined that Polly must come to him, and in August he had set down in a letter to Francis Eppes the arrangements he felt it necessary to make.

First, he stipulated that Polly should travel in a good vessel sailing from Virginia in April, May, June, or July only. She must not sail at the time of the equinoxes, the time of violent storms.

The boat should have made at least one voyage, he told his brother-in-law, but must not be more than four or five years old. All vessels lost at sea, he explained, are either on their first voyage or are more than five years old. He suggested, also, that Polly be entrusted to the care of "some good lady passing from America to France, or even England, . . . who has had the smallpox. . . ." He ended his letter with "kisses for dear Poll, who hangs on my mind night and day."[1]

Pirates were another ever-present threat to American ships, and he worried about that also. His anxiety about her safety was that of a father *and* a mother: "No event of your life has put it into your power to conceive how I feel when I reflect that such a child, and so dear to me, is to cross the ocean, is to be exposed to all the sufferings and risks, great and small, to which a situation on board a ship exposes everyone. I drop my pen at the thought—but she must come. My affections have me balanced between the desire to have her with me, and the fear of exposing her; but my reason tells me the dangers are not great, and the advantages to her will be considerable."[2]

From the time just after his arrival in Paris when he had first learned of the death of "Little Lu" and had resolved to have Polly come to France, he had been trying to convince her to make the journey. But he hadn't reckoned with the little girl's determination to remain with the aunt and uncle who had shown her unconditional love and affection. He wrote to her, telling her:

> I wish so much to see you, that I have desired your uncle and aunt to send you to me. I know, my dear Polly, how sorry you will be, and ought to be, to leave them and your cousins; but your sister and myself cannot live without you, and after a while we will carry you back again to see your friends in Virginia. In the mean time you shall be taught here to play on the harpsichord, to draw, to dance, to read and talk French, and such other things as will make you more worthy of the love of your friends; but above all things, by our care and love of you, we will teach you to love us more than you will do if you stay so far from us. . . . when you come here you shall have as many dolls and playthings as you want for yourself, or to send to your cousins whenever you shall have opportunities. . . . We shall hope to have you with us next summer, to find you a very good girl, and to assure you of the trust of our affection for you. Adieu, my dear child. Yours affectionately,
>
> Th. Jefferson.[3]

Polly, living happily at Eppington with her loving aunt, uncle, and cousins, was reluctant to leave the only mother she ever really knew and the comfort of their sprawling white frame house to cross the ocean alone to be with the father and sister about whom she knew very little. She wrote back:

> Dear Papa—I want to see you and sister Patsy, but you must come to Uncle Eppes house.
>
> Polly Jefferson[4]

And then she wrote:

> Dear Papa—I long to see you, and hope that you and sister Patsy are well; give my love to her and tell her that I long to

see her, and hope that you and she will come very soon to see us. I hope that you will send me a doll. I am very sorry that you have sent for me. I don't want to go to France, I had rather stay with Aunt Eppes. Aunt Carr, Aunt Nancy and Cousin Polly Carr are here. Your most happy and dutiful daughter.

Polly Jefferson.[5]

It was going to be very difficult, Jefferson saw, to lure this child to France, away from the family she loved. And the Eppes were no more anxious to let her go than Polly was to leave them. They had grown to love her as their own and were still clinging to the hope that her father would change his mind.

Sensitively, tactfully, Jefferson appealed to them, stressing the "importance to the future happiness of the child that she should neither forget nor be forgotten by her sister and myself."[6]

Eventually, Francis Eppes devised a plan whereby Polly was tricked into going. A party was planned aboard a ship that had tied up at the dock at Eppington, to which Polly and her young cousins were invited. The children played together on the decks and in the cabins until Polly began to feel comfortable on the vessel. When she finally curled up in a corner and fell asleep from sheer exhaustion after all the games and good food, the others crept away, leaving Polly with a beautiful young servant named Sally Hemings,* and in the charge of Andrew Ramsay, captain of the vessel. Her favorite cousin, Jack Eppes, and Aunty Eppes were the last to tear themselves away.

Tucked in with her belongings was a note to her father from her anxious aunt: "This will, I hope, be handed you by my dear Polly, who I most ardently wish may reach you in the health she is in at present. I shall be truly wretched till I hear of her being safely landed with you. . . . For God's sake give us the earliest intelligence of her arrival."[7]

While Polly slept the captain gave the order to weigh anchor, and by the time she awoke, the ship had already set sail. Polly Jefferson

---

* fourteen-year-old sister of James, who had accompanied Tom to France

was bound for France. She was first bewildered, then heartbroken when she began to comprehend what had happened. But Captain Ramsay's kindness and his devotion to her soon helped her adjust, and in the five weeks that they were at sea the two became very attached to one another. Polly ate at his table and often walked the deck with him, holding tightly to his hand. She was a sweet little girl, with a sunny disposition, and she eventually came to enjoy her time on board the ship.

But the problem of separation repeated itself when she arrived in England. There, Captain Ramsay delivered her to Abigail Adams in London, who had offered to look after her until her father could come for her. Once again, Polly cried at having to leave the captain, whom she had grown to trust and to love. Abigail quickly won her heart, though, and Polly spent three happy weeks with her, awaiting her father's arrival.

Jefferson, just back from his three-month trip, and overwhelmed by the backlog of important paperwork that had accumulated during his absence and was waiting for his attention, decided to send his trusted French steward, Petit, to collect Polly instead of making the trip to London himself.

Once again, the little girl was devastated. Knowing no French, she was frightened of Petit—a strange man who spoke a strange language. She told Mrs. Adams that, as she had left all her friends in Virginia to come over the ocean to see her father, she thought he would have taken the pains to come to England for her.

Polly finally arrived in Paris for a joyful reunion with her father and sister in the middle of July, two months after she had left Eppington. Patsy was given a week's holiday from school, and the two girls stayed with their father. Patsy took her sister to the convent from time to time to familiarize her with it. When the little girl seemed comfortable there, Jefferson enrolled her, and she and Patsy returned together. Polly soon became the favorite of the girls and the mistresses and, within a year, was speaking and reading French easily, was learning to draw and to play the harpsichord, and was about to begin to study Spanish. The girls visited their father once or twice a week.

It was at the convent that Polly was first called "Maria," the name by which she chose to be known for the rest of her life.

Polly never ceased talking about Eppington, and her face lit up whenever she heard the name of her Aunt Eppes mentioned. She missed all the Eppes terribly, and while she eventually became happy in Paris, she longed for the day when they would be reunited.

Although she grew to love her father, she never became her father's daughter in the sense that Patsy was. Her ties were always to the family at Eppington.

Jefferson, though, became fully reconciled to life in France only after this child of his had crossed the ocean to him. He loved her deeply and was completely happy only when both his daughters were about. He considered them his jewels and enveloped them in a kind of motherly softness. He was firm with them, yet kind and always just. He never lost patience with them and considered no need of theirs too small to attend to. He insisted on buying them all their clothes. In return, they, and ultimately all their children, revered and adored him.

XVII
"For the public good"

During his years in France, Jefferson was a diligent and skillful diplomat. He was dealing, now, with problems facing the United States, not simply those of Virginia. He was becoming more aware of the value of a strong central government, which could require individual states to honor America's treaty obligations, to protect the country's vulnerable northern and southern borders and secure the allegiance of the area west of the Allegheny Mountains, and to garner the respect of foreign countries.

He struggled to solve the question of America's debt to France for aid during the Revolutionary War by negotiating favorable treaties of navigation and commerce with Prussia and Morocco. He worked hard to obtain the commercial rights for his country that would make it possible for her to pay off all her debts to Europe. He worked out a plan whereby a league of nations would restrain pirates on the high seas, he gained a lowering of French duties on American products, and he tried to do away with an existing French monopoly on tobacco.

During the summer of 1787 the fight to ratify the Constitution was rocking the Pennsylvania State House, where the Constitutional Convention was sitting, and Madison kept Jefferson up to date on developments. Many of the ideas in the Constitution had originally been Jefferson's, and he was happy for that, but he was disturbed at the omission of a bill of rights, which provided for "freedom of religion, freedom of the press, protection against standing armies, restriction against monopolies, . . . habeas corpus laws, and trials by jury." He added that "a bill of rights is what the people are entitled to against every government on earth . . . & what no just government should refuse."[1]

He also feared the exclusion of the principle of rotation in office, particularly in the case of the president. Unless the Constitution expressly prohibited it, he reasoned, the president might be reelected for his lifetime. He wrote Madison long letters expressing his views.

While he was in France, many Frenchmen looked to him for advice on the rapidly approaching revolution in that country. He watched carefully as the French people groped toward freedom, and to their leaders he preached moderation. The monarchy, he told Lafayette and his other French friends, must not be overthrown all of a sudden. There must be a gradual movement toward individual freedom and self-government. Reforms must be worked out patiently. Sudden change could be dangerous. He cautioned his liberal-minded friends to make haste slowly. Here, once again, he showed himself to be an idealist who tempered his idealism with common sense, a dreamer who dreamed with his eyes open.

When asked by a French friend to explain what he meant by "government by the people," he replied that people should be introduced into every department of government to the extent that they are capable. He went on to explain that they are not qualified to *be* the executive, but they are qualified to *choose* the executive; they are not qualified to legislate, but they are qualified to *choose* the legislators; they are not qualified to judge questions of *law*, but they are capable of judging questions of *fact*.[2]

In Europe this was the time of the full flowering of the Enlightenment, and Jefferson agreed with the prevailing thought that men could be free and happy if they came to know more about everything. He seemed to recognize that the eighteenth century in which he was living was a time of possibilities. To his old friend George Wythe he wrote, "Preach, my dear Sir, a crusade against ignorance; establish and improve the law for educating the common people."[3]

He was never again as happy as he was during the last years he spent in France. It was one of the richest periods of his life in terms of personal friendships and freedom to indulge in cultural and intellectual pursuits. Yet the longer he remained there, the more his pride in America asserted itself. Paris, to him, was "empty bustle." The great mass of the people were oppressed, and even the nobility did not have the happiness "which is enjoyed in America by every class of people," he told his friends. Paris, he thought, was a purposeless society, and life for Thomas Jefferson was empty when not purposeful.

A stream of young men whose fathers had written to Jefferson from America, requesting counsel for their sons, came to his house. To all of them he extended hospitality, advice, and inspiration. This stemmed in part from his innate kindness, but it was motivated also by a strong sense of duty. He believed that he was training these young men to serve their country. They, in turn, appreciated his consideration of their opinions and his treatment of them as equals.

One of these was Thomas Mann Randolph, Jr., the tall, dark son of Jefferson's cousin and lifelong friend since his days at Tuckahoe. Young Randolph came to Paris in the summer of 1788, after having studied at the University of Edinburgh, in Scotland, for three years. During that period Jefferson had been writing to him, counseling him in his studies.

Now, having graduated with honors, Randolph wrote to Jefferson, telling him that he had decided on a career in politics. Jefferson responded happily that his country would have much for him to do. "It will remain . . . to those now coming on the stage of public affairs, to perfect what has been so well begun by those going off it," he wrote.[4]

It was while Randolph was in Paris that he saw Patsy for the first time since they were children. She was now a tall, attractive sixteen-year-old with reddish hair in tiny curls that framed her face and deep blue eyes. He, said to have descended on his mother's side from the Indian princess Pocahontas, was, at twenty-one, a handsome young man—no longer the playmate who had climbed trees with her. They were immediately attracted to one another.

Soon after Tom Randolph left to return to Virginia, Patsy wrote her father a very disturbing letter. She told him that she had decided to remain in the convent and become a Catholic nun and would like his permission to do so. As a Protestant, Jefferson was dismayed.

Characteristically, he did nothing for a few days. Then he went to the convent, spoke quietly to Mother Louise-Therese, and withdrew both Patsy and Polly. Then he found his girls, greeted them warmly, and told them simply that he had come to take them out of school. They immediately drove home together. The subject of Patsy's letter was never mentioned by father or daughter.

Jefferson soon saw to it that Patsy was introduced into society at the brilliant court of Louis XVI. As usual, he shopped for the new wardrobe that was required, selecting beautiful gowns with extremely good taste. Patsy, on her part, moved easily and happily from her role as student to her new role as Mademoiselle Martha, mistress of her father's household. Added to her duties was one she seemed to love also, tutoring her younger sister.

Polly was not as happy. She missed the attention of the adoring Sisters and her classmates at the convent. She began to spend a part of most days in the home of the Lafayettes and became the special friend of their daughter Anastasie.

Both Patsy and Polly met many diplomats in their father's home. Patsy, in addition to being her father's hostess, occasionally filled in as secretary when William Short was away. As a result, she came to understand what was happening in France.

That winter was a severe one, and hundreds of people died of starvation. The girls witnessed mobs of hungry people roaming the streets, searching for food, and Patsy could see why the people might revolt. They had lost faith in their king and in the newly convened Assembly of Notables, which had been called into session for the emergency.

Back in America, on April 14, 1789, George Washington was notified by Charles Thompson, secretary of the Continental Congress, that he had been unanimously elected the first president of the United States. John Adams was named vice president, an office that Benjamin Franklin thought should have carried the title "His Superfluous Excellency."

When the news reached Jefferson, knowing that Washington much preferred the quiet of Mount Vernon to the turmoil of politics,

George Washington as first president of the United States.

he wrote to him, "Nobody who has tried both public and private life can doubt that you were much happier on the banks of the Potomac than you will be at New York."*⁵

His respect for George Washington amounted almost to reverence. He knew Washington would accept the position out of the same sense of duty toward his country that he had. He wrote to Francis Hopkinson of "our great leader whose executive talents are superior to those, I believe, of any man in the world, and who alone, by the authority of his name and the confidence reposed in his perfect integrity, is fully qualified to put the new government so under way, as to secure it against opposition."⁶

Shortly before four o'clock on the afternoon of July 4, 1789, many of the Americans in Paris gathered for a gala dinner at the Jeffersons' house. A radiant Patsy was her father's hostess, and the Lafayettes were the honored guests. Coffee was poured for the first time from a silver coffee pot that Jefferson had designed. Ten days later the Bastille, the Paris prison that was the hateful symbol of feudal tyranny in France, fell. The French Revolution had begun.

Just three days before, Lafayette, who had been elected vice president of the Assembly of Notables, presented his "Declaration of Rights of Man and of the Citizen," in which he had incorporated many of Thomas Jefferson's suggestions. This declaration would ultimately become the basis for a French constitution as well as for similar statements of law in other European nations.

On the day of the fall of the Bastille, Polly, returning to their house on the Champs Élysées from a visit to the Lafayettes', witnessed firsthand the violence of the mob. It was a frightened little girl who finally ran into her father's arms. She was so disturbed by what she had seen that she became ill and spent several days in a darkened upstairs room, the shutters closed against the noise outside.

All the Jeffersons became prisoners in their own home. Food and candles grew scarce. Some of the servants fled. And Jefferson began to fear for the safety of his daughters.

He had already written to John Jay, the American secretary for

* New York was then the seat of the new government.

foreign affairs, explaining that he had been away from Monticello for five years and had not attended to any of his personal affairs in that time. He had requested a leave of absence to attend to these and, most important, "to carry my children back to their own country."[7] He could return to France within six months, he told the secretary, but he would leave his daughters in America, in the care of their loving Aunt Eppes. "Their future welfare," he wrote to his sister-in-law, depended on this.

When his letter to Mr. Jay went unanswered, Jefferson appealed to George Washington, adding, "there has never been a moment at which the presence of a minister here could be so well dispensed with. . . ."[8]

Washington's permission for a six-month leave of absence finally arrived at the end of August, and Jefferson immediately busied himself with preparations for the trip home.

On October 8, 1789, all the Jeffersons and their servants, along with eighty-six packing cases filled with furnishings, books, wine, drawings, paintings, generous and thoughtful gifts for family and friends, a heavy marble pedestal for the bust of Lafayette, which had already been shipped to Virginia, and all the papers of Thomas Jefferson, left Paris for Le Havre. William Short remained in France in charge of American affairs and the Jeffersons' house.

In France Tom had collected a gallery of portraits of Americans to take home with him. He had commissioned paintings of Washington, Adams, Franklin, Madison, and Thomas Paine, as well as of his friend Lafayette. The years in Paris had had a profound impact on his tastes in all the arts.

James Hemings, who could have remained in France as a free man, chose to accompany his master home. He had Mr. Jefferson's promise that if he taught a servant at Monticello the art of French cooking, which his master had come to love, he would be granted his freedom.* Sally and Petit accompanied them also, Petit going only as far as Le Havre.

At Havre they were delayed by raging winds—the wildest weather Jefferson had ever seen. Finally, on the twenty-second of October,

---

* James was freed in 1796 and given money to go from Monticello to Philadelphia, where he wanted to live.

he and his family embarked on the *Clermont,* the British vessel that John Trumbull had arranged to have pick them up. They were her only passengers. Jefferson was on deck at daybreak to hand a last letter to the pilot and to take a last, long look at the receding shoreline as the ship, "in company with upwards of thirty vessels which had collected there and been detained, as we were, by contrary winds," weighed anchor and headed toward America.[9] The American minister to France was on his way home.

Jefferson's affection for France would never waver, and his French friendships would be unaffected by the course of French politics, but he was returning to his own country with even stronger ties to it than when he had left, and with his faith in a democratic government renewed.

The Clermont arrived near the Virginia Capes after a pleasant voyage of just less than a month, in fog so thick it was impossible to see. After standing off for three days, the captain, a bold and experienced seaman, determined to venture into Chesapeake Bay in spite of the weather. They beat against a strong head wind, lost their topsails, and were almost run down by a brig coming out of port and sailing before the wind. But they arrived safely at Norfolk about noon on November 23. Other ships whose captains were not as daring were kept at sea for another month by a storm that came up suddenly.

When the Jeffersons debarked, they were astonished to find a delegation from the legislature waiting to greet them. It was then that they learned that Mr. Jefferson had been nominated by President Washington and confirmed by the Senate as secretary of state. His cousin and good friend Edmund Randolph had been named attorney general at the same time. John Jay was chief justice.

Jefferson's reply to the delegation was gracious but noncommittal. He did not accept the post, nor did he categorically refuse it: "That my country should be served is the first wish of my heart; I should be doubly happy indeed, were I to render it a service."[10]

The Jeffersons borrowed four horses from friends to draw their carriage and began a leisurely journey home, stopping along the way to visit relatives and friends. Polly, calling herself Maria now, was overjoyed to be reunited with Aunty Eppes and all her young cousins, particularly Jack Eppes, who was now sixteen. Jack accompanied them on the remainder of the trip to Monticello.

It was at Eppington that an express rider caught up with them and handed Jefferson the official notification from George Washington of his appointment as secretary of state. He was not happy about it. He had hoped to return to France for a short period to complete his work there and then to retire from the political scene altogether. His family, his farm, his books called to him irresistibly.

But, in the end, "I found it better . . . to sacrifice my own inclinations to those of others." He couldn't refuse Washington: "But it is not for an individual to choose his post. You are to marshal us as may be best for the public good."[11]

When the servants at Monticello learned that their master was on his way home, they went wild with joy and requested a holiday on the day that he was expected. The overseer granted this, and two days before Christmas they assembled at Monticello from all of Jefferson's farms. Young and old, men, women, and children, dressed in their finest, the women wearing their brightest turbans, all gathered to greet him. Some, growing impatient, started walking down the mountain and met the carriage just as it reached Shadwell, four miles away.

"Such a scene I never witnessed," Patsy wrote of it. They crowded around the carriage, then unhitched the horses and pulled and pushed the vehicle up the mountain to the front door of Monticello, shouting and singing all the way.

"When the door of the carriage was opened, they received him in their arms and bore him to the house, crowding around and kissing his hands and feet—some blubbering and crying—others laughing. It seemed impossible to satisfy their anxiety to touch and kiss the very earth which bore him."[12]

When the girls alighted from the carriage, the people stood back respectfully, many holding their children up to see them, and quietly cleared a way for them. These two girls had left Monticello when they were only children. Now they were returning as young ladies, as Martha and Maria, one a mature and stately young woman of seventeen, witty and graceful, and skilled in the ways of court life, the other a "fairy-like" fragile eleven year old, even more beautiful and lovable than when she had left, whose haunting resemblance to her mother grew stronger with the passing of time.

Thomas Jefferson and his daughters had come home to Monticello.

XVIII
"I have no ambition to govern men"

Jefferson's respect for George Washington would not allow him to refuse the president anything, and he reluctantly accepted the post that was offered to him. On a windy Sunday morning, March 21, 1790, wearing the red breeches and red waistcoat that were the fashion then in Paris, his reddish hair beginning to turn an untidy gray, the forty-seven-year-old Thomas Jefferson stepped off the Hudson River ferry and made his way through the narrow, crooked streets of lower Manhattan in New York, then the capital city, to the executive residence on "the Broadway," where he presented himself to President Washington, ready to assume his duties as secretary of state.

But he knew little of the conservative reaction that had been taking place in America while he was in France. He was not prepared for the organized and brilliantly led fight against democracy that was about to take place.

As secretary of state in George Washington's cabinet, he became embroiled in a bitter conflict with the young, brilliant Alexander Hamilton, then secretary of the treasury. When Jefferson and Hamilton first met in New York, they had only respect for each other's reputation. But this was short lived. Their disagreements began on foreign policy issues, Jefferson favoring close ties with France, Hamilton with England. Jefferson, fearing the concentration of power in the hands of the national government that existed in England, was shocked by Hamilton's admiration for the British monarchy.

But their disagreements quickly went beyond this to basic ideological and constitutional considerations. The best government was the one that governed the least, Jefferson believed. He had always had faith in the enlightened judgment of the people. Hamilton was con-

Thomas Jefferson as secretary of state, December 1791.

temptuous of the common man. This became the basis for their feud. While Jefferson strove at the outset to cooperate, he was distressed to find himself in an atmosphere of distrust of a republican system of government. He saw Hamilton, who coveted personal as well as national power, betraying the Revolution and moving the country toward monarchy.

Alexander Hamilton, secretary of the treasury in George Washington's cabinet.

The two men came into conflict, also, over Hamilton's financial system. When Hamilton suggested that the federal government assume the states' war debts, Jefferson, along with Madison and others, foresaw that such a policy would strengthen the central government and thus weaken the role of the states. He argued, also, that the Bank of the United States that Hamilton proposed would further jeopardize states' rights and was unconstitutional. There was, he said, no specific authorization in the Constitution for a national bank. The states, not Congress, had the power to charter banks. He believed that the Constitution should be interpreted "literally," or "strictly." In this way only, he felt, could the Constitution be preserved and liberty ensured.

Members of Congress began to take sides. Hamiltonians were called Federalists, while those who sympathized with Thomas Jefferson called themselves Republicans. But the idea of loyal opposition had not yet developed in America, and people considered organized political opposition to be dangerous. Political parties had not been anticipated by the framers of the Constitution, and no provision had been made for them.

While Jefferson was the senior cabinet member, he had none of the glittering personal magnetism of the aggressive young Hamilton, and his persistent shyness made him appear cold. His simple clothes, his "laxity of manner," and his lack of "the firm collected deportment" expected of a cabinet minister were in sharp contrast to the erect military bearing of Hamilton and the brightly colored satins and expensive ruffles and laces worn by the secretary of the treasury. But Jefferson felt that finery was out of place in a republican government.

When, in the autumn of 1792, Hamilton published a series of ferocious attacks on his colleague in the *Gazette of the United States* in an attempt to drive him out of office, Jefferson made no reply. But his friends did that for him.

Never a manipulator or an intriguer like Hamilton, Jefferson was scrupulous as an official. Although he opposed Hamilton's policies, his loyalty to President Washington was far more important to him. Despite the fact that he was unable to convince the president of the unconstitutionality of a national bank, and Washington signed the bill establishing one, Jefferson reluctantly agreed to the president's strong urging that he remain in office.

Washington, unwilling to admit the existence of political parties, valued both Hamilton and Jefferson and recognized the important service rendered by each.

Jefferson always had a strong distaste for personal controversy, and he understood that compromise was necessary for the preservation of the Union. He was a skilled diplomat, and now he remembered Benjamin Franklin's rule: "Never contradict anybody." He tried hard to tolerate differences of opinion. It was far better, he believed, to use the technique of asking questions and planting doubts and to look for ways to cooperate. In this way he continued to battle quietly for principles and policies, but never for his own interests.

He labored diligently in his role as secretary of state and fully justified Washington's confidence in him. But his most notable accomplishment was calling attention to the dangers of Hamilton's policies and inspiring others to modify them in the years to come.

Soon after the Jeffersons' return from France, Martha had announced to her father that she had fallen in love with her cousin Thomas Mann Randolph, Jr., and wanted to marry him. She had just turned seventeen; he was twenty-one. Jefferson was delighted with her choice.

Before he embarked on his career as secretary of state, he gave her away in marriage at Monticello. The wedding, a small affair with only the immediate families attending, took place on February 23, 1790. The white gown she wore had been purchased for her by her father in Paris. The Reverend Mr. James Maury, Jefferson's old friend from his school days, performed the ceremony.

While her father was gone, Maria divided her time among the Eppes; her Aunt Martha Carr and her Carr cousins who were living at Monticello; and her newly married sister and brother-in-law at Varina, the estate given to the couple by Thomas Mann Randolph, Sr.

Once again, letters exchanged between father and daughters allow us a glimpse of their remarkable relationship. The lonely secretary of state wrote to Patsy from New York: "Having had yourself & dear Poll to live with me so long, to exercise my affections and cheer me in the intervals of business, I feel heavily the separation from you." Then he went on, "the happiness of your life now depends on the continuing to please a single person. to [sic] this all other objects must be secondary; even your love to me."[1]

Martha's reply was reassuring: "I assure you My Dear papa my happiness can never be compleat [sic] without your company. . . . I have made it my study to pleas [sic] [Mr. Randolph] in every

"I . . . consider all other objects as secondary [to her husband] *except* my love for you," Martha wrote to her father shortly after her marriage.

thing and do consider all other objects as secondary to that *except* my love for you."[2]

In fact, Martha's bond with her father was so strong that her husband never did displace him in her affections.

When, early in May of 1791, hoping to rid himself of a recurring "violent" headache and to make scientific observations, Jefferson took advantage of an interval of relative quiet in the cabinet and set out with James Madison on a holiday trip up the Hudson River, he delighted Maria by writing a letter to her on a piece of birch bark, "supposed to be the same used by the antients [sic]."[3] This, she told him, was "prettier than paper."[4] She loved the fabric her father sent her, but she was not interested in the geography lesson he included.

She was much more interested in her new niece: "My sweet Anne grows prettier every day," she reported to her father.[5] Martha had made Thomas Jefferson a grandfather in January.

In the fall of 1791, just after Maria had turned thirteen, her father spent a month at Monticello with her and then took her to Philadelphia with him. The federal government had just moved there. On the way, father and daughter stopped for a brief visit with President and Mrs. Washington at Mount Vernon. Here Maria and Nellie Custis, Mrs. Washington's granddaughter, became close friends, and Maria stayed on after her father left, continuing her trip to Philadelphia in the president's coach.

In Philadelphia Jefferson enrolled Maria in boarding school, but she spent several days each week with him in the small house he had rented on the banks of the Schuylkill River. There they spent many hours together under the trees that surrounded the house. Under them they had breakfast and dinner, wrote, read, and received company. "What would I not give that the trees planted nearest round the house at Monticello were full grown," he wrote to Martha.[6]

Maria's nineteen-year-old cousin Jack Eppes was now living with them also and pursuing his studies under his uncle's supervision. Jack was reading law and attending classes periodically at the University of Pennsylvania. He somehow managed to arrange his schedule so that his time in Schuylkill coincided with Maria's visits there.

It was at this time that George Washington designated Thomas Jefferson unofficial assistant in laying out the as-yet-unnamed new capital city on the Potomac River. Once again Jefferson would utilize ideas accumulated during his years in France.

"Whenever it is proposed to prepare plans for the Capitol," he wrote to Major Pierre Charles L'Enfant, the first architect involved in planning the new city, "I should prefer the adoption of some one of the models of antiquity which have had the approbation of thousands of years." Somehow, the new nation's architecture must have in it a "ring of eternity." The best building examples that civilization had to offer must be the models.[7]

To Washington he suggested that the government circulate, free of charge, inexpensive copies of prints of outstanding architecture that Jefferson had brought home from Europe, in order to educate, and elevate, the taste of the citizens of nearby Georgetown. And he worked closely with the architect Benjamin H. Latrobe to design and build the Capitol building.

Years later Washington, D.C., would be considered by art historians to be the birthplace of the profession of architecture in America.

Thomas Jefferson resigned as secretary of state at the end of 1793, arriving home by mid-January certain that this was to be a permanent retirement. He was only fifty years old, but he was weary and sick of politics, and he revealed his true feelings to James Madison:

"There has been a time when . . . the esteem of the world was of higher value in my eye than everything in it," he wrote. But "the motion of my blood no longer keeps time with the tumult of the world. It leads me to seek for happiness in the lap and love of my family, in the society of my neighbors and my books, in the wholesome occupations of my farms and my affairs, in an interest or affection in every bud that opens, in every breath that blows around me, in an entire freedom of rest, of motion, of thought."[8]

Now he gathered his family around him at Monticello and pictured himself spending the rest of his days repairing his ravaged farms, gardening, and enjoying his family. His farms had been neglected for many years, and his debts ran to many thousands of pounds.

He began to redesign Monticello, his restless mind already planning the changes he would make. "The length of my tether is now fixed for life from Monticello to Richmond,"* he wrote to a friend. "My private business can never call me elsewhere, and certainly politics will not, which I have ever hated both in theory & in practice."[9]

But this was not to be.

In 1796, when an exhausted President Washington determined not to run for a third term, the Republicans made Jefferson their candidate for president against his old friend John Adams. Reluctantly,

---
* a distance of about seven miles

he agreed to run, but he would do nothing to aid the campaign. Using the metaphor of the sea to express his sentiments, he told Madison he would be willing to go into the presidency for a while, in order "to put our vessel on her republican tack before she should be thrown too much to leeward of her true principles."[10] But he remained on his mountaintop—a silent candidate.

"I have no ambition to govern men," he wrote to John Adams in December.[11]

Jefferson had already indicated his hope that Adams would be elected president. He would be satisfied with second place, although he would prefer the third—his rejection—since then he would be free to remain at home, he said. In the case of a tie, it was important, he cautioned Madison, that he request, on Jefferson's behalf, that Adams be preferred. Mr. Adams, he told him, had always been his senior and had always "ranked" him in public life, both in France and in America.

He knew, too, that Benjamin Franklin had been bitterly attacked after his death and that George Washington himself had come under public attack. Nor had he forgotten the bitter and unmerited abuse to which he had been subjected when governor of Virginia. "Before my God, I shall from the bottom of my heart, rejoice at escaping," he wrote to Edward Rutledge. He was certain that "no man will ever bring out of that office the reputation which carries him into it."[12]

Soon word reached him confirming that Adams had received three more votes than he in the electoral college, thereby designating John Adams president and Thomas Jefferson vice president.

Never anticipating that the president and the vice president might represent antagonistic points of view (as in this case, Adams, a Federalist, and Jefferson, a Republican), the framers of the Constitution had provided simply that the ablest man would become president, and the one who received the second highest number of votes would be vice president.

Jefferson, wishing to avoid the elaborate ceremonies planned for the inauguration in Philadelphia, looked up the Constitution and decided that the oath of office could be administered anywhere—at Charlottesville, even at Monticello. But he finally decided to go to

Philadelphia out of respect for the public and braved the long winter journey over muddy roads. This time the delicate Maria did not accompany him. More and more Maria reminded Tom of her mother, and he was fearful that the trip at this time of year would prove too strenuous for her.

Now Jefferson, who hated the cold, traveled ten days in weather so cold that the ink froze in his pen. Jupiter accompanied him for part of the way, but his master soon sent him home in order to spare him and the horses the hard trip. Jefferson completed the journey by stage. His fellow passengers might have been surprised to learn that the bag he carried with him contained the fossilized bones of a prehistoric mastodon that had once roamed the western part of Virginia. They had been given to him by an Indian chief, and now he planned to present them to the American Philosophical Society, which met in Philadelphia.

Jefferson had hoped to arrive in the capital unnoticed, but he was met by a military delegation carrying a banner inscribed: JEFFERSON, THE FRIEND OF THE PEOPLE.

On March 4, 1797, Thomas Jefferson was inaugurated as the second vice president of the United States.

The evening before he had been installed as president of the American Philosophical Society. He succeeded the noted astronomer and mathematician David Rittenhouse, who had succeeded Benjamin Franklin. The society's meetings, and Jefferson's contacts with its members, would help considerably to diminish his loneliness in Philadelphia. His election attested to his national recognition as a man of science, or knowledge, the broad sense in which the word *science* was used. He later referred to his installation as president of the society as the "most flattering incident" of his life.

The vice presidency provided Jefferson with relative leisure and enabled him to divide his time between Monticello and Philadelphia. He played no part in the conduct of the administration—President Adams ignored him in all political matters—although he was frequently the target of the Federalist press, which continued to consider him the personification of Republicanism. He kept a remarkably cool head in the midst of the turmoil swirling around him, hopeful that his country would not be drawn into the hazards of a war with France.

But the differences between Adams and Jefferson began, by painful degrees, to undermine their old friendship.

It was during Jefferson's vice presidency that the Alien and Sedition Laws were pushed through Congress in an attempt by the Federalists to suppress public criticism of their policies. Jefferson regarded these Acts as "an experiment on the American mind to see how far it will bear an avowed violation of the constitution."[13] The Alien Acts extended the term of residence required for naturalization from five to fourteen years, gave the president the right to expel any alien whose presence he considered dangerous, and to expel the nationals of any state with which the United States might be at war. The Sedition Act was an attempt by the Federalists to crush free speech and silence the opposition. It was a direct slap at two freedoms guaranteed by the Bill of Rights, freedom of speech and freedom of the press.

As vice president, Jefferson was powerless to act against these. He, too, could be prosecuted for sedition if he spoke out against them. Yet he recognized that if the Federalists managed to stifle free speech, the country might well become a dangerous one-party monarchy.

Ten years before, referring to Shays' Rebellion in Massachusetts, he had said, "The people are the only censors of their governors . . . and were it left to me to decide whether we should have a government without newspapers or newspapers without a government, I should not hesitate to choose the latter. But I should mean that every man should receive those papers and be capable of reading them."[14] What he was saying here was that the mind of man must be left free. There must be freedom of discussion. The security of society is dependent on the free dissemination of knowledge. To Thomas Jefferson a free press was an essential feature of a republican government. This was one of his deepest convictions.

So he and James Madison secretly wrote the Kentucky and Virginia resolutions, which were passed by the Kentucky and Virginia legislatures, respectively, in November and December 1798. The resolutions reaffirmed natural rights and states' rights and challenged the constitutionality of the Alien and Sedition Acts. Freedom of speech would become an important issue in the next campaign.

* * *

The first duty of the vice president is to preside over the Senate, but Jefferson's recollection of the rules of parliamentary procedure had grown rusty over the years. As a young lawyer and member of the Virginia legislature he had prepared a *Parliamentary Pocket Book,* and this he now studied, then revised and expanded it. *A Manual of Parliamentary Practice* remains today the standard book of rules that govern American deliberative bodies.

In June of 1797, Jefferson received news that couldn't have surprised him but must surely have delighted him. Maria was engaged to marry Jack Eppes. Over the years, and particularly in Philadelphia, Jefferson had watched as friendship blossomed into love. He was "inexpressibly" pleased, he confided to Martha, and couldn't have found a better person "if I had the whole earth free to have chosen a partner for her."[15]

Later he would advise his young daughter, "Harmony in the married state is the very first object to be aimed at . . . a determination in each to consider the love of the other as of more value than any object whatever."[16]

Maria and Jack were married at Monticello on a glorious autumn day, the brilliant fall foliage a foil for her delicate beauty. Tradition says that she wore her mother's white satin wedding gown. Her Uncle Eppes nearly drowned himself attempting to pick pond lilies for her bridal bouquet.

Maria Jefferson had finally become an Eppes in name—as she had long been in spirit.

Jefferson continued to divide his time between Philadelphia and Monticello, but his time away from his family always caused him to be homesick. He constantly counted the days until he could return to his mountain and his family. During the intervals when he was at Monticello, its joy was lessened if his daughters weren't there to share it. "The bloom of Monticello is chilled by my solitude. It makes me wish the more that yourself and sister were here to enjoy it."[17]

Waiting impatiently for Maria's and Jack's arrival when he was home for a holiday during the summer of 1798, he wrote, "We have been . . . imagining that every sound we heard was that of the carriage which was once more to bring us together."[18] But when he learned that Maria was ill and unable to travel, he cautioned her not to undertake the journey until she was strong enough and then only by very short stages.

"Nurse yourself, therefore, with all possible care for your own sake, for mine, and that of all those who love you,"[19] he entreated her. He would be uneasy, he told her in another letter the next day, until he knew the "truth of your situation."[20]

Maria came as soon as she recovered.

XIX
"We are all republicans
—we are all federalists"

During his tenure as secretary of state, Jefferson had worked closely with George Washington in planning the new "Federal City" on the Potomac River. Now, in June of 1800, the government was moved there, and President and Mrs. John Adams took up residence in the half-finished "President's House." Jefferson returned to Monticello and tried to remain aloof from the political storms swirling around him.

At this time he drew up a list of services he had rendered to his country that he considered worthy of remembrance. The list went back to his efforts as a young man to improve the navigation of the Rivanna, which had, since then, been carrying produce to market. It included the writing of the Declaration of Independence, the Statute of Virginia for Religious Freedom, and the act for the more general diffusion of knowledge. And it included the sending of olive plants and upland rice to Georgia and South Carolina from Italy. But it mentioned nothing about his diplomatic or political labors. And when he asked himself if his country were better for his having lived, he answered that he was not sure it was. Others could have done what he had.

A hardening of the line between parties had been gradually taking place over the last two years, and now the Republican Party was welded together on a platform of states' rights as opposed to the increasing power of the federal government. By late fall Jefferson found himself nominated for the presidency as the Republican Party candidate. Aaron Burr, a senator from New York, would be his running mate for vice president. The Federalists nominated John Adams and

Charles Coatsworth Pinckney of South Carolina. A bitter campaign was under way.

Invectives hurled at Thomas Jefferson were fierce. In some states the clergy denounced him as an atheist. They hoped to see the formation of an established church in the United States as in England. To Jefferson, this would undermine the freedom of religion guaranteed by the Bill of Rights. In his view the Sedition Act had already destroyed freedom of speech and of the press. He couldn't allow the same to happen to freedom of religion.

"They [the clergy] believe that any portion of power confided to me will be exerted in opposition to their schemes; and they believe rightly," he wrote in a letter to his friend Dr. Benjamin Rush, "for I have sworn upon the altar of God, eternal hostility against every form of tyranny over the mind of man."[1]

December 3, 1800, was designated "election day." But it would take two and a half months for the results of this election to be final. Actually, December 3 was the day on which *electors* were to cast their votes. The electors themselves had been chosen by the people in their respective states in November.

Jefferson knew that in his own state of Virginia the freeholders supported him solidly. In fact, from the time he had first been elected a burgess for the county of Albemarle more than thirty years before, he had never suffered defeat at the Virginia polls.

When he arrived in Washington at the end of November, he took lodgings at the boardinghouse of Conrad and McMunn, often called simply Conrad's. Here he took his meals at a common table with anywhere from twenty-four to thirty people, all of them political friends. From Conrad's, he walked to the still-unfinished Capitol building, where, as vice president, he presided over the Senate.

Within two weeks of his arrival, Jefferson knew that his party was victorious. The Republicans had a clear victory over John Adams and the Federalist Party. But his own victory was not assured. A tie had developed between Thomas Jefferson and his running mate, Aaron Burr. Each man had received seventy-three electoral votes against sixty-five for Adams and sixty-four for Pinckney. This sort of tie within the same party had never been foreseen.

In accordance with the Constitution the tie could be broken only by a vote in the House of Representatives.

Neither John Adams nor Alexander Hamilton trusted Aaron Burr. Now, with Adams no longer in the running, both he and Hamilton urged support of Thomas Jefferson. Despite this, a deadlock continued in the Federalist-dominated House of Representatives through thirty-five ballots, over a period of six days. Throughout, Jefferson maintained his traditional calm and dignity.

When told that if he would agree to certain conditions of the Federalists some members of the House of Representatives would change their votes, he flatly refused. He would make no attempt to sway the voters, and he would make no political compromises.

On the thirty-sixth ballot the tie was broken, and on February 17, Thomas Jefferson was elected president of the United States.

His faith in his countrymen was evident two weeks later when he announced in a letter to his old friend Lafayette: "The storm we have passed through proves our vessel indestructible."[2]

During the weeks in which the outcome of the election had remained uncertain, President Adams had filled every office under his control with Federalists loyal to him. By March 3 he had appointed 216 new officials in what came to be known as the "midnight appointments." The most distressing of these was his appointment of John Marshall, a bitter political foe of Jefferson's, as chief justice of the Supreme Court. In that role, Marshall could defeat many of Jefferson's cherished aims.

Then, on the eve of the inauguration, in the middle of the night, John Adams left town.

At ten o'clock on Wednesday morning, March 4, 1801, a tall, lanky, and plainly dressed Thomas Jefferson, having declined Jupiter's offer to call a coach, left his boardinghouse and, accompanied by a few friends, strolled the short distance to the Capitol to be inaugurated as the third president of the United States.

For Jefferson, his election to the presidency signaled a turning point in the history of the young nation. Subtle attempts to twist its Constitution into a monarchy had been defeated, and he had been carried into office on a great tide of public feeling. The right of political opposition had been affirmed. It was apparent that the spirit of '76 was still alive.

He vowed there would be no reprisals. He was not vindictive. He had always been a harmonizer, a pacifier. He would not prolong party strife. He would attempt to calm the political passions of the past ten years. His inaugural address, audible only to those seated at the front of the crowded Senate Chamber, made this abundantly clear.

"Every difference of opinion is not a difference of principle. We have called by different names brethren of the same principle. We are all republicans—we are all federalists."[3]

In more than one sense this was the most characteristic and the most masterly of Thomas Jefferson's political statements.

He went on with a brilliant definition of minority rights: "If there be any among us who would wish to dissolve this Union or to change its republican form, let them stand undisturbed as monuments of the safety with which error of opinion may be tolerated where reason is left free to combat it."[4]

To him, the sum of good government was to be "wise and frugal," to "restrain men from injuring one another," and to "leave them otherwise free to regulate their own pursuits."[5] This he succeeded in doing throughout his tenure in office.

When President Jefferson returned to Conrad's for dinner following the inauguration ceremonies, he took his usual seat far from the fire, at the coldest end of the table.

Washington, at this time, was little more than a swamp, with a few shapeless, unfinished buildings. There were no shops, no amusements of any kind. But the members of Congress who came exhibited a faith in a government and in a way of life they knew they were building. Thomas Jefferson had the distinction of being the first president to be inaugurated in Washington, in the first year of the new century.

Politically, his first term as president was a brilliant success. He had, surrounding him, men of extraordinary intellect and loyalty. Among these, he had named James Madison, his closest political colleague and personal friend, secretary of state. Albert Gallatin, who combined financial and administrative talent with political wisdom, was his secretary of the treasury. Harmony was important to their leader, all his Cabinet members knew, and they made a particular effort to cooperate. Jefferson, in turn, frequently sought their advice and was willing to alter his own views when he was presented with a better argument.

By the end of 1803 most of his party's political program had been accomplished. In close collaboration with Congress, Jefferson had begun to pay off the national debt, he had cut taxes, reduced the standing army, and ensured that the oceans were safe for American shipping.

During his presidency, he refused to sanction any alterations in the Constitution. The only change he would endorse was the Twelfth Amendment, which corrected the irregularities that had occurred in the elections of 1796 and 1800 by providing that separate electoral ballots be cast for president and vice president.

The hated Alien and Sedition Acts had already expired, and now Jefferson pardoned the "martyrs" serving sentences under the Sedition Law, and the government returned many fines. In 1802, a new naturalization law was enacted, reducing the requirement of fourteen years of residence to the original five.

Jefferson had determined as soon as he took office that he would change any of the social practices that savored of anti-republicanism. In keeping with this he shocked a visiting minister from Great Britain when he received him in his "usual morning-attire" and wearing slippers. The minister was in "full dress." Nor did Mr. Jefferson ever observe any formality at his table. He seated his guests indiscriminately and denied that there was ever a guest of honor. And he abolished the formal receptions that President Washington had instituted. When a group of ladies called on him despite this, the president, who had just returned from his morning ride, greeted them in his muddy riding boots. But he was never rude. His manners were easy, if not polished, and his simplicity was the naturalness of one who had achieved enough to dare to be himself.

Most dramatic of all, his long-standing fascination with the western wilderness inspired his brilliant purchase of the vast Louisiana Territory from France in 1803. This contained 828,000 square miles of virgin land west of the Mississippi River, including the strategic port of New Orleans. Not only did this double the size of the United States at less than three cents an acre, but it opened up the port of New Orleans, "through which the produce of three-eighths of our territory must pass to market. . . ."[6]

When the opportunity to strike this magnificent real estate bargain presented itself, Jefferson was in a quandary. The strict construction-ist—this literal interpreter of the Constitution—wrestled with the realist and public servant that he was. He knew the Constitution did not authorize the president to negotiate treaties for acquiring new land. But he knew, also, that it was a wise move, best taken advantage of quickly. So a conscience-stricken Jefferson submitted the treaties to the Senate, which promptly and enthusiastically approved them. The Louisiana Purchase is considered the single greatest achieve-ment of his presidency.

The subsequent expedition of Meriwether Lewis and William Clark across the far West to map the Missouri River, and then west "even to the Western Ocean," became another of the glories of the Jefferson administration.

Such was his popularity that, after his reelection to the presidency in 1805, it was said, half in jest, that he had a "prospect of reelection for life." None but his closest friends knew that he was determined that his second term would be his last.

He continued to hunger for his family. "It is in the love of one's family only that heartfelt happiness is known. I feel it . . . beyond what can be imagined. . . . I count from one meeting to another as we do between port and port at sea: and I long for the moment with the same earnestness," he wrote to Maria.[7]

During the autumn of 1799, Maria and Jack had told him that Maria was expecting a baby. By this time Martha already had four children and seemed to have no difficulty bearing them. But Maria, so like her mother, filled her father with dread at the thought of what might be in store for her. His fear was justified. Maria's baby was born at Eppington, prematurely, on New Year's Eve and died less than a month later. The grief-stricken Maria had a long and painful convalescence.

Medallion portrait
of Thomas Jefferson,
1805, considered by
his family to be the
best likeness of him.

"How deeply I feel it in all its bearings I shall not say—nor attempt consolation when I know that time and silence are the only medicines. I shall only observe, as a source of hope to us all, that you are young, and will not fail to possess enough of these dear pledges which bind us to one another and to life itself," her distraught father wrote to her. In the same letter he told her of the untimely death of Jupiter, his faithful servant and traveling companion, whom Martha's little daughter Ellen lovingly referred to as "Uckin Juba." "He leaves a void . . . which cannot be filled."[8]

Two years later Maria did have another of "these dear pledges." Francis Wayles Eppes, named for his paternal grandfather, was born at Monticello while his maternal grandfather was enjoying a long summer vacation from the presidency there. Jefferson always made it a practice to spend the two sickly months (August and September) on his mountain, where the air was free of infection. At this time he had his family and slaves inoculated against smallpox and brought vaccine from Washington to Albemarle for the use of his neighbors. In this way he unofficially established vaccination as a public health procedure in Virginia.

Martha had also given birth at Monticello to her fifth child, Virginia, just a month before. This newest daughter proved to be the largest and healthiest Martha ever had. She ultimately gave birth to twelve children overall, of whom all but one survived. Martha herself remained amazingly strong and healthy throughout her life.

Martha was content to move between her own homes and Monticello—to spend, in fact, the greater portion of her time at her father's house. Jefferson had also helped his son-in-law purchase Edgehill, just a few miles from Monticello, from Randolph, Sr. "It is essential to my happiness, our living near together," the president explained to his son-in-law.

Martha's husband apparently had no objections to this, moving easily between the houses. When he was elected to the House of Representatives, he willingly added the trip to Washington to his itinerary as well.

During the winter of 1802 to 1803, Maria's strength had returned, and she and Martha, together with some of the older children, were able to make the arduous journey from Virginia to Washington to visit their father and their husbands.* This was the only time Jefferson had both his daughters together in Washington. The solicitous president was happy to pay all their traveling expenses and delighted in taking them to the new shops for the latest fashions. His generosity to his daughters and their husbands and children never ceased.

He was overjoyed to have them all together in the presidential mansion, despite the lack of plaster on some of the ceilings and the cold—thirteen fires had to be kept going in order to provide even minimum warmth, and the children were bundled up in coats as though they were out-of-doors.

All of Washington was charmed by the president's daughters. Martha's friendliness and intelligence and Maria's beauty and sweetness were frequently remarked upon. But the modest Maria hated allusions to her beauty. She wished for the kind of intelligence her sister had, in order—she told her father—to be more worthy of his love. This, in spite of her father's reassurances that there could never be a difference in his feelings for them. But Maria was not convinced.

* * *

---

* Jack Eppes, like his brother-in-law, had been elected to the House of Representatives.

Jefferson doted on his grandchildren and served them ice cream for the first time in Washington: he had brought the recipe from France. In fact, to Thomas Jefferson goes the credit for introducing to America not only ice cream but macaroni and waffles as well.

An official caller who found the president of the United States on the floor, playing with his grandchildren, was disarmed when Jefferson asked if he also were a father. "If so," said the president, "I need offer no apology."

Late in 1803, as his first term of office was drawing to a close, Thomas Jefferson's popularity was as its highest peak, and the nation was prospering. His daughters were temporarily living together in Albemarle while their husbands and their father were in Washington, waiting for Congress "to rise." Martha had had a sixth child, and Maria, ill once again, was fearfully awaiting the birth of her third.

The baby, a girl whom they named Maria, arrived on February 15, 1804—before the arrival of her father or her grandfather. Jefferson sent "A thousand joys to you, My dear Maria, on the happy accession to your family."[9]

But their joy was short-lived. Jefferson soon learned from Martha that her fragile sister was dangerously ill. When Maria's milk dried up as a result, Martha simply took over the job of nursing the infant along with her own.

"Nothing but the impossibility of Congress proceeding a single step in my absence" prevented his "instant departure to join you," the president wrote to his daughter. "God bless you my ever dear daughter and preserve you safe to be the blessing of us all."[10]

By the time Jefferson arrived at Monticello, where, at his suggestion, Maria had been gently carried on a man-borne litter in the hope that the change of air would do her some good, he found her "so weak as to be barely able to stand, her stomach so disordered as to reject almost every thing she took into it, a constant small fever, & an imposthume [abscess] rising in her breast."[11] She grew steadily weaker.

Four days after his own sixty-first birthday, when the first bloom of spring was just beginning on the mountainside, Thomas Jefferson entered in his *Account Book:* "This morning between 8 & 9 o'clock my dear daughter Maria Eppes died." She was not yet twenty-six.

While Jefferson may never have fully acknowledged the clash of loyalties that constantly beset Maria, she was, in fact, more an Eppes than a Jefferson. But in death he claimed her as his own. He buried her in the lonely hillside graveyard at Monticello, near her mother and the tiny children they had lost.

His grief, he said, was "inexpressible." Replying to a letter of condolence from his old friend John Page, he wrote, "Others may lose of their abundance, but I, of my want, have lost even the half of all I had. My evening prospects now hang on the slender thread of a single life."[12]

Abigail Adams, who never quite forgave Jefferson for what she considered his political offenses against her husband, read of Maria's death in the Quincy, Massachusetts, newspapers. Poignant memories of the tearful little girl who had clung to her in London prompted her to write to her old friend, "The powerful feelings of my heart burst through the restraint, and called upon me to shed the tear of sorrow over the departed remains of your beloved and deserving daughter."[13]

Francis and Elizabeth Eppes took the little Maria and Francis—all they had left of their precious Polly—back to Eppington to care for them there. Little Maria's life, too, was brief. She lived only three and a half years. But Francis grew up to be a source of pride and joy to his grandfather and remained a living link with this cherished daughter.

Politically, Jefferson's second term in office did not end on the same optimistic note as his first. The last years of his presidency were dominated by the problem of maintaining American neutrality in the face of a war between France and Great Britain. Both countries interfered with American trade. England had gone so far as to seize American seamen and had attacked the American naval frigate *Chesapeake* off the coast of Norfolk, Virginia, claiming that it harbored four British deserters. When the British fired at close range, three Americans were killed and eighteen wounded.

Determined to avoid war, Jefferson recommended, and Congress speedily adopted, an embargo on foreign trade. It has been described as an original and daring act of statesmanship but a practical failure. While it did avoid war and encourage American manufacturing, there was widespread opposition to it, particularly in New England and in parts of the Middle Atlantic States, where shipping was an important industry, and methods were found to evade it.

At first Jefferson did not realize the full extent of the economic distress the embargo was causing. When he did, he acceded to the will of the people and lifted the embargo. He signed the law repealing it during his last days in office. But he left the presidency disheartened. James Madison succeeded him.

Jefferson described himself then as a wave-worn mariner approaching the shore and as a prisoner emerging from shackles. In a letter to a friend he wrote, "Nature intended me for the tranquil pursuits of science, by rendering them my supreme delight. But the enormities of the times in which I have lived have forced me to take a part in resisting them, and to commit myself on the boisterous ocean of political passions."[14]

XX
A tangled web

On September 1, 1802, during the first term of Jefferson's presidency, a feature article had appeared in the Richmond, Virginia, *Recorder,* a weekly newspaper, that kindled a scandal that would haunt Thomas Jefferson for the rest of his life and that, in fact, seems not to have died even near the end of the twentieth century. Its embers are fanned periodically.

> It is well known that [Thomas Jefferson] the man, whom it delighteth the people to know, keeps, and for many years past has kept, as his concubine, one of his own slaves. Her name is SALLY. The name of her eldest son is Tom. His features are said to bear a striking although sable resemblance to those of the president himself. The boy is ten or twelve years of age. His mother went to France in the same vessel with Mr. Jefferson and his two daughters.* The delicacy of this arrangement must strike every person of common sensibilitys [sic]. . . .
> By this wench Sally, our president has had several children. . . . The AFRICAN VENUS is said to officiate, as housekeeper at Monticello.

The story was written by James Callender, the notoriously unscrupulous editor of the *Recorder,* whom Thomas Jefferson had previously, unwisely, befriended. Its motive was clear. Callender wanted revenge.

Callender was a Scot who had fled his native country in 1793 in order to escape a jail sentence for sedition and libel. In the United States he used his literary talents in the newspaper battle then waging

---
* Callender later admitted that this was, in fact, *not* the case.

between the Federalists and the Republicans. Political rivalries then were strong, and Jefferson, unaware of Callender's lack of scruples, seemed at first to welcome his support. Naively, he did not anticipate that Callender might later use blackmail to extract payment from him.

Then, in 1798, Callender was tried and convicted under the Sedition Act for defaming President John Adams. He was sentenced to nine months in jail and fined two hundred dollars. Three years later, when Thomas Jefferson became president, Callender was one of the "martyrs" he pardoned. When the government was unable to refund Callender's fine immediately, Jefferson paid part of it out of his own pocket. But Callender was not satisfied.

Now he demanded an appointment as postmaster in Richmond as a reward. Jefferson refused, and Callender took his revenge in the stinging attack in the *Recorder*. Its accusations have echoed down the centuries.

Jefferson, Callender claimed, had seduced Sally Hemings, his young slave, in Paris when she was just fifteen years old, and Sally was pregnant when she returned to America with him and his two daughters. Callender further alleged that Jefferson kept Sally as his mistress—having six children by her—over the next fifteen years, even while he was president of the United States.

Facts have come to light that prove that Sally was *not* pregnant when she returned to America. Her first child was born in 1795 and died two years later. This was documented by Jefferson in his *Farm Book*, in which he recorded detailed statistics about *all* his slaves and made it possible to trace the genealogy of many of them through four generations. This *Farm Book* lay unnoticed in the Massachusetts Historical Society from 1898 until 1953, when it was reprinted in facsimile.

Furthermore, it seems impossible to believe that Thomas Jefferson, traveling home from France with his two teenage daughters, would include in this intimate family group a pregnant teenage mulatto mistress. "There are such things, after all, as moral impossibilities."[1]

Jefferson himself steadfastly refused to reply to the accusations.

"As to federal slanders, I never wished them to be answered, but by the tenor of my life, half a century of which has been on a theatre at which the public have been spectators, and competent judges of its merit. Their approbation has taught a lesson, useful to the world, that the man who fears no truths has nothing to fear from lies. I should have fancied myself half guilty had I condescended to put pen to paper in refutation of their falsehoods, or drawn to them respect by any notice from myself," he wrote to a friend years later.[2]

His silence in the face of the attacks can be understood even more clearly when we recognize that in order to defend himself he would have had to reveal who Sally Hemings was and how she came to be at Monticello. He would writhe under the attacks and keep quiet rather than reveal this.

His acceptance of full responsibility for all the Hemings immediately upon the death of John Wayles, his determination to give them the fullest measure of his own protection as members of his family, with every opportunity to grow up as self-respecting individuals, and his resolve to train the boys in a trade whereby they could support themselves, and then to offer them their freedom, made his actions toward the family appear suspicious to anyone who did not fully comprehend the situation.

He knew full well that Sally was the youngest of John Wayles's children by his mistress, Betty Hemings. Thus, Sally and her five brothers and sisters were his wife Martha's half-brothers and sisters.

But the "Dusky Sally story" was further complicated. Sally's children "resembled Mr. Jefferson so closely that it was plain that they had his blood in their veins." In fact, the resemblance was so great in one of her sons that, from a distance and in the right clothes, the slave might have been mistaken for Jefferson. Visitors to Monticello were frequently startled by this similarity.

Documents have been discovered that explain this and shed light on a situation that knotted the lives of three generations of blacks and whites into a tangled web.

Jefferson's policy of freeing the Hemings boys if they desired it did not apply to the girls, especially to Sally. Sally was unusually beautiful. Her upbringing as a companion to Patsy and Polly, her years in France absorbing the culture around her, her education, all contributed to a style of behavior that set her apart from other slaves. By birth and upbringing, she was a socially displaced person in the

America of 1790. If she had been freed, there would have been no place for her to go. To free her would have been akin to abandoning a child. So Jefferson kept her in his own family—safe, he hoped, from the hazards of sexual exploitation she would have faced outside, safe from suffering the same wrong he felt had been practiced on her mother by John Wayles.

But Sally and Peter Carr, Jefferson's favorite nephew, who lived at Monticello, developed a deep and lasting emotional involvement. Peter became Sally's lover and remained so for fifteen years. There is no evidence that Sally, who had accepted middle-class standards of monogamy, ever developed an attachment to another man. Peter, though, while sustaining his love for Sally, married the daughter of a distinguished Baltimore family and seemed a devoted husband and father to the four children his wife bore him. But for at least ten years after his marriage, Peter and Sally remained lovers, and she had three more children by him.

When Edmund Bacon, overseer at Monticello, told the story of his years at Monticello, it was incorporated into a little book called *Jefferson at Monticello,* published in 1862. The book, reprinted more than a century later, substantiates the fact that Peter Carr was the father of Sally's children. Bacon stated that he had seen Peter come out of Sally's room "many a morning when I went up to Monticello very early."[3]

And Jefferson's granddaughter Ellen Randolph Coolidge, writing to her husband while she was visiting her brother Thomas Jefferson Randolph long after her grandfather had died, refuted the accusations against him: "The four children of Sally Hemmings [sic] were *all* the children of Col. Carr."[4] Thomas Jefferson Randolph also wrote that Peter Carr had admitted his paternity to him in 1813 or 1814.

Jefferson always loved Peter as a son and had great hopes for him. This was one instance in which Peter disappointed his uncle. But Jefferson would never attempt to absolve himself by implicating his sister's son.

Nor is it reasonable to believe that he would keep Sally as his mistress in a house that was always overflowing with grandchildren whom he adored. This is inconsistent with everything we have learned about the real Thomas Jefferson.

"Such a ruthless exploitation of the master-slave relationship re-volted his whole being," one of his biographers has written.[5]

Callender, a moody and ill-tempered drunkard who frequently threatened to commit suicide, was found drowned in the James River, in three feet of water, in July of 1803. But his lurid allegations about "Dusky Sally" had been broadcast to the world and would remain to haunt the memory of Thomas Jefferson.

XXI
Man on a
mountain

It was when Jefferson had resigned his duties as secretary of state and returned to his mountaintop in 1793 that he had determined to begin the radical alterations of Monticello that he had been considering since he had first been captivated by the ancient architecture he saw in France.

No doubt, also, Monticello as it stood in 1793 served as a poignant, bittersweet reminder of the happy days when his wife had been alive, and this played a large part in his decision to change it. And perhaps his statement to a visitor, "architecture is my delight, and putting up and pulling down, one of my favorite amusements,"[1] was a basis for his decision as well.

As he surveyed his own Monticello after his stay in Paris, it began to look provincial to him. So he decided not only to make the necessary repairs but to enlarge the house as well. And he would alter it to reflect French taste. He determined that from the outside the house would *appear* to be one story only. But he would double its size in the manner of "all the new and good houses" in Paris. He would use native American materials and traditions of craftsmanship to transform his home into something new. Roman and French classicism would be interpreted in red brick and white painted wood. It was a project that he would pursue for the next sixteen years.

He decided to erect a dome, constructed of wooden ribs and radiating panes of glass, in the center of the structure, over the front parlor. It would be reminiscent of the Halle aux Bles in Paris—and of that delightful afternoon in the summer of 1786 when he met Maria Cosway.

Construction of the dome began in 1800. Although an advanced design for its day, it was remarkably simple to build. In 1805 the single sheet of glass that became its large circular window was put in place, and Mr. Jefferson's "sky-room" was completed.

The entrance hall of Monticello, just inside the front portico, faces the Southwest Mountains. In time it became a museum, reflecting the broad scope of Jefferson's interests and included one of the most important private collections of natural history specimens and American Indian artifacts in America at that time.

Jefferson's interest in the Native Americans was long-standing. He had studied their language and grappled with their problems. In fact, fascinated by the Indian language, he had, over the years, collected fifty Indian vocabularies. He had planned to have them printed side by side in columns, in order to compare them with each other and with Russian, which he found in some ways similar. He had hoped to discover a common origin. But this was never accomplished. At the close of his presidency, the papers were packed in a trunk to be shipped back to Monticello from Washington. Some wharf hands, thinking the trunk heavy enough that it might contain gold, made off with it. When they opened it and discovered that it contained nothing but papers, they were so angry they ripped the sheets and

tossed them into the James River. A few of the papers that were later discovered were soaked and muddy and completely useless. It was an irreparable loss.

The dining room at Monticello, where the entire family gathered for dinner at three-thirty every afternoon, perhaps best exemplifies the life there in the later years of Jefferson's life. The Wedgewood inserts on the mantel, and the silver candlesticks on the Chippendale dining table, a gift from his old friend George Wythe, impart a sense of the quiet elegance of the man and the surroundings. The small candlestand and chair near the fireplace, and the selection of books on the mantel, attest to his habit of reading while waiting for the family to assemble for dinner. This was a man who never wasted a minute.

Mechanical dumbwaiters on either side of the mantel allowed wine and fruit to be sent up from the cellar below. Small rectangular tables, also called dumbwaiters, placed between guests enabled them to serve themselves, reducing the number of servants necessary in the room. This allowed for more privacy for conversation during dinner.

Watercolor of Monticello in 1826, showing Jefferson's granddaughters.

Monticello

Jefferson's deep need for privacy is reflected in his own suite of rooms, which included his bedroom; his cabinet, or study, where he did all his writing; and his library, which he called his "bookroom." A greenhouse adjoined. This wing was always locked and was considered his sanctuary. No one entered without an invitation. It was the only place at Monticello where he could escape from the incessant swarm of visitors, to read and to carry on his voluminous correspondence.* It was, in fact, the heart of his private world. His books, his telescope, his measuring devices were all there, centered around his chair with candlesticks in its arms for light and a chaise longue to accommodate his long legs. A desk, drawn up over the chair, held his writing materials and the polygraph he used to make file copies of his letters. The little portable desk on which he had written the Declaration of Independence was kept on a shelf in the study, at just the proper height for writing while standing.

His bed, set in an alcove in the French style, was open on both

---

* It is estimated that in his lifetime Thomas Jefferson wrote and received 50,000 letters.

sides, providing ventilation and allowing him to rise on either side—his bedroom or his cabinet. Making things with his hands was always a relaxing hobby for Jefferson, so he had a room with a carpenter's workbench and a large assortment of tools. But perhaps the greatest convenience that Monticello could boast were the indoor privies (bathrooms) that he had seen in France.

So Thomas Jefferson built a home that met his family's practical, social, and emotional needs, as well as a house that reflected the same human dignity and scholarship that he strove for throughout his life. It became a symbol of his ideal for the country he helped to build.

Jefferson's perpetual longing for Monticello—and all that it symbolized for him—the pull that existed throughout most of his life between what he saw as his duty to his country and domestic peace and tranquility in the bosom of his family—finally ended with his retirement from the presidency and his return to Monticello in 1809.

Now he was able to give free reign to his plans to revitalize his gardens, and in this his granddaughter Anne, whom he once compared to a gleam of sunshine, was his enthusiastic assistant, his keeper of the flowers, as she had been all the time he was in Washington. Then, letters had flowed between them filled with talk of flowers. Anne's younger sister Ellen took over this job when Anne married.

Jefferson was always essentially a scientist, and his gardens and groves were his laboratory. If they proved suitable, he passed cuttings on to interested neighbors and friends. The greatest service one could render any country was to add a useful plant to its culture, he had said some years before. Now he planted two hundred and fifty varieties of vegetables and one hundred and fifty varieties of fruit trees. Peas were his favorite food, and he grew twenty-two varieties.

In a radical departure from the customs of the times, he planted trees close to the house when southern houses had their lawns swept clean.

The weather continued to interest him, so he made careful note of the amount of rainfall, the severity of the winds, the dates of the first and last killing frosts, and the range in the temperature. That he found the time to make such an enormous number of observations

Jefferson's study

in his *Garden Book* attests to the fact that observing nature was something he loved to do.

"No occupation is so delightful to me as the culture of the earth, and no culture is comparable to that of the garden. . . . But though an old man, I am but a young gardener."[2] His perpetual cheerfulness manifested itself most visibly here.

In the greenhouse off his suite of rooms he had his favorite bird, the mockingbird, in a cage suspended over his flowers. He often allowed it to fly free, and it would at times sit on his table and sing for him or perch on his shoulder and take food from his lips. His grandchildren loved to watch it hop up the stairs after him.

The setting of his house on his mountaintop with its unobstructed, spectacular views in all directions attests to the importance of nature in his thinking. The changing moods and seasons of nature served as a constant spark for his imagination.

The Marquis de Chastellux had been among the first to recognize this many years before—and to understand the special relationship between Thomas Jefferson and Monticello—when he had said that

Mr. Jefferson's house, like his mind, was placed in an elevated position so that he could calmly view the world at a distance. He had, indeed, set himself and his house upon a mountain.

Jefferson had at one time planned to build a home for Maria at Pantops, near Monticello. When Maria died, he abandoned the plan and decided to build instead in Bedford County, a three-day carriage ride away, on land he had inherited from his wife. It would be his legacy to Maria's son, Francis.

The house, which he had named Poplar Forest for the 190 tulip poplar trees he planted there, became the first octagonal house in the New World and one of the most imaginative. Jefferson believed then—and architects have since confirmed—that the octagonal floor plan used space economically and allowed maximum flow of light and air. In both Poplar Forest and Monticello, he was particularly concerned that there be large rooms and large windows.

It was only at Poplar Forest that Jefferson, always accompanied by one or two grandchildren, could escape the steady stream of visitors at Monticello, exchanging it for "his favorite pursuits—to think, to study, to read—whilst the presence of his family took away all the character of solitude from his retreat."[3] He made at least three visits there annually and the grandchildren who were chosen each time to accompany him considered it a special treat.

XXII
"The venerable corps of grandfathers"

"I receive with real pleasure your congratulations on my advancement to the venerable corps of grandfathers, and can assure you with truth that I expect from it more felicity than any other advancement ever gave me. I only wish for the hour when I may go and enjoy it entire."[1]

So Thomas Jefferson had responded to Elizabeth Eppes after the birth of his first grandchild on January 23, 1791, the little girl born to Martha and Tom Randolph, whom the grandfather was privileged to name Anne. This birth ushered in a period of his life that brought him untold joy—as well as unexpected sorrow.

During his years after the presidency, when he was able, finally, to "go and enjoy it entire," he derived his greatest happiness from his grandchildren. While his natural reserve and his superior intellect may have made him appear withdrawn or intimidating to some adults, he was always at ease with children. His warmth toward them is evident in all their reminiscences about him and in the letters they exchanged with him as soon as they were old enough to read and to write.

He thoughtfully responded to *all* their questions—both serious and trifling—so that they felt comfortable going to him with all their problems. He devoted as much time and effort to selecting a new dress or a toy for a young child as he did to outlining a course of study for an older child.

His sense of family was strong. Like his father before him, he cared for the fatherless, and his home was always filled with nieces and nephews as well as with his own children and grandchildren.

He even strove to keep his slave families together, occasionally buying or selling a slave *only* to keep a marriage or a family intact.

But the constant stream of visitors, the workmen who continued to swarm through the as yet unfinished house, in addition to all the children, often brought problems as well as happiness. Including children, there could be more than twenty people in the house at one time. An entire beef might be consumed in two days. Frequently there weren't enough beds to sleep in, nor were there stables enough for the horses.

He described his life at Monticello then in a letter to a friend: "My mornings are devoted to correspondence. From breakfast to dinner I am in my shops, my garden, or on horseback among my farms; from dinner to dark, I give to society and recreation with my neighbors and friends; and from candle-light to early bed-time I read. My health is perfect, and my strength considerably reinforced by the activity of the course I pursue. . . . A part of my occupation, and by no means the least pleasing, is the direction of the studies of such young men as ask it. They . . . have the use of my library and counsel, and make a part of my society."[2]

But it is the reminiscences of his grandchildren, written years later when they were grown men and women, that best depict his life then and attest to the place he held in their hearts, and they in his.

Ellen Wayles Randolph, the second and possibly the favorite of his granddaughters, described the times the grandchildren had spent with him in the garden:

> I remember well, when he first returned to Monticello, how immediately he began to prepare new beds for his flowers . . . with . . . a crowd of younger grandchildren clustering round to see the progress, and inquire anxiously the name of each separate deposit.
>
> Then, when spring returned, how eagerly we watched the first appearance of the shoots above ground. . . . and what joy it was for one of us to discover the tender green breaking through the mould, and run to grandpapa to announce that we really believed Marcus Aurelius* was coming up. . . . With how much

* a deep purple tulip

pleasure, compounded of our pleasure and his own . . . he would immediately go out to verify the fact, and praise us for our diligent watchfulness.[3]

His granddaughter Virginia remembered that they raced after him delightedly, yet

not one of us, in our wildest moods, ever placed a foot on one of the garden beds, for that would violate one of his rules, and yet I never heard him utter a harsh word to one of us, or speak in a raised tone of voice, or use a threat. He simply said, "Do," or "Do not."[4]

These moments that the grandchildren spent with him amid the flowers were among the happiest of all their lives.

Reminiscing about her grandfather on another occasion, Ellen wrote:

As a child, girl, and woman, I loved and honored him above all earthly beings. And well I might. From him seemed to flow all the pleasures of my life. To him I owed all the small blessings and joyful surprises of my childish and girlish years. . . . Our grandfather seemed to read our hearts, to see our invisible wishes . . . to wave the fairy wand, to brighten our young lives by his goodness and his gifts."[5]

Virginia, five years younger than Ellen, lamented the fact that she was born the year her grandfather was elected president, and was, therefore, too young to correspond with him during his years in Washington. But, when he was home, she remembered:

On winter evenings, when it grew too dark to read, in the half hour which passed before candles came in, as we all sat round the fire, he taught us several childish games, and would play them with us.

When the candles were brought, all was quiet immediately, for he took up his book to read; and we would not speak out

Jefferson's granddaughter Anne—his keeper of the flowers—whom he once described as a "gleam of sunshine."

of a whisper, lest we should disturb him, and generally we followed his example and took a book. . . . When the snow fell, we would go out, as soon as it stopped, to clear it off the terraces with shovels, that he might have his usual walk on them without treading in snow.[6]

For many years Ellen was the belle and pride of the family. While not as beautiful as Anne, Ellen had also inherited the fair skin and rosy complexion of the Jeffersons. She was intelligent, reflective, and unusually articulate. Her grandfather is reputed to have said once that had she been a man she would have been a great one. But because she was a woman in the early nineteenth century, and particularly a granddaughter of the president of the United States, her role was sorely limited.

"My dear Ellen," as he called her, remained her grandfather's constant companion during his later years, until her marriage to Joseph

Coolidge, Jr., in the drawing room at Monticello on May 27, 1825. The story is told that when Ellen married and moved with her husband to Boston, whenever her sisters saw their grandfather looking at her empty chair, one of them hastened to sit in it, although they knew that nobody could fill her place.

Shortly after Ellen and Joseph arrived in Boston, they learned that the ship carrying her baggage had been lost at sea. The loss was a great one for her. Not only did her luggage contain personal items, wedding gifts, and furniture for her new home, but it contained, as well, a handsome writing desk that had been a gift from her grandfather and in which she had placed some of her most treasured possessions—letters and other memorabilia she had received from him over the years.

The writing desk had been designed and crafted by John Hemings, Jefferson's carpenter at Monticello. Hemings, particularly fond of Ellen—she was his favorite among the grandchildren—and anxious to create something special for her, had combined several woods in unusual patterns and had produced an exceptionally beautiful piece of furniture.

Jefferson understood the wrenching pain this must have caused the lonely young bride and sent Ellen and Joseph as consolation the writing box on which he had written the Declaration of Independence so many years before. "It claims no merit of particular beauty. It is plain, neat, convenient. . . . Its imaginary value will increase with years, and if [Mr. Coolidge] lives . . . another half-century, he may see it carried in the procession of our nation's birthday,"[7] he wrote to Ellen.

He wrote out an affidavit attesting to its history and to its link to the "Great Charter of our Independence."

The lap desk remained in the Coolidge family until 1880, after the deaths of both Ellen and Joseph, when their children decided to present it to the nation.

Thomas Jefferson Randolph, the second of Martha's children, was Thomas Jefferson's first grandson. He had been born at Monticello in September of 1792, while Martha was living there and her father

"My dear Ellen" was Jefferson's favorite granddaughter. Her sisters knew that nobody could fill her place.

was vacationing there from his duties as secretary of state. Named for his grandfather, he was an enormous baby and grew to be a huge man, resembling in many ways his great-grandfather, Peter Jefferson. He would become an adored and adoring grandson, the mainstay of his grandfather's later life. Jefferson, as his grandfather called him, became his favorite grandchild and ultimately took the place of the son he had never had.

It was to this grandson, just beginning college, that Jefferson wrote a letter that is remarkable for the advice it offered. He had already provided for young Jefferson all the things that he thought a boy going off to college should have, had given him pocket money, and had paid his tuition. But he was concerned with more than material things. His grandson was only fifteen and alone in Philadelphia for the first time.

Thrown on a wide world, among entire strangers, without a friend or guardian to advise, so young too and with so little experience of mankind, your dangers are great, and still your

Thomas Jefferson Randolph, cherished grandson, whom Jefferson considered "the greatest of the God-sends which heaven has granted to me."

safety must rest on yourself. A determination never to do what is wrong, prudence and good humor, will go far towards securing to you the estimation of the world. When I recollect that at fourteen years of age, the whole care and direction of myself was thrown on myself entirely, without a relation or friend qualified to advise or guide me, and recollect the various sorts of bad company with which I associated from time to time, I am astonished I did not turn off with some of them, and become as worthless to society as they were. I had the good fortune to become acquainted very early with some characters of very high standing, and to feel the incessant wish that I could ever become what they were. Under temptation and difficulties, I would ask myself what would Dr. Small, Mr. Wythe, Peyton Randolph do in this situation? . . .

I must not omit the important [rule] of never entering into dispute or argument with another. I never saw an instance of one or two disputants convincing the other by argument. . . . When I hear another express an opinion which is not mine, I say to myself, he has a right to his opinion, as I to mine; why should I question it? . . . Be a listener only, keep within yourself, and endeavor to establish with yourself the habit of silence, especially on politics.[8]

To this cherished grandson, he wrote near the end of his life, "Yourself particularly, dear Jefferson, I consider as the greatest of the God-sends which heaven has granted to me."[9]

His feelings were evident when, as an old man, he learned late one evening that this grandson had been in a serious accident. He immediately had his horse, Eagle, brought to the door and, despite the fact that he was too feeble to mount the mare without help, and against the pleas of his family, he struck the animal such a blow that it bounded off down the dark mountain at full gallop and got its master the four miles to Charlottesville and his grandson in record time.

The relationship between Thomas Jefferson and his namesake grew stronger and stronger over the years, and the older man came to rely heavily on the younger.

XXIII
"The last service
I can render my country"

During his retirement, Jefferson was gradually coming to the conclusion that a collection of books such as his should be in public rather than in private hands. Late in the summer of 1814, while he was contemplating this on his mountain, something happened in Washington that made him decide to act: The invading British army burned the Capitol during the War of 1812. The congressional library, housed in the building, was destroyed.

Jefferson immediately offered his own magnificent collection as a replacement, at any fee deemed appropriate by Congress. His only condition was that it must be accepted in its entirety. He recognized that the country was at war and in debt, and that many congressmen would object to spending any money on books, particularly those books that did not deal specifically with legislation. His library covered the entire field of human knowledge. It was far superior to the original owned by Congress and, at 6,700 volumes, was more than twice its size.

Jefferson had begun to classify his books in 1783, after his wife had died, and had continued to add titles to the catalogue over the next thirty years. Now he carefully revised it and had labels pasted to the spine of each book that corresponded to its listing in the catalogue.

Congress deliberated about accepting his offer for four months. Eventually the deliberations became partisan, and some of his political enemies mocked both him and his books. When the resolution finally did pass, it was only by a narrow margin. But in April, when the ten wagons carrying pine boxes filled with books wended their way to Washington, it marked the beginning of a great national library, one of the finest and most accessible in the world. While Thomas Jefferson never claimed that he founded the Library of Congress, certainly the institution that emerged out of the ashes was his creation.

He used the money he received from Congress, $23,950, to pay off troubling old debts. Then he immediately began assembling another library at an astonishing rate. "I cannot live without books," he wrote to his old friend John Adams.

The friendship between these two venerable patriots had recently been renewed after eleven years of silence between them when, in 1812, they began a correspondence that has become a classic in American letters and an unrivaled record of an extraordinary friendship. Their mutual friend, Dr. Benjamin Rush, was responsible for bringing about the reconciliation by repeatedly reminding them of their past comradeship and urging them to renew communication.

When Jefferson learned that John Adams had said, "I always loved Jefferson, and still do," he loosened the tight rein he generally kept on his emotions and declared that he would express his unchanged affection as soon as the right moment presented itself. They had been young rebels together, and Jefferson had never forgotten his friend's support of him in 1776 or his closeness to the entire Adams family while in France.

"A letter from you calls up recollections very dear to my mind," he wrote. "It carries me back to the times when, beset with difficulties and dangers, we were fellow-laborers in the same cause, struggling for what is most valuable to man, his right of self-government."[1]

He was ready to forgive.

Actually, John Adams made the first move, but Jefferson responded immediately. Both agreed that they ought not to die before they had explained themselves to one another.

Their correspondence began, appropriately, with an exchange of books, and their letters over the next fourteen years continued to be filled with references to their reading. The letters are memorable for their discussions of politics, history, philosophy, religion, and psychology. But as these two old friends reviewed the past and surveyed the present, they revealed the special warmth of feeling they had for one another.

*   *   *

When Thomas Jefferson offered his books to the Library of Congress, he was giving substance to his faith in learning. Throughout his long life he had advocated public education, convinced that freedom and knowledge were inseparable. He had always believed that the common people must be educated.

When he first set down in the Declaration of Independence his belief in the right to life, liberty, and the pursuit of happiness, he knew that education was the only sure foundation for the preservation of freedom and happiness.

Now, near the end of his life, he found the opportunity to make his dream a reality. In the spring of 1814, when Mr. Jefferson was seventy-one years old, he was invited to become a member of the Board of Trustees of a small, unorganized private school known as Albemarle Academy. His first suggestion was that it be transformed into Central College, and from this came the nucleus out of which the University of Virginia would develop.

A few months later, in a letter to his nephew Peter Carr, who was also on the board of Central College, Jefferson outlined his views on education. These ultimately became his Bill for Establishing a System of Public Education. That bill was sent to the Virginia legislature in October 1817 and passed both houses in February 1818.

Soon Jefferson was appointed a member of a group organized to recommend a site for a state university. He "did his homework," and gained a victory for the site of Central College in Charlottesville.

At the meeting of this group he took from his pocket a card cut into the shape of Virginia, with the proposed site of the university indicated by a dot. By balancing the dot on the point of a pencil, he proved that Charlottesville was in fact near the geographic center of the state. Then he produced another cardboard map of Virginia on which he had written, in his precise, minute handwriting, the population of every part of the state. Again, it quickly became clear that Charlottesville was centrally located.

His report also included his ideas of what a liberal university should be and remains one of his great educational papers. Characteristically, he then went to work quietly behind the scenes to have the paper adopted, and the University of Virginia was chartered the following year.

Suddenly, he had a new zest for living. There was a new spring

The University of Virginia: Mr. Jefferson's school—"the last service I can render my country."

to his step. His mind teemed with ideas and plans that had been simmering for years. He quickly made his old friend James Madison, who had recently retired from the presidency, his right-hand man, and swung into action.

Mr. Jefferson became the architect of the university at every level. It was he who chose its site, supplied its bricks, and saw to its construction. It was he who designed its buildings, laid out its paths, and supervised its plantings. He wrote its curriculum and recruited its faculty. And it was he who provided the library with the books he had acquired after selling his first collection to the Library of Congress. Perhaps most important, because of him the University of Virginia became the first university to have no religious affiliation. It was "based on the illimitable freedom of the human mind."[2]

Not only did he plan and personally supervise all aspects of the university, he struck the very first peg into the ground. Then, using the little ruler he always carried in his pocket, he measured off the ground and marked off the foundation. From that time until the university's completion, Jefferson could always be found at the building site. Early every morning he would mount his horse Eagle and canter down the mountain to Charlottesville. Once there, he used a walking stick of his own invention made of three sticks which, when spread out and covered with a cloth, became a seat. Late afternoons, after dinner back at Monticello, he could continue to watch what was going on there through the lens of his telescope set up on a terrace.

In 1822, when he was seventy-nine, a visitor to the construction site was amazed to see him take a chisel from the hand of an Italian stonecutter and show the craftsman how to model an ornament on a column.

The university was laid out as a rectangle open at one end. At the closed end was the Rotunda, modeled after the Pantheon in Rome. The dome room in the Rotunda would become the library.

Jefferson separated the functions of the university into distinct buildings, bringing to fruition an ideal of education that had been maturing throughout his life. This plan for what he called an "academical village" created a setting in which learning would be an integral part of living, and was totally his own. No model has ever been found for it. Both architecturally and intellectually, the creation of the university became the crowning achievement of his life. He himself referred to it as "the last service I can render my country."[3]

When the school finally opened on March 7, 1825, Mr. Jefferson was its first rector and chairman of the board of trustees. The University of Virginia, which has been called "the lengthened shadow of one man,"[4] made possible a perpetuation of his dream of an educational system and academic excellence in his native Virginia. He had set an example for the state universities that play such an important role in education today. He was in truth, its "father."

Shortly before the official opening of the university, Jefferson learned with joy that his old friend Lafayette was returning to America after thirty-five years and would visit him at Monticello. On a glorious November morning, Lafayette and his colorful entourage entered Albemarle County, where he was met by Jefferson Randolph, who accompanied him the rest of the way up the mountain to Monticello. Crowds lined the way: citizens on one side, brightly plumed cavalrymen on the other.

As they neared the house and Lafayette, now lame and broken in health by a long imprisonment during the French Revolution, caught sight of his old friend waiting on the portico, he gave the order to halt his carriage, and he stepped out. Each moved forward to greet the other, feebly at first, then quickening to a shuffling run as the two old men approached one another. Tears were shed by both as they embraced, saying, "My dear Jefferson." "My dear Lafayette." This was one of the rare instances in Jefferson's lifetime of a public display of emotion.

Lafayette found Mr. Jefferson "much aged" after thirty-five years but "marvelously well" at eighty-one and "in full possession of all the vigor of his mind and heart."[5]

The following day Lafayette was honored at a dinner in the Rotunda of the university, the first public dinner to be given there.

Throughout his life, aside from a few bouts with rheumatism and periodic attacks of migraine headaches, Jefferson had remained remarkably healthy. He rarely, if ever, had a cold. His life was a temperate one, orderly and industrious, and he exercised regularly. From the time he was a tall, lanky, red-haired boy of sixteen he had always considered walking the best exercise. As an old man he continued to believe that two hours of hard exercise every day was essential. Health, he had always contended, was worth even more than learning.

By the spring of 1826, as he approached his eighty-third birthday, he began to realize that his long life was coming to a close. His precarious financial situation no doubt hastened the end.

His son-in-law Thomas Mann Randolph unfortunately had been forced to declare bankruptcy, and the care and support of Martha and all her children fell to Jefferson. Then, too, an incident that occurred in 1819 had completely ruined him financially and took its toll physically as well. Jefferson, already in dire financial straits himself, had endorsed a note for twenty thousand dollars for his friend Wilson Cary Nicholas, ex-governor of Virginia and father of his grandson Jefferson's wife, Jane. When Nicholas went bankrupt, Thomas Jefferson was called on to pay. His loyalty was remarkable. He honored his guarantee and never allowed one word to be uttered against his longtime friend, nor did he ever hint at the disaster in the presence of his granddaughter-in-law.

By now, Jefferson Randolph had assumed the management of his grandfather's farms and attempted to relieve him of all the unpleasantness that developed from the fluctuation in the value of money and the continued depression of farming, both of which made it increasingly more difficult to pay off long-standing debts. In the end, after his grandfather had died, it was young Jefferson who personally saw to it that all these debts were paid.

As his debts, and the accumulated interest on them, continued to mount, his health steadily declined. While debt was the rule rather than the exception in the society in which he lived, "To owe what I cannot pay is a constant torment," he said. He tried in vain to find a purchaser for his lands. But he refused to accept the offer of an interest-free loan because, he said, that would cost the taxpayers money. Then, early in 1826, he hit upon the idea of holding a lottery to dispose of some of his lands.

Finally, with the help of his grandson Jefferson, he secured permission for the lottery from the Virginia legislature. But when the public protested against this indignity and some voluntary contributions were made, the project was abandoned.

His grandsons and his nephews rallied round him, offering what support they could. A heartbroken young Francis Eppes wrote to his grandfather from Poplar Forest at the end of February 1826:

> It was with infinite pain My Dr. Grandfather, that I saw your application to the legislature . . . and I write . . . to express, My unfeigned grief [and] to assure you that I return to your funds with the utmost good will, the portion of property [Poplar Forest] which you designed for me. . . . You have been to me ever, an affectionate, and tender Father, and you shall find me ever, a loving, and devoted son . . . I shall remain ever, as deeply indebted, as though your kind intentions had been completely fulfilled. . . . May God bless and long preserve you My dearest Grandfather, my best friend, with most sincere love your grandson, Frans. Eppes.[6]

His grandfather declined the offer.

Happily, Jefferson never knew that Monticello would soon pass out of the hands of his heirs forever.

*   *   *

It was March of 1826 before Jefferson Randolph first realized that his grandfather might be seriously ill. It was then that Thomas Jefferson, speaking of an event scheduled to take place in midsummer, said that he *might* live until that time. He had been suffering from a severe case of diarrhea for several weeks, and his strength was steadily declining. But he had not revealed this to his family.

He continued to ride Eagle—alone. When his family begged him to allow a servant to accompany him, he reminded them that he had ridden alone since childhood, that he must converse with nature alone, and that he had always "helped himself." He dreaded a dotty old age, he told them.

By early June he was so weak that he could mount the horse only by standing on one of the terraces and lowering himself into the saddle. His crippled wrist had grown worse as he grew older, and he had difficulty holding the reins. Eagle seemed to understand and, although it was generally a fiery and impatient horse, it stood perfectly still while its master mounted, then moved slowly and quietly down the path.

Late in June Jefferson received an invitation to join in the celebration of the fiftieth anniversary of American independence, to be held in Washington. As he thought back to those memorable days, some of the old spirit surged through his body and he found the strength to reply—with an eloquence reminiscent of his Declaration:

It adds sensibly to the sufferings of sickness, to be deprived by it of a personal participation in the rejoicings of that day. . . . I should indeed, with peculiar delight, have met and exchanged there congratulations personally with the small band, the remnant of that host of worthies, who joined with us on that day, in the bold and doubtful election we were to make for our country, between submission or the sword. . . . May it be to the world . . . the signal of arousing men to burst the chains under which monkish ignorance and superstition had persuaded them to bind themselves, and to assume the blessings and security of self-government. . . . All eyes are opened, or opening, to the rights of man. . . . For ourselves, let the annual return of this day, forever refresh our recollections of these rights, and an undiminished devotion to them.[7]

How much the celebration meant to him and how much he would have liked to participate in the festivities become clear when we know that some years before he had refused to divulge the date of his birthday to a committee intent on designating it a national holiday. He suggested, instead, that they honor him by celebrating the Fourth of July as the nation's birthday.

Soon after he wrote his reply, Jefferson became too weak to leave his bed. Members of his family prevailed upon him to allow them to stay with him, but he would not allow Martha to sit up at night. Jefferson Randolph and Nicholas Trist, his granddaughter Virginia's husband and grandson of his old friend Elizabeth Trist, maintained the vigil. He suffered no pain, but grew steadily weaker. Throughout, he remained calm and composed and concerned for his family. He reassured them that he had no fear of dying, that he was "like an old watch, with a pinion worn out here, and a wheel there, until it can go no longer."

On July 2 he called his family to his bedside and spoke to each of them briefly, characteristically offering advice—admonishing them to be good and truthful. He told young Jefferson that all the bitterness that had been hurled at him over the years by his enemies had in truth not abused him. His enemies, he said, had never known *him*. They had created an imaginary being to whom they had given his name.

To Martha he said that in an old pocketbook in a particular drawer she would find something for herself.

That night he lapsed into unconsciousness. He awoke briefly on the evening of July 3, and whispered, "This is the Fourth?" Nicholas Trist, sitting with him, had been constantly turning his eyes from the clock in the corner of the room to his grandfather-in-law's face. Now he couldn't bear to say, "No." He pretended not to hear.

"This is the Fourth?" he repeated. Although it was not quite eleven o'clock, Nicholas nodded yes.

"Ah, just as I wished," he murmured, and sank back asleep again.

Jefferson and Nicholas watched anxiously as the hands of the clock moved slowly round to midnight. "At fifteen minutes before twelve we stood noting the minute hand of the watch, hoping a few minutes of prolonged life." Soon, they knew, he would "see his own glorious Fourth."

At four A.M. he called out for his servant Burwell in a clear strong voice. He did not speak again.

"He ceased to breathe, without a struggle, fifty minutes past meridian* —July 4th, 1826. I closed his eyes with my own hands," Jefferson Randolph recalled.[8]

At just that time, bells were ringing and cannons booming in every city and town throughout the country in celebration of the anniversary of his Declaration. He would have liked that.

A few hours later, in Braintree, Massachusetts, a dying John Adams uttered his last words, "Thomas Jefferson still survives."

Thomas Jefferson was buried at five o'clock the next day beneath the old oak tree on the side of his mountain, between his beloved wife and daughter and near his dear friend Dabney Carr, without pomp, in a simple grave-side ceremony. His gardener Wormley dug the grave. John Hemings had made the coffin. No invitations were sent, but Albemarle neighbors and students came in droves, in spite of a soft summer rain.

Martha, too distraught to cry, found her father's parting gift, a little poem he had written for her entitled, "A Death-bed Adieu from Th.J to M.R."

> Life's visions are vanished, its dreams are no more;
> Dear friends of my bosom, why bathed in tears?
> I go to my fathers, I welcome the shore
> Which crowns all my hopes or which buries my cares.
> Then farewell, my dear, my lov'd daughter, adieu!
> The last pang of life is parting from you!
> Two seraphs await me long shrouded in death;* *
> I will bear them your love on my last parting breath.

Toward the end of his life, Thomas Jefferson had written out, on the torn back of an old letter, specific instructions for a monument to be erected after his death. His family found them among his papers.

* 12:50 P.M.
* " Martha and Maria

He had described a simple stone, then ordered: "On the face of the obelisk the following inscription and not a word more:

HERE WAS BURIED
THOMAS JEFFERSON
AUTHOR OF THE DECLARATION OF INDEPENDENCE,
OF THE STATUTE OF VIRGINIA FOR RELIGIOUS FREEDOM,
AND FATHER OF THE UNIVERSITY OF VIRGINIA

because by these, as testimonials that I have lived, I wish most to be remembered."

Thomas Jefferson had long ago revealed to his friend James Madison his desire for "the esteem of the world." This he had earned. But political achievements had never been important to him. He had accepted his assignments as simply his duty, and he had done his best. His contribution to his country, he knew, went far beyond politics. He had always championed the rights of the people. Now he recognized that they would be freer because he had lived. He needed no other monument.

He had truly set himself and his house on a mountaintop. But he strove all his life to lift his fellow human beings to the same lofty heights. Now he could be content that his personal dream had come true:

I am as happy nowhere else, and in no other society, and all my wishes end, where I hope my days will, at Monticello.[9]

Chapter notes

Prologue
1. Wirt, *Patrick Henry*, 59.

I. On the edge of the wilderness
1. Jefferson, *Notes on Virginia*, in *Basic Writings*, 144.
2. Cripe, *Jefferson and Music*, 13.
3. *Albemarle County Will Book*, No. 2, 32.
4. *Ibid.*
5. Jefferson, *Autobiography*, in *Basic Writings*, 409.
6. Jefferson to John Harvie, January 14, 1760, *Writings of Thomas Jefferson*, ed. Lipscomb and Bergh, vol. 4, 268–269.

II. A restless mind
1. Jefferson, *Notes on Virginia*, in *Basic Writings*, 152.
2. Malone, *Jefferson the Virginian*, 50.
3. Jefferson to Harvie, January 14, 1760, *Papers of Thomas Jefferson*, ed. Boyd, vol. 1, 3.
4. Harvie to Jefferson, July 1850, *Virginia Historical Register*, vol. 3, 151.
5. From John Page to Jefferson, July 1850, *Virginia Historical Register*, vol. 3, 147–150.
6. Jefferson to Dr. Benjamin Rush, August 17, 1811, *Basic Writings*, 693.
7. Burk, *History of Virginia*, vol. 3, 333.
8. Jefferson, *Autobiography*, in *Basic Writings*, 410.
9. Jefferson to John Adams, June 11, 1812, *Writings of Thomas Jefferson*, ed. Lipscomb and Bergh, vol. 13, 160.
10. Laslett, ed., *Locke: Two Treatises*, 289.

III. Old Coke
1. Jefferson to Bernard Moore, n.d., *Writings of Thomas Jefferson*, ed. Ford, vol. 9, 480.
2. Jefferson to Dr. Thomas Cooper, February 10, 1814, *Writings of Thomas Jefferson*, ed. Lipscomb and Bergh, vol. 14, 85.
3. Euripides, *Orestes*, v. 694, in Jefferson, *Literary Bible*, 92.
4. Jefferson to Page, December 25, 1762, *Basic Writings*, 488.
5. Jefferson to Page, January 20, 1763, *Basic Writings*, 491.
6. Jefferson to Page, December 25, 1762, *Basic Writings*, 489.
7. Jefferson to Page, January 20, 1763, *Basic Writings*, 491.
8. Jefferson to Fleming, 1763, *Basic Writings*, 494.
9. Jefferson to P. S. Dupont de Nemours, March 2, 1809, *Jefferson Profile*, 179.
10. Jefferson to Page, October 7, 1763, *Basic Writings*, 495.
11. Euripides, *Medea*, 573.
12. Euripides, *Medea*, 616.
13. Euripides, *Orestes*, v. 1155.

14. Jefferson to Page, June 25, 1804, *Basic Writings,* 666.
15. Jefferson to Peter Carr, 1787, *Writings of Thomas Jefferson,* ed. Lipscomb and Bergh, vol. 6, 257.

IV. Listening at the door
1. Jefferson to Page, April 9, 1764, *Papers of Thomas Jefferson,* vol. 1, 17.
2. Burk, *History of Virginia,* vol. 3, 299.
3. Wirt, *Patrick Henry,* 74–75.
4. *Ibid.,* 83.
5. *Ibid.,* 78–79.

V. Lawyer on horseback
1. Jefferson, *Autobiography,* in *Basic Writings,* 412.

VI. An imaginative leap
1. Jefferson, August 3, 1767, *Garden Book,* 6.
2. *Ibid.,* May 15, 1760, 12 (quoting *Account Book*).

VII. First assignment: first failure
1. Jefferson, *Autobiography,* in *Basic Writings,* 411.
2. Jefferson to L. H. Girordin, January 15, 1815, *Writings of Thomas Jefferson,* ed. Lipscomb and Bergh, vol. 14, 231.
3. *Journals of the House of Burgesses, 1766–1769,* March 21, 1768.
4. Edmund Randolph, "Essay," *Virginia Magazine of History and Biography,* 122.
5. *Journals of the House of Burgesses, 1766–1769,* May 8, 1769, 187–189.
6. Jefferson, May 8, 1769, *Writings of Thomas Jefferson,* ed. Ford, vol. 1, 369.
7. *Journals of the House of Burgesses, 1766–1769,* April 14, 1768, 174.
8. *Ibid.,* May 17, 1769, 214.
9. *Ibid.,* 218.
10. Jefferson, *Garden Book,* 6.
11. Jefferson to Ogilvie, February 20, 1771, *Writings of Thomas Jefferson,* ed. Lipscomb and Bergh, vol. 3, 231.
12. Jefferson to Page, February 21, 1770, *Writings of Thomas Jefferson,* ed. Ford, vol. 1, 370.
13. T. Nelson, Jr., to Jefferson, March 6, 1770, Coolidge Collection, Massachusetts Historical Society.
14. T. Nelson, Sr., *ibid.*
15. Wythe to Jefferson, March 9, 1770, Jefferson, *Garden Book,* 20.
16. Jefferson, Howell vs. Netherland, April 1770, *Cases Determined in the General Court,* 90–96.
17. Laslett, ed., *Locke: Two Treatises,* 287.

VIII. "Worthy . . . of the lady . . ."
1. Jefferson to Thomas Adams, June 1, 1771, *Writings of Thomas Jefferson,* ed. Lipscomb and Bergh, vol. 4, 235–236.
2. Virginia *Gazette,* January 2, 1772.
3. Jefferson Papers, Library of Congress (R to G, #172–173).
4. Jefferson to T. M. Randolph, October 19, 1792, LC 78:1346555.
5. Jefferson, *Autobiography,* in *Basic Writings,* 412.
6. *Journals of the House of Burgesses, 1773–1776,* March 12, 1773, 28.

7. Parton, *Life of Jefferson*, 125.
8. Jefferson, *Garden Book*, 44.
9. *Ibid.*
10. Jefferson, *Autobiography*, in *Basic Writings*, 411.

IX. Aristocrat turned rebel

1. Jefferson, *Autobiography*, in *Basic Writings*, 413.
2. *Ibid.*
3. Wirt, *Patrick Henry*, 116.
4. Jefferson, *Autobiography*, in *Basic Writings*, 413–414.
5. Jefferson, *A Summary View of the Rights of British America*, in *Basic Writings*, 5–19.
6. Edmund Randolph, "Essay," *Virginia Magazine of History and Biography*, 216.
7. Jefferson, *Autobiography*, in *Writings of Thomas Jefferson*, Appendix C, ed. Lipscomb and Bergh, vol. 1, 183.
8. Edmund Randolph, "Essay," *Virginia Magazine of History and Biography*, 216.
9. Adams, *Works*, vol. 2, 366–367.
10. Washington, *Writings of George Washington*, vol. 3, 246–247.

X. "The ball of revolution"

1. Jefferson, *Autobiography*, in *Writings of Thomas Jefferson*, ed. Ford, vol. 1, 82.
2. Jefferson to John Bernard, Padover, *Thomas Jefferson*, 25.
3. Jefferson to T. M. Randolph, *Writings of Thomas Jefferson*, ed. Lipscomb and Bergh, vol. 6, 167.
4. Wirt, *Patrick Henry*, 138–141.
5. Edmund Randolph, "Essay," *Virginia Magazine of History and Biography*, 223.
6. Jefferson, *Writings of Thomas Jefferson*, ed. Ford, vol. 9, 340.
7. Jefferson to Wirt, August 14–15, 1814, Wirt, *Patrick Henry*, 143.
8. *Journals of the House of Burgesses, 1773–1776*, July 31, 1775, 17.
9. Jefferson to William Small, May 7, 1775, *Writings of Thomas Jefferson*, ed. Ford, vol. 1, 453–454.
10. Edmund Randolph, "Essay," *Virginia Magazine of History and Biography*, 223.
11. Jefferson, *Account Book*, spring 1775, in *Garden Book*.
12. Adams, *Works*, 357–358.
13. *Journals of Congress 1777*, vol. 7, 147–148.
14. Jefferson to John Randolph, August 25, 1775, *Writings of Thomas Jefferson*, ed. Lipscomb and Bergh, vol. 4, 28–31.
15. Jefferson to Francis Eppes, November 7, 1775, *ibid.*, 250.
16. T. Nelson, Jr., to Jefferson, February 4, 1776, *New England Historical and Genealogical Register*, vol. 56, 54.
17. Conway, ed., *Writings of Thomas Paine*, vol. 1, *Common Sense*, 84.
18. *Ibid.*

XI. Reclaiming a birthright

1. Jefferson to Page, April 6, 1776, *New England Historical and Genealogical Register*, vol. 56, 55.
2. John Adams, *Works*, vol. 9, 374.
3. Jefferson to T. Nelson, May 16, 1776, *Writings of Thomas Jefferson*, ed.

Lipscomb and Bergh, vol. 4, 253–256.

4. *Journals of the House of Burgesses 1773–1776,* June 7, 1776.
5. Jefferson, *Autobiography,* in *Basic Writings,* 421.
6. Boyd, "New Light on Jefferson," *New York Times Magazine,* April 13, 1947, 65.
7. Jefferson, *Autobiography,* in *Basic Writings,* 421.
8. Adams, *Works,* vol. 2, 512.
9. Jefferson, R. H. Lee, May 8, 1825, *Basic Writings,* 802.
10. Jefferson, *Declaration of Independence.*
11. Jefferson to Page, July 20, 1776, *Writings of Thomas Jefferson,* ed. Lipscomb and Bergh, vol. 4, 268.
12. Jefferson to Madison, 1823, *Becker, Declaration of Independence,* 136.
13. Jefferson, *Writings of Thomas Jefferson,* vol. 9, 337–378.
14. Adams, *Works,* 418, 420.
15. Jefferson, *Writings of Thomas Jefferson,* ed. Ford, vol. 10, 120 (written in 1818).
16. Becker, *Declaration of Independence,* 212.
17. *Ibid.*
18. Jefferson, *Autobiography,* in *Basic Writings,* 422.
19. Becker, *Declaration of Independence.*
20. Fowler, *The Baron of Beacon Hill,* 213.
21. Parton, *Life of Jefferson,* 192.
22. R. H. Lee to Jefferson, July 21, 1776, Ballagh, *Letters of Richard Henry Lee,* vol. 1, 210, quoted in Kimball, *Jefferson: The Road to Glory,* 304.
23. Page to Jefferson, July 20, 1776, *New England Historical and Genealogical Register,* vol. 56, 210.

XII. "Public service and private misery"
1. Jefferson to Francis Eppes, July 15, 1776, *Writings of Thomas Jefferson,* ed. Lipscomb and Bergh, vol. 4, 260.
2. Jefferson to Pendleton, July 1776, *Writings of Thomas Jefferson,* ed. Ford, vol. 2, 61.
3. Jefferson to R. H. Lee, July 8, 1776, *Writings of Thomas Jefferson,* ed. Lipscomb and Bergh, vol. 3, 34.
4. R. H. Lee to Jefferson, September 27, 1776, *ibid.*
5. Jefferson to Hancock, October 11, 1776, *Writings of Thomas Jefferson,* ed. Ford, vol. 2, 91–92.
6. John Adams to Jefferson, May 26, 1777, *Declaration of Independence,* vol. 2, 20–22.
7. Jefferson, Report of Committee of Revisors, *Writings of Thomas Jefferson,* ed. Ford, vol. 2, 220ff.
8. Jefferson, Bill for Establishing Religious Freedom, *Basic Writings,* 49.
9. Jefferson, *Autobiography,* in *Basic Writings,* 438.
10. Jefferson to Henry, March 27, 1779, *Writings of Thomas Jefferson,* ed. Lipscomb and Bergh, vol. 4, 45.
11. Jefferson to Bellini, Kimball, *Jefferson: War and Peace,* 18.
12. Jefferson to R. H. Lee, June 17, 1779, ed. Ford, vol. 2, 192.
13. Peterson, *Jefferson and the Revolution,* 42.
14. *Time,* July 4, 1976, 65.

15. Fleming to Jefferson, *Jefferson Papers*, Library of Congress.
16. Monroe to Jefferson, Hamilton, *Writings on Monroe, I,* 8–11 (quoted in Bowers, *Young Jefferson,* 256).
17. Jefferson to David Jameson, April 16, 1781, *Official Letters,* vol. 2, 479 (quoted in Kimball, *Jefferson: War and Peace*).
18. Jefferson to Monroe, May 20, 1782, *Papers of Thomas Jefferson,* vol. 6, 186.
19. Jefferson to Washington, May 28, 1781, *Writings of Thomas Jefferson,* ed. Lipscomb and Bergh, vol. 4.
20. Washington to Jefferson, June 8, 1781, Malone, *Jefferson the Virginian,* 354.
21. Davis, *Monticello Scrapbook,* 40.
22. Jefferson to Dr. William Gordon, July 16, 1788, *Writings of Thomas Jefferson,* ed. Ford, vol. 5, 39.

XIII. "That eternal separation"
1. *House of Delegates Journal,* December 19, 1787 (quoted in Kimball, *Jefferson: War and Peace*).
2. Jefferson to Monroe, May 20, 1782, Randall, *Life of Jefferson,* vol. 1, 377.
3. Jefferson to Washington, October 28, 1781, *Writings of Thomas Jefferson,* ed. Ford, vol. 3, 51.
4. Jefferson to Edmund Randolph, September 16, 1781, *Writings of Thomas Jefferson,* ed. Ford, vol. 3, 49–50.
5. Edmund Randolph to Jefferson, October 9, 1781, LC 7:1162
6. Jefferson, *Notes on Virginia,* in *Basic Writings,* 160.
7. Chastellux, *Travels in North America,* vol. 2, 41–42.
8. *Ibid.*
9. *Ibid.*
10. John Tyler to Jefferson, May 16, 1782, LC 8:1235–1236.
11. Jefferson to Monroe, May 20, 1782, *Writings of Thomas Jefferson,* ed. Ford, vol. 3, 56–60.
12. Sarah Randolph, *Domestic Life,* 62–63.
13. *Ibid.,* 63.
14. *Ibid.*
15. Jefferson, *Autobiography,* in *Basic Writings,* 441.
16. Jefferson to Elizabeth Eppes, October 3, 1782, *Papers of Thomas Jefferson,* vol. 6, 198.
17. Sarah Randolph, *Domestic Life,* 67.
18. *Ibid.,* 68.
19. Jefferson, *Autobiography,* in *Basic Writings,* 441.
20. Jefferson to Marbois, December 5, 1783, Malone, *Jefferson the Virginian,* 405.
21. Jefferson to Martha (Patsy), November 28, 1783, *Papers of Thomas Jefferson,* vol. 6, 359.
22. Washington's Farewell Address to Congress, *Papers of Thomas Jefferson,* vol. 6, 411–412.
23. Jefferson, ed., *Writings of Thomas Jefferson,* ed. Ford, vol. 3, 364.
24. Jefferson to Martha (Patsy), December 22, 1783, *Papers of Thomas Jefferson,* vol. 6, 41.
25. Jefferson to Count Hogendorp, undated (probably summer 1784), Kimball, *Jefferson: War and Peace,* 328.

26. Jefferson to Madison, January 1, 1784, *Papers of Thomas Jefferson,* vol. 6, 436.

XIV. **"Behold me on the vaunted scene of Europe"**
1. Martha (Patsy) to Elizabeth Trist, Edgehill Randolph Collection, Alderman Library, University of Virginia.
2. Jefferson to Bellini, September 30, 1785, *Papers of Thomas Jefferson,* vol. 8, 568–570.
3. Jefferson to Nathaniel Greene, January 12, 1785, *Writings of Thomas Jefferson,* ed. Ford, vol. 4, 25.
4. Abigail Adams, *Letters of Mrs. Adams,* 216, quoted in Kimball, *The Scene of Europe.*
5. Jefferson to Dr. James Currie, Malone, *Jefferson and the Rights of Man,* 12.
6. Jefferson to Francis Eppes, February 5, 1785, *Papers of Thomas Jefferson,* vol. 7, 635–636.
7. Elizabeth Eppes to Jefferson, October 31, 1784, *Papers of Thomas Jefferson,* vol. 7, 441.
8. Beloff, *Jefferson and American Democracy,* 102.
9. Jefferson to Madison, June 1787, *Writings of Thomas Jefferson,* ed. Lipscomb and Bergh, vol. 6, 134.
10. Abigail Adams, *Letters of Mrs. Adams,* 240–241.
11. Jefferson to Madison, May 1785, *Writings of Thomas Jefferson,* ed. Ford, vol. 4, 46–47.
12. Jefferson, *Autobiography,* in *Basic Writings,* 451.
13. Jefferson to Elizabeth Eppes, September 22, 1785, in Sarah Randolph, *Domestic Life,* 105.
14. Abigail Adams, *Letters of Mrs. Adams,* 191.
15. *Ibid.,* 207.
16. Jefferson to Monroe, *Writings of Thomas Jefferson,* ed. Ford, vol. 4, 11–12.
17. Jefferson to Thomas Turpin, from Shadwell, February 5, 1769, quoted in Malone, *Jefferson the Virginian,* 67.
18. Jefferson to Madison, December 16, 1786, *Basic Writings,* 545–546.

XV. **"Dialogue between the head and the heart"**
1. Jefferson to Madison, September 20, 1785, *Writings of Thomas Jefferson,* ed., Lipscomb and Bergh, vol. 5, 136–137.
2. Bullock, *My Head and My Heart,* 14.
3. Jefferson to Maria Cosway, October 12, 1786, *ibid.,* 31–32.
4. John Trumbull, *Autobiography,* 101–102.
5. Maria Cosway to Jefferson, about September 20, 1786, Sarah Randolph, *Domestic Life,* 85.
6. Jefferson to Maria Cosway, probably September 21, 1786, Butterfield and Rice, *William and Mary,* 31–32.
7. Maria Cosway to Jefferson, n.d. Sarah Randolph, *Domestic Life,* 86.
8. Jefferson to Maria Cosway, October 12, 1786, *ibid.,* 87.
9. Jefferson to S. Smith, October 22, 1786, *Writings of Thomas Jefferson,* ed. Ford, vol. 4, 325.
10. Malone, *Jefferson and the Rights of Man,* 76.
11. Bullock, *My Head and My Heart,* 30.

12. *Ibid.*, 41–42.
13. Jefferson to Maria Cosway, n.d., *Writings of Thomas Jefferson,* ed. Lipscomb and Bergh, vol. 5, 448–449.
14. Jefferson to Madison, January 30, 1787, *A Jefferson Profile,* 45–46.
15. Jefferson to Maria Cosway, December 25, 1786, Alderman Library, University of Virginia.
16. Jefferson to Lafayette, April 11, 1787, *Writings of Thomas Jefferson,* ed. Lipscomb and Bergh, vol. 6, 106–109.
17. Jefferson to Martha (Patsy), March 28, 1787, Betts and Bear, *Family Letters,* 34.
18. Martha (Patsy) to Jefferson, April 9, 1787, *ibid.,* 37–38.
19. Jefferson to Martha (Patsy), May 5, 1787, *ibid.,* 40.
20. Jefferson to Maria Cosway, July 1, 1787, Kimball, *Scene of Europe,* 177.
21. Maria Cosway to Jefferson, December 1787, Coolidge Collection, Massachusetts Historical Society.
22. Jefferson to Maria Cosway, January 1788, Coolidge Collection, Massachusetts Historical Society.
23. Jefferson to Maria Cosway, September 26, 1788, University of Virginia.
24. *Ibid.*

XVI. "She must come"
1. Jefferson to Francis Eppes, August 30, 1785, Kimball, *Scene of Europe,* 304.
2. Jefferson to Elizabeth Eppes, September 22, 1785, *ibid.*
3. Jefferson to Mary (Polly), September 20, 1785, Betts and Bear, *Family Letters,* 29.
4. Mary (Polly) to Jefferson, about September 13, 1785, *ibid.,* 29.
5. Mary (Polly) to Jefferson, about May 22, 1786, *ibid.,* 31.
6. Jefferson to Elizabeth Eppes, January or February 1786, Sarah Randolph, *Domestic Life,* 107.
7. Elizabeth Eppes to Jefferson, March 1787, *ibid.,* 124.

XVII. "For the public good"
1. Jefferson to Madison, December 20, 1787, *Basic Writings,* 563–564.
2. Jefferson to M. l'Abbé Arnoud, Paris, July 19, 1789, ed. Lipscomb and Bergh, vol. 7, 422.
3. Jefferson to Wythe, August 13, 1786, *Basic Writings,* ed. Foner, 532.
4. Jefferson to T. M. Randolph, Jr., *Writings of Thomas Jefferson,* ed. Lipscomb and Bergh, vol. 6, 165.
5. Jefferson to Washington, *Writings of Thomas Jefferson,* ed. Lipscomb and Bergh, vol. 7, 349–350.
6. Jefferson to Hopkinson, *Writings of Thomas Jefferson,* ed. Lipscomb and Bergh, vol. 7, 301–302.
7. Jefferson to Jay, November 1788, Hall, *Ladies,* 99.
8. Jefferson to Washington, spring 1789, ed. Lipscomb and Bergh, vol. 7, 349–350.
9. Martha, Sarah Randolph, *Domestic Life,* 151.
10. Malone, *Jefferson and the Rights of Man,* 244. Printed in *Gazette of the United States,* December 16, 1789.

11. Jefferson to Washington, December 15, 1789, *Basic Writings*, 592–593.
12. Sarah Randolph, *Domestic Life*, 152.

XVIII. "I have no ambition to govern men"
1. Jefferson to Martha, April 4, 1790, Betts and Bear, *Family Letters*, 50–51.
2. Martha to Jefferson, April 25, 1790, *ibid.*, 52–53.
3. Jefferson to Maria, May 30, 1791, *ibid.*, 83.
4. Maria to Jefferson, July 10, 1791, *ibid.*, 87.
5. *Ibid.*
6. Jefferson to Martha, July 7, 1793, *ibid.*, 121–122.
7. Jefferson to L'Enfant, 1791, Peterson, *Reference Biography*, 143.
8. Jefferson to Madison, June 1793, Sarah Randolph, *Domestic Life*, 218–219.
9. Jefferson to Horatio Gates, February 3, 1794, LC 16747.
10. Jefferson to Madison, January 1, 1797, *Writings of Thomas Jefferson*, ed. Ford, vol. 7, 98.
11. Jefferson to John Adams, December 28, 1796, *Basic Writings*, 633.
12. Jefferson to Rutledge, December 27, 1796, *Writings of Thomas Jefferson*, ed. Ford, vol. 7, 93–94.
13. Padover, *Thomas Jefferson*, 258.
14. Jefferson to Carrington, January 16, 1787, *Writings of Thomas Jefferson*, ed. Ford, vol. 4, 359.
15. Jefferson to Martha, June 8, 1797, Betts and Bear, *Family Letters*, 145–147.
16. Jefferson to Maria, January 7, 1798, *ibid.*, 151–153.
17. Jefferson to Martha, March 27, 1797, *ibid.*, 142.
18. Jefferson to Maria, July 13, 1798, *ibid.*, 166–167.
19. *Ibid.*
20. Jefferson to Maria, July 14, 1798, *ibid.*, 167–168.

XIX. "We are all republicans—we are all federalists"
1. Jefferson to Rush, September 23, 1800, *Writings of Thomas Jefferson*, ed. Ford, vol. 7, 460.
2. Jefferson to Lafayette, March 6, 1801, *Writings of Thomas Jefferson*, ed. Lipscomb and Bergh, vol. 10, 214.
3. Jefferson, First Inaugural Address, March 4, 1801, *Basic Writings*, 332–335.
4. *Ibid.*
5. *Ibid.*
6. Jefferson to Robert Livingston, April 1802, Beloff, *Jefferson and American Democracy*, 203–204.
7. Jefferson to Maria, October 26, 1801, Betts and Bear, *Family Letters*, 210–211.
8. Jefferson to Maria, February 12, 1800, *ibid.*, 185–186.
9. Jefferson to Maria, February 26, 1804, *ibid.*, 258.
10. Jefferson to Maria, March 3, 1804, *ibid.*
11. Jefferson to Madison, April 9, 1804, Papers of James Madison, Library of Congress.
12. Jefferson to Page, June 25, 1804, *Basic Writings*, 665–666.
13. Abigail Adams to Jefferson, May 20, 1804, Sarah Randolph, *Domestic Life*, 304–305.
14. Jefferson to Dupont de Nemours, March 2, 1809, *ibid.*, 323.

XX. A tangled web
1. Ellen Randolph Coolidge to Joseph Coolidge, October 24, 1858, Malone, "Mr. Jefferson's Private Life," 7.
2. Jefferson to Dr. George Logan, June 20, 1816, *Writings of Thomas Jefferson,* ed. Ford, vol. 10, 27.
3. Bear, *Jefferson at Monticello,* 102.
4. Ellen Randolph Coolidge to Joseph Collidge, October 24, 1858, Malone, "Mr. Jefferson's Private Life," 7.
5. Peterson, *Thomas Jefferson and the New Nation,* 707.

XXI. Man on a mountain
1. Malone, *Ordeal of Liberty,* 222. (From B. L. Rayner, *Sketches of the Life, Writings, and Opinions of Thomas Jefferson,* 1832, 524.)
2. Jefferson to Charles Wilson Peale, August 20, 1811, *Writings of Thomas Jefferson,* ed. Lipscomb and Bergh, vol. 13, 79.
3. Ellen R. Coolidge to Randall, February 18, 1856, Randall, *Life of Jefferson,* vol. 3, 342.

XXII. "The venerable corps of grandfathers"
1. Jefferson to Elizabeth Eppes, May 15, 1791, Sarah Randolph, *Domestic Life,* 201.
2. Jefferson to Kosciusko, February 26, 1810, *ibid.,* 331–332.
3. Ellen R. Coolidge to Randall, about 1850, *ibid.,* 340–343.
4. Virginia J. Trist to Randall, May 26, 1839, *ibid.,* 345–346.
5. Ellen R. Coolidge to Randall, *ibid.,* 344.
6. Virginia J. Trist to Randall, *ibid.*
7. Jefferson to Ellen R. Coolidge, November 14, 1825. Coolidge Collection, Massachusetts Historical Society.
8. Jefferson to T. J. Randolph, November 24, 1808, Betts and Bear, *Family Letters,* 362–365.
9. Jefferson to T. J. Randolph, February 8, 1826, *ibid.,* 469–470.

XXIII. "The last service I can render my country"
1. Jefferson to John Adams, early in 1812, n.d., Sarah Randolph, *Domestic Life,* 354–355.
2. Jefferson to William Roscoe, December 27, 1820, *Writings of Thomas Jefferson,* ed. Lipscomb and Bergh, vol. 15, 303.
3. Jefferson to Correa, October 24, 1820, *Garden Book,* 590.
4. Bruce, *History of the University of Virginia: The Lengthened Shadow of One Man,* from Emerson, "An institution is the lengthened shadow of one man."
5. November 8, 1924, Chinard, *Letters of Lafayette and Jefferson,* 358–359.
6. Francis Eppes to Jefferson, February 23, 1826, Betts and Bear, *Letters,* 470–472.
7. Jefferson to Roger C. Weightman, June 24, 1826, *Basic Writings,* 807 (Jefferson's last extant letter).
8. Randall, *Life of Jefferson,* vol. 3, 543–548.
9. Jefferson to George Gilmer, August 12, 1787, *Papers of Thomas Jefferson,* vol. 12, 26.

Bibliography

Secondary Sources

Adair, Douglas. *Fame and the Founding Fathers*. New York: W. W. Norton & Co., 1974.

Adams, William Howard. *Jefferson's Monticello*. New York: Abbeville Press, 1983.

Adams, William Howard, ed. *The Eye of Thomas Jefferson*. Washington, D.C.: National Gallery of Art, 1976.

Bailey, Thomas A., and David M. Kennedy. *The American Pageant: A History of the Republic*. Lexington, Mass.: D. C. Heath & Co., Sixth Ed., 1979.

Bear, James A., Jr., ed. *Jefferson at Monticello*. Charlottesville: University Press of Virginia, 1967.

Becker, Carl. *The Declaration of Independence: A Study in the History of Political Ideas*. New York: Vintage Books, 1958.

Bedini, Silvio A. *Declaration of Independence Desk: Relic of Revolution*. Washington, D.C.: Smithsonian Institution Press, 1981.

Beloff, Max. *Thomas Jefferson and American Democracy*. London: The English Universities Press, 1948.

Betts, Edwin Morris, and James A. Bear, Jr., eds. *The Family Letters of Thomas Jefferson*. Columbia: University of Missouri Press, 1966.

Betts, Edwin M., and Hazlehurst Bolton Perkins. *Thomas Jefferson's Flower Garden at Monticello*. Richmond: The Dietz Press, 1941.

Biddle. *Eulogium on Thomas Jefferson*. (del. 1827)

Binger, Carl. *Thomas Jefferson: A Well-Tempered Mind*. New York: W. W. Norton & Co., 1970.

Boorstin, Daniel J. *The Lost World of Thomas Jefferson*. Boston: Beacon Press, 1948.

Bowen, Catherine Drinker. *John Adams and the American Revolution*. Boston: Little Brown and Co., 1950.

Bowers, Claude G. *Making Democracy a Reality: Jefferson, Jackson, and Pope*. Memphis: Memphis State College Press, 1954.

———. *The Young Jefferson, 1743–1789*. Cambridge, Mass.: Riverside Press, 1945.

Boyd, Julian. *The Spirit of Christmas at Monticello*. New York: Oxford University Press, 1964.

Boykin, Edward. *To the Girls and Boys. Being the delightful, little-known letters of Thomas Jefferson to and from his children and grandchildren*. New York: Funk & Wagnalls Co., 1964.

Brodie, Fawn M. *Thomas Jefferson: An Intimate History*. New York: W. W. Norton & Co., 1974.

Bruce, Philip Alexander. *History of the University of Virginia 1819–1919, Volume I*. New York: Macmillan Co., 1920.

Bullock, Helen Duprey. *My Head and My Heart*. New York: G. P. Putnam's Sons and the University of Virginia, 1945.

Burk, John. *The History of Virginia from the First Settlement to the Present Day*. Petersburg, Va.: Dickenson & Pescud, 1805.

Burnett, Edmund Cody. *The Continental Congress*. New York: Macmillan Co., 1941.

Burns, Jehane, ed. *The World of Franklin and Jefferson*. New York: Metropolitan Museum of Art, 1976.

Bush, Alfred L. *The Life Portraits of Thomas Jefferson*. Princeton, N.J.: Princeton University Press, 1962.

Chastellux, Marquis de. *Voyages dans l'Amerique*. 2 Vol. Paris, 1786.

Chinard, Gilbert. *Letters of Lafayette and Jefferson*. Baltimore: Johns Hopkins Press, 1929.

———. *Thomas Jefferson, The Apostle of Americanism*. Boston: Little, Brown and Co., 1929.

Conway, Moncure Daniel. *Omitted Chapters of History Disclosed in the Life and Papers of Edmund Randolph*. New York and London: Putnam's, 1888.

Conway, Moncure Daniel, ed. *The Writings of Thomas Paine, Vol. I, 1774–1779*. New York, London: Knickerbocker Press, 1894.

Cripe, Helen. *Thomas Jefferson and Music*. Charlottesville: University Press of Virginia, 1974.

Dabney, Virginius. *The Jefferson Scandals: A Rebuttal*. New York: Dodd, Mead & Co., 1981.

Davis, Betty Elise. *Monticello Scrapbook*. Charlottesville, Va.: Michie Co., 1939.

Donovan, Frank. *The Thomas Jefferson Papers*. New York: Dodd, Mead & Co., 1963.

Fleming, Thomas. *The Man from Monticello*. New York: William Morrow Co., 1969.

Fowler, William M., Jr. The *Baron of Beacon Hill: A Biography of John Hancock*. Boston: Houghton Mifflin Co., 1980.

Freudenberg, Anne. *Malone and Jefferson*. Charlottesville, Va.: The University of Virginia Library, 1981.

Hall, Gordon Langley. *Mr. Jefferson's Ladies*. Boston: Beacon Press, 1966.

Kimball, Fiske. *Life Portraits of Thomas Jefferson*. Charlottesville, Va.: The Thomas Jefferson Memorial Foundation, 1962.

Kimball, Marie. *Jefferson: The Road to Glory*. Westport, Conn.: Greenwood Press, 1977.

_____. *Jefferson: War and Peace*. New York: Coward McCann, 1947.

_____. *Jefferson: The Scene of Europe*. New York: Coward McCann, 1950.

Klapthor, Margaret. *Story of the Declaration of Independence Desk*. Smithsonian Institution, Annual Report, 1953.

Koch, Adrienne, ed. *The American Enlightenment*. New York: George Braziller, 1965.

Koch, Adrienne. *The Philosophy of Thomas Jefferson*. New York: Columbia University Press, 1943.

Laslett, Peter, ed. *John Locke: Two Treatises of Government*. London: The Cambridge University Press, 1960.

Lewis, Jan. *The Pursuit of Happiness: Family and Values in Jefferson's Virginia*. Cambridge: Cambridge University Press, 1983.

Malone, Dumas, and William H. B. Thomas. *A Miracle of Virginia—The School for Statesmen*. Charlottesville, Va.: Ben Franklin Publishing of Charlottesville, 1984.

Malone, Dumas. *Jefferson and His Time*. Boston: Little, Brown and Co.
  Vol. 1. *Jefferson the Virginian*. (1948).
  Vol. 2. *Jefferson and the Rights of Man*. (1951).
  Vol. 3. *Jefferson and the Ordeal of Liberty*. (1962).
  Vol. 4. *Jefferson the President: First Term, 1801–1805*. (1970).
  Vol. 5. *Jefferson the President: Second Term, 1805–1809*. (1974).
  Vol. 6. *The Sage of Monticello*. (1981).

Mayo, Bernard. *Another Peppercorn for Mr. Jefferson*. Charlottesville, Va.: The Thomas Jefferson Memorial Foundation, 1977.

Mazzei, Philip. *Memoirs, 1730–1816*. Trans. by Howard R. Marraro. New York: Columbia University Press, 1942.

Mellon, Matthew T. *Early American Views on Negro Slavery*. New York: Bergman Publishers, 1969.

Moscow, Henry, with Dumas Malone. *Thomas Jefferson and His World*. New York: American Heritage Publishing Co., 1960.

Munves, James. *Thomas Jefferson and the Declaration of Independence*. New York: Charles Scribner's Sons, 1978.

Nichols, Frederick D., and James A. Bear, Jr. *Monticello: A Guidebook*. Monticello, Va.: Thomas Jefferson Memorial Foundation, 1982.

Nutting, Wallace. *Virginia Beautiful*. New York: Garden City Publishing Co., 1935.

Padover, Saul K. *Thomas Jefferson*. New York: Harcourt, Brace & Co., 1942.

Parton, James. *Life of Thomas Jefferson*. Boston: James R. Osgood and Co., 1874. (Reprint, N.Y.: Da Capo Press, 1971).

Peterson, Merrill D. *Thomas Jefferson and the American Revolution*. Williamsburg:

Virginia Independence Bicentennial Commission, 1976.

_____. *The Jefferson Image in the American Mind*. New York: Oxford University Press, 1960.

_____. *Thomas Jefferson and the New Nation: A Biography*. New York: Oxford University Press, 1970.

_____, ed. *Thomas Jefferson: A Reference Biography*. New York: Charles Scribner's Sons, 1986.

Pierson, Rev. Hamilton W., D. D. *Jefferson at Monticello*. New York: Charles Scribner, 1862.

Randall, Henry S. *The Life of Thomas Jefferson, Vols. 1, 2, 3*. Freeport, New York: Books for Libraries Press, 1970. (First published 1857.)

Randolph, Sarah N. *The Domestic Life of Thomas Jefferson*. New York: Frederick Ungar Publishing Co., 1958.

Rawlings, Mary. *The Albemarle of Other Days*. Charlottesville: Michie Co., 1925.

Rosenberger, Francis Coleman, ed. *Jefferson Reader*. New York: E. P. Dutton & Co., 1953.

Russell, Phillips. *Jefferson, Champion of the Free Mind*. New York: Dodd, Mead & Co., 1956.

Sanford, Charles B. *Thomas Jefferson and His Library*. Hamden, Conn.: Archon Books, 1977.

Sydnor, Charles S. *American Revolutionaries in the Making*. New York: Free Press, 1965.

Tripp, Valerie. *An Introduction to Williamsburg*. Wisconsin: Pleasantry Press, in cooperation with the Colonial Williamsburg Foundation, 1985.

Weymouth, Lally, ed. *Thomas Jefferson: The Man . . . His World . . . His Influence*. New York: G. P. Putnam's Sons, 1973.

Whitehill, Walter Muir. *"The Many Faces of Monticello,"* Address at Monticello, April 13, 1964. Charlottesville, Va.: The Thomas Jefferson Memorial Foundation, 1965.

Whitney, Jeanne, ed. *The Colonial Williamsburg Interpreter Handbook*. Williamsburg, Va.: The Department of Interpretive Education, 1985.

Willis, Garry. *Inventing America*. Garden City, N.Y.: Doubleday & Co., 1978.

Wilstach, Paul. *Jefferson and Monticello*. New York: Doubleday, Doran & Co., 1939.

Wirt, William. *The Life of Patrick Henry*. New York: McElrath & Bangs, 1831.

Woodfin, Maude. "Contemporary Opinion in Virginia of Thomas Jefferson," in *Essays in Honor of William E. Dodd*. Ed. Avery Croner. Chicago: Chicago University Press, 1935.

The Writings of Thomas Jefferson

The Basic Writings of Thomas Jefferson. Ed. Philip S. Foner. New York: Wiley Book Co., 1944.

The Commonplace Book of Thomas Jefferson. A Repertory of His Ideas on Government. Introduction and Notes by Gilbert Chinard. Baltimore: Johns Hopkins Press, 1926.

The Declaration of Independence. The Evolution of the Text as Shown by Facsimilies of Various Drafts by its Author, Thomas Jefferson. Julian P. Boyd. Revised edition, Princeton: Princeton University Press, 1945.

The Founding Fathers: Thomas Jefferson: A Biography in His Own Words. Introduction by Joseph L. Gardner. New York: Newsweek, 1974.

The Jefferson Cyclopedia. A comprehensive collection of the views of Thomas Jefferson, classified and arranged in alphabetical order. Ed. J. P. Foley. New York and London: Funk & Wagnalls, 1900.

A Jefferson Profile (As Revealed in His Letters). Ed. Saul K. Padover. New York: The John Day Co., 1956.

The Literary Bible of Thomas Jefferson. His Commonplace Book of Philosophers and Poets. With an introduction by Gilbert Chinard. Baltimore: Johns Hopkins Press, 1928.

Thomas Jefferson's Architectural Drawings. With commentary and a checklist by Frederick Doveton Nichols. Charlottesville: The Thomas Jefferson Memorial Foundation and University Press of Virginia, 1961.

Thomas Jefferson's Farm Book, with commentary and relevant extracts from other writings. Ed. Edwin Morris Betts. Charlottesville: University Press of Virginia, 1976. (Originally owned by the Massachussetts Historical Society.)

Thomas Jefferson's Garden Book. Annotated by Edwin Morris Betts. Philadelphia: The American Philosophical Society, 1981.

The Papers of Thomas Jefferson. Vols. 1–20. Ed. Julian P. Boyd. Vols. 21—Index ed. Charles Cullen. Princeton, N.J.: Princeton University Press, 1953.

The Writings of Thomas Jefferson, 10 Volumes. Ed. Paul Leicester Ford. New York, G. P. Putnam's Sons, 1892–1899.

The Writings of Thomas Jefferson, 20 Vols. Ed. A. A. Lipscomb, and A. E. Bergh. Washington: Thomas Jefferson Memorial Association, 1903.

Original Sources

Albemarle County Will Book, No. 2. University of Virginia.

The Carr and Cary Papers. University of Virginia Press.

Catalogue of the Library of Thomas Jefferson. Compiled with annotations by E. Millicent Sowerby. Washington, D.C.: Library of Congress, 1952.

The Collected Papers to Commemorate Fifty Years of the Monticello Association of the Descendents of Thomas Jefferson. Ed. George Green Shackelford. Published by the Monticello Association. Princeton: Princeton University Press, 1965.

The Coolidge Collection. Massachusetts Historical Society.

The Edgehill Randolph Collection. Alderman Library, University of Virginia.

Facsimile of the Olive Branch Petition, July 8, 1775. From the original in II. M. Public Record Office, London.

The Jefferson Papers. Library of Congress.

Journals of Congress.

Journals of the House of Burgesses.

The New England Historical and Genealogical Register.

Report of the Committee of Revisors [Jefferson, George Wythe and Edward Pendleton]. Appointed by the General Assembly of Virginia in 1776. Richmond: 1784.

Reports of Cases Determined in the General Court of Virginia from 1768 to 1772. Charlottesville: published by the legatee of Jefferson's manuscript papers, 1829. This work contains a few of his own cases.

The Virginia Gazette.

Virginia Historical Register, Vol. 3.

Writings of Jefferson's Contemporaries

Adams, Abigail. *Letters of Mrs. Adams.* Ed. Charles Francis Adams, Boston: 1848.

Adams, John. *Works.* Ed. C. F. Adams. 10 vols. Boston: 1856.

Madison, James. *Papers of James Madison.* Library of Congress.

Madison, James. *Writings.* Ed. Gaillard Hunt. 9 vols. New York: 1900–1910.

Trumbull, John. *Autobiography, Reminiscences and Letters.* New York: 1841.

Washington, George. *Writings.* Ed. J. C. Fitzpatrick. 39 vols. Washington: Government Printing Office, 1931–1941.

Periodicals

Bierne, Francis F. "A Visit to Shadwell." *The Evening Sun,* Baltimore, Md. (April 13, 1943).

Boyd, Julian P. "New Light on Jefferson and His Great Task." *New York Times Magazine* (April 13, 1947).

Butterfield, L. H., and H. C. Rice, Jr. "Jefferson's Earliest Note to Maria Cosway with Some New Facts and Conjectures on His Broken Wrist." *William and Mary,* 3 ser., Vol. 5, pp. 31–32.

Chinard, Gilbert. "Thomas Jefferson as Classical Scholar." *Johns Hopkins Alumni Magazine.* Vol. 18, pp. 291–303 (Baltimore, 1930).

Ellis, Edward S. "Thomas Jefferson, a Character Sketch." *The Patriot,* Vol. I, No. 1, April 1898 (Chicago: The University Association).

Keslo, William M. "Digging on Jefferson's Mountain." *World Book Encyclopedia—1985 Yearbook,* pp. 100–117 (Chicago: World Book, 1985).

Kimball, Marie. "In Search of Jefferson's Birthplace." *Virginia Magazine of History and Biography,* Vol. 51, October 1943, pp. 313–325.

_____. "Jefferson, Patron of the Arts." *Antiques,* Vol. 43, No. 4 (April 1943) pp. 164–167.

_____. "The Epicure of the White House." *Virginia Quarterly Review* (January 1933).

Malone, Dumas. "Jefferson Goes to School in Williamsburg." *Virginia Quarterly Review,* Vol. 33, No. 4 (Autumn 1957).

_____. "Mr. Jefferson's Private Life." *Proceedings of the American Antiquarian Society,* Vol. 84 (1974).

_____. "Polly Jefferson and Her Father." *Virginia Quarterly Review.* (January 1931) pp. 81–95.

Penrice, Daniel. "Jeffersonian Architecture." *Bostonian Magazine,* Vol. 59, No. 4, July/August 1985. (A Boston University Publication.)

Time (July 4, 1976) (Special 1776 Issue).

Randolph, Edmund. "Edmund Randolph's Essay on the Revolutionary History of Virginia (1774–1782)." *Virginia Magazine of History and Biography,* Vol. 43, No. 2 (April 1935). (Published by the Virginia Historical Society, Richmond, Va.)

Rowse, A. L. "The Other Jefferson House." *The New York Times,* Travel section (July 6, 1986).

Webster, Donald, Jr. "The Day Jefferson Got Plastered." *American Heritage* (June 1963), Volume XIV, no. 4.

Willis, Gary. "Uncle Thomas' Cabin." *New York Review of Books* (April 18, 1974).

Films

The Eye of Thomas Jefferson. National Gallery of Art, 1976.

Williamsburg—The Story of a Patriot. Colonial Williamsburg Foundation, 1957.

Index